T0136454

MACROANALYSIS

TOPICS IN THE DIGITAL HUMANITIES

Humanities computing is redefining basic principles about research
and publication. An influx of new, vibrant, and diverse communities of
practitioners recognizes that computer applications are subject to continual
innovation and reappraisal. This series publishes books that demonstrate the
new questions, methods, and results arising in the digital humanities.

SERIES EDITORS
Susan Schreibman
Raymond C. Siemens

MACROANALYSIS
DIGITAL METHODS AND LITERARY HISTORY

MATTHEW L. JOCKERS

UNIVERSITY OF ILLINOIS PRESS

Urbana, Chicago, and Springfield

Additional material referred to in this book, including
confusion matrices, an expanded stop-words list, and
additional graphs and color images, can be found at
http://www.matthewjockers.net/macroanalysisbook/.

Library of Congress Cataloging-in-Publication Data
Jockers, Matthew Lee, 1966–
Macroanalysis : digital methods and literary
history / Matthew L. Jockers.
pages cm. — (Topics in the digital humanities)
Includes bibliographical references and index.
ISBN 978-0-252-03752-8 (hardcover) —
ISBN 978-0-252-07907-8 (pbk.) —
ISBN 978-0-252-09476-7 (e-book)
1. Literature—Research—Methodology.
2. Literature—Research—Data processing.
I. Title.
PN73.J63   2013
807'.2—dc23   2012032491

For my father,

Maestro Artigiano

CONTENTS

PART III. PROSPECTS

ACKNOWLEDGMENTS

Without initial support from John Bender, Lois Brooks, Mike Keller, Makoto Tsuchitani, and Ramón Saldívar, this work would not have been started. Without ongoing support from the Stanford University Department of English and the Stanford University Library, this work would not have continued. For years Glen Worthey has been my text *pusher*, my sounding board, my trusted digital humanities colleague, and my friend. His contributions to the completion of this project are innumerable. From Franco Moretti I have learned and been given much. Our partnership over the past seven years has been the most rewarding collaboration of my career. A special thank-you goes to Susan Schreibman, who convinced me to put these ideas into a book and then read drafts and offered kind and honest feedback. I thank Alan Liu for being such a generous and thoughtful reader of an early draft of the first few chapters; we should all be such gracious scholars. Stéfan Sinclair provided a careful and expert review of the entire manuscript, and I could not have asked for a better reader of the work. For chapter 8, David Mimno was essential; he indulged my layman's questions about latent Dirichlet allocation with kindness and good humor. For chapter 9, Elijah Meeks was similarly tolerant and gave his time, energy, and expertise to help me understand and leverage the power of Gephi. For patient advice with R in particular and statistics more generally, I acknowledge indirect contributions from Vijoy Abraham, Claudia Engel, Ken Romeo, and Daniela Witten. For their direct and essential contributions to the final manuscript, I thank my copy editor, Annette Wenda, along with the top-notch University of Illinois Press team, especially Bill Regier and Tad Ringo, who fostered this project through to completion. A special and personal thank-you to my wife, Angela, who has been a patient reader, thoughtful editor, and tolerant friend for more than twenty years.

Importantly, enthusiastically, and with deep appreciation, I acknowledge my debt to the students who enrolled in my first course in "macroanalysis" at Stanford. I doubt that a future group of students could ever capture the enthusiasm and excitement of that year. Their energy and earnestness were the catalyst behind the founding of the Stanford Literary Lab, and they have been in my mind most often in the writing of this book: Richard Alvarez, Cameron Blevins, Ryan Heuser, Nadeen Kharputly, Rachel Kraus, Alison Law, Long Le-Khac, Rhiannon Lewis, Madeline Paymer, Moritz Sudhof, Amir Tevel, Ellen Truxaw, Kathryn VanArendonk, and Connie Zhu, you are all, quite simply, the best a teacher could hope for.

PART I   FOUNDATION

1 REVOLUTION

The digital revolution is far more significant
than the invention of writing or even of printing.
—Douglas Carl Engelbart

An article in the June 23, 2008, issue of *Wired* declared in its headline "Data
Deluge Makes the Scientific Method Obsolete" (Anderson 2008). By 2008 computers, with their capacity for number crunching and processing large-scale data
sets, had revolutionized the way that scientific research gets done, so much so
that the same article declared an end to theorizing in science. With so much data,
we could just run the numbers and reach a conclusion. Now slowly and surely,
the same elements that have had such an impact on the sciences are revolution-
izing the way that research in the humanities gets done. This emerging field we
have come to call "digital humanities"—which was for a good many decades
not emerging at all but known as "humanities computing"—has a rich history
dating back at least to Father Roberto Busa's concordance work in the 1940s,
if not before.* Only recently, however, has this "discipline," or "community of
practice," or "field of study/theory/methodology," and so on, entered into the
mainstream discourse of the humanities, and it is even more recently that those
who "practice" digital humanities (DH) have begun to grapple with the challenges of big data.† Technology has certainly changed some things about the
way literary scholars go about their work, but until recently change has been

---

* Roberto Busa, a Jesuit priest and scholar, is considered by many to be the founding
father of humanities computing. He is the author of the *Index Thomisticus,* a lemmatized
index of the works of Thomas Aquinas.

† Some have already begun thinking big. In 2008 I served on the inaugural panel reviewing applications for the jointly sponsored National Endowment for the Humanities
and National Science Foundation "Digging into Data" grants. The expressed goals of the
grant are to promote the development and deployment of innovative research techniques
in large-scale data analysis; to foster interdisciplinary collaboration among scholars in

mostly at the level of simple, even anecdotal, search. The humanities computing/ digital humanities revolution has now begun, and big data have been a major catalyst. The questions we may now ask were previously inconceivable, and to answer these questions requires a new methodology, a new way of thinking about our object of study.

For whatever reasons, be they practical or theoretical, humanists have tended to resist or avoid computational approaches to the study of literature.* And who could blame them? Until recently, the amount of knowledge that might be gained from a computer-based analysis of a text was generally overwhelmed by the dizzying amount of work involved in preparing (digitizing) and then processing that digital text. Even as digital texts became more readily available, the computational methods for analyzing them remained quite primitive. Word-frequency lists, concordances, and keyword-in-context (KWIC) lists are useful for certain types of analysis, but these staples of the digital humanist's diet hardly satiate the appetite for more. These tools only scratch the surface in terms of the infinite ways we might read, access, and make meaning of text. Revolutions take time; this one is only just beginning, and it is the existence of digital libraries, of large electronic text collections, that is fomenting the revolution. This was a moment that Rosanne Potter predicted back in the digital dark ages of 1988. In an article titled "Literary Criticism and Literary Computing," Potter wrote that "until everything has been encoded, or until encoding is a trivial part of the work, the everyday critic will probably not consider computer treatments of texts" (93). Though not "everything" has been digitized, we have reached a tipping point, an event horizon where enough text and literature have been encoded to both allow and, indeed, force us to ask an entirely new set of questions about literature and the literary record.

———

the humanities, social sciences, computer sciences, information sciences, and other fields around questions of text and data analysis; to promote international collaboration; and to work with data repositories that hold large digital collections to ensure efficient access to these materials for research. See http://www.diggingintodata.org/.

* I suspect that at least a few humanists have been turned off by one or more of the very public failures of computing in the humanities: for example, the Donald Foster Shakespeare kerfuffle.

2 EVIDENCE

Scientists scoff at each other's theories but agree
in basing them on the assumption that evidence,
properly observed and measured, is true.

—Felipe Fernández-Armesto

While still graduate students in the early 1990s, my wife and I invited some friends to share Thanksgiving dinner. One of the friends was, like my wife and me, a graduate student in English. The other, however, was an outsider, a graduate student from geology. The conversation that night ranged over a wine-fueled spectrum of topics, but as three of the four of us were English majors, things eventually came around to literature. There was controversy when we came to discuss the "critical enterprise" and what it means to engage in literary research. The very term *research* was discussed and debated, with the lone scientist in the group suggesting, asserting, that the "methodology" employed by literary scholars was a rather subjective and highly anecdotal one, one that produced little in terms of "verifiable results" if much in the way of unsupportable speculation.

I recall rising to this challenge, asserting that the literary methodology was in essence no different from the scientific one: I argued that scholars of literature (at least scholars of the idealistic kind that I then saw myself becoming), like their counterparts in the sciences, should and do seek to uncover evidence and discover meaning, perhaps even truth. I dug deeper, arguing that literary scholars employ the same methods of investigation as scientists: we form a hypothesis about a literary work and then engage in a process of gathering evidence to test that hypothesis.

After so many years it is only a slightly embarrassing story. Although I am no longer convinced that the methods employed in literary studies are exactly the same as those employed in the sciences, I remain convinced that there are a good many methods worth sharing and that the similarities of methods exist in concrete ways, not simply as analogous practices.

The goal of science, we hope, is to develop the best possible explanation for some phenomenon. This is done via a careful and exhaustive gathering of evidence. We understand that the conclusions drawn are only as good as the evidence gathered, and we hope that the gathering of evidence is done both ethically and completely. If and when new evidence is discovered, prior conclusions may need to be revised or abandoned—such was the case with the Ptolemaic model of a geocentric universe. Science is flexible in this matter of new evidence and is open to the possibility that new methods of investigation will unearth new, and sometimes contradictory, evidence.

Literary studies should strive for a similar goal, even if we persist in a belief that literary interpretation is a matter of opinion. Frankly, some opinions are better than others: better informed, better derived, or just simply better for being more reasonable, more believable. Science has sought to derive conclusions based on evidence, and in the ideal, science is open to new methodologies. Moreover, to the extent possible, science attempts to be exhaustive in the gathering of the evidence and must therefore welcome new modes of exploration, discovery, and analysis. The same might be said of literary scholars, excepting, of course, that the methods employed for the evidence gathering, for the discovery, are rather different. Literary criticism relies heavily on associations as evidence. Even though the notions of evidence are different, it is reasonable to insist that some associations are better than others.

The study of literature relies upon careful observation, the sustained, concentrated reading of text. This, our primary methodology, is "close reading." Science has a methodological advantage in the use of experimentation. Experimentation offers a method through which competing observations and conclusions may be tested and ruled out. With a few exceptions, there is no obvious corollary to scientific experimentation in literary studies. The conclusions we reach as literary scholars are rarely "testable" in the way that scientific conclusions are testable. And the conclusions we reach as literary scholars are rarely "repeatable" in the way that scientific experiments are repeatable. We are highly invested in interpretations, and it is very difficult to "rule out" an interpretation. That said, as a way of enriching a reader's experience of a given text, close reading is obviously fruitful; a scholar's interpretation of a text may help another reader to "see" or observe in the text elements that might have otherwise remained latent. Even a layman's interpretations may lead another reader to a more profound, more pleasurable understanding of a text. It would be wasteful and futile to debate the value of interpretation, but interpretation is fueled by observation, and as a method of evidence gathering, observation—both in the sciences and in the humanities—is flawed. Despite all their efforts to repress them, researchers will have irrepressible biases. Even scientists will "interpret" their evidence through a lens of subjectivity. Observation is flawed in the same way that generalization from the specific is flawed: the generalization may be good, it may even explain a total population, but the selection of the sample is always something less than perfect, and so the observed results are likewise imperfect. In the sciences, a great deal of time and energy goes into the proper construction of "representative samples," but even with good sampling techniques and careful statistical calculations, there remain problems: outliers, exceptions, and so on. Perfection in sampling is just not possible.

Today, however, the ubiquity of data, so-called big data, is changing the sampling game. Indeed, big data are fundamentally altering the way that much science and social science get done. The existence of huge data sets means that many areas of research are no longer dependent upon controlled, artificial experiments or upon observations derived from data sampling. Instead of conducting controlled experiments on samples and then extrapolating from the specific to the general or from the close to the distant, these massive data sets are allowing for investigations at a scale that reaches or approaches a point of being comprehensive. The once inaccessible "population" has become accessible and is fast replacing the random and representative sample.

In literary studies, we have the equivalent of this big data in the form of big libraries. These massive digital-text collections—from vendors such as Chadwyck-Healey, from grassroots organizations such as Project Gutenberg, from nonprofit groups such as the Internet Archive and HathiTrust, and from the elephants in Mountain View, California, and Seattle, Washington*—are changing how literary studies get done. Science has welcomed big data and scaled its methods accordingly. With a huge amount of digital-textual data, we must do the same. Close reading is not only impractical as a means of evidence gathering in the digital library, but big data render it totally inappropriate as a method of studying literary history. This is not to imply that scholars have been wholly unsuccessful in employing close reading to the study of literary history. A careful reader, such as Ian Watt, argues that elements leading to the rise of the novel could be detected and teased out of the writings of Defoe, Richardson, and Fielding. Watt's study is magnificent; his many observations are reasonable, and there is soundness about them.† He appears correct on a number of points, but he has observed only a small space. What are we to do with the other three to five thousand works of

---

* That is, Google.com and Amazon.com.

† A similar statement could be made of Erich Auerbach's *Mimesis*. It is a magnificent bit of close reading. At the same time, Auerbach was acutely aware of the limitations of his methodology. In the epilogue to *Mimesis,* he notes the difficulties of dealing with "texts ranging over three thousand years" and how the limitations of his library in Istanbul made it "probable that [he] overlooked things which [he] ought to have considered." Interestingly, however, he says at the same time that "it is quite possible that the book owes its existence to just this lack of a rich . . . library." If it had been possible to access the greater archive, he "might never have reached the point of writing" (1953).

fiction published in the eighteenth century? What of the works that Watt did not observe and account for with his methodology, and how are we to now account for the works not penned by Defoe, by Richardson, or by Fielding? Might other novelists tell a different story? Can we, in good conscience, even believe that Defoe, Richardson, and Fielding are representative writers? Watt's sampling was not random; it was quite the opposite. But perhaps we only need to believe that these three (male) authors are representative of the trend toward "realism" that flourished in the nineteenth century. Accepting this premise makes Watt's magnificent synthesis into no more than a self-fulfilling project, a project in which the books are stacked in advance. No matter what we think of the sample, we must question whether in fact realism really did flourish. Even before that, we really ought to define what it means "to flourish" in the first place. Flourishing certainly seems to be the sort of thing that could, and ought, to be measured. Watt had no such yardstick against which to make a measurement. He had only a few hundred texts that he had read. Today, things are different. The larger literary record can no longer be ignored: it is here, and much of it is now accessible.

At the time of my Thanksgiving dinner back in the 1990s, gathering literary evidence meant reading books, noting "things" (a phallic symbol here, a biblical reference there, a stylistic flourish, an allusion, and so on) and then interpreting: making sense and arguments out of those observations.* Today, in the age of digital libraries and large-scale book-digitization projects, the nature of the "evidence" available to us has changed, radically. Which is not to say that we should no longer read books looking for, or noting, random "things," but rather to emphasize that massive digital corpora offer us unprecedented access to the literary record and invite, even demand, a new type of evidence gathering and meaning making. The literary scholar of the twenty-first century can no longer be content with anecdotal evidence, with random "things" gathered from a few, even "representative," texts.† We must strive to understand these things we find interesting in the context of everything else, including a mass of possibly "uninteresting" texts.

---

* Yes, a simplification, but close enough to serve as a heady foil in this introductory polemic. Along similar lines, Susan Hockey writes of the "somewhat serendipitous noting of interesting features" (2000, 66).

† When writing of "anecdotal" here, I am not thinking of the use made of anecdote in the new historical tradition that we find expressed in, for example, Greenblatt's "cultural poetics." Rather, I use the word in the sense of "anecdotal evidence": that is, evidence that is atypical, informally gathered, speculative, or purely interpretive, which is to say not empirical. On this point, the type of literary data I am exploring allows me to adopt a fundamentally empirical position. Having said that, there is a place for anecdotal evidence in literary study, and I do not intend here a critique of anecdotalism per se, but rather to simply make a distinction and separation between two types of evidence.

"Strictly speaking," wrote Russian formalist Juri Tynjanov in 1927, "one cannot study literary phenomena outside of their interrelationships" (1978, 71). Unfortunately for Tynjanov, the multitude of interrelationships far exceeded his ability to study them, especially with close and careful reading as his primary tools. Like it or not, today's literary-historical scholar can no longer risk being *just* a close reader: the sheer quantity of available data makes the traditional practice of close reading untenable as an exhaustive or definitive method of evidence gathering. Something important will inevitably be missed. The same argument, however, may be leveled against the macroscale; from thirty thousand feet, something important will inevitably be missed. The two scales of analysis, therefore, should and need to coexist. For this to happen, the literary researcher must embrace new, and largely computational, ways of gathering evidence. Just as we would not expect an economist to generate sound theories about the economy by studying a few consumers or a few businesses, literary scholars cannot be content to read literary history from a canon of a few authors or even several hundred texts. Today's student of literature must be adept at reading and gathering evidence from individual texts and equally adept at accessing and mining digital-text repositories. And *mining* here really is the key word in context. Literary scholars must learn to go beyond search. In search we go after a single nugget, carefully panning in the river of prose. At the risk of giving offense to the environmentalists, what is needed now is the literary equivalent of open-pit mining or hydraulicking. We are proficient at electronic search and comfortable searching digital collections for some piece of evidence to support an argument, but the sheer amount of data now available makes search ineffectual as a means of evidence gathering. Close reading, digital searching, will continue to reveal nuggets, while the deeper veins lie buried beneath the mass of gravel layered above. What are required are methods for aggregating and making sense out of both the nuggets and the tailings. Take the case of a scholar conducting research for a hypothetical paper about Melville's metaphysics. A query for *whale* in the Google Books library produces 33,338 hits—way too broad. Narrowing the search by entering *whale* and *god* results in a more manageable 3,715 hits, including such promising titles as *American Literature in Context* and *Melville's Quarrel with God*. Even if the scholar could further narrow the list to 1,000 books, this is still far too many to read in any practical way. Unless one knows what to look for—say, a quotation only partially remembered—searching for research purposes, as a means of evidence gathering, is not terribly practical.*
More interesting, more exciting, than panning for nuggets in digital archives

---

* In revising this section before publication, I went back to Google Books and discovered that the number of hits for this particular search had grown significantly since I first tested. No doubt readers will find even higher numbers today.

is the ability to go beyond the pan and exploit the trommel of computation to process, condense, deform, and analyze the deeper strata from which these nuggets were born, to unearth, for the first time, what these corpora really contain. In practical terms, this means that we must evolve to embrace new approaches and new methodologies designed for accessing and leveraging the electronic texts that make up the twenty-first-century digital library.

This is a book about evidence gathering. It is a book about how new methods of analysis allow us to extract new forms of evidence from the digital library. Nevertheless, this is also a book about literature. What matter the methods, so long as the results of employing them lead us to a deeper knowledge of our subject? A methodology is important and useful if it opens new doorways of discovery, if it teaches us something new about literary history, about individual creativity, and about the seeming inevitability of influence.

3 TRADITION

Talents imitate, geniuses steal.
—[Oscar Wilde?]

As noted previously, there is a significant tradition of researchers employing computational approaches to the study of literature and an even longer tradition of scholars employing quantitative and statistical methods for the analysis of text. The specifically computational tradition dates back to the work of Father Roberto Busa, and since that time momentum has been building, exponentially, so that now, somewhat suddenly, the trend line has rocketed upward and the "digital humanities" have burst upon the scene and become a ubiquitous topic of discussion in humanities programs across the globe.* Notwithstanding the fact that there is no general agreement as to what exactly the term *digital humanities* defines, the sudden popularity of this thing called digital humanities has occurred with such rapidity that even we who consider ourselves natives of the tribe have been taken by surprise. Some have suggested that the reason stock in digital humanities is skyrocketing is because literary studies are in a general state of crisis and that we are yearning for a new theoretical construct that would ground our inquiries in science (see, for example, Gottschall 2008). This may be the case, for some, but I am not a member of that club. As someone who has studied diasporas, I understand that there can be pushes and pulls to any migration. For the Irish, British oppression made for an imposing stick and the promise of opportunity in America an enticing carrot. Here, however, the migration to digital humanities appears to be mostly about opportunity. In fact, the sudden motivation for scholars to engage in digital humanities is more than likely a direct by-product of having such a wealth of digital material with which to engage. With apologies to the indigenous, I must acknowledge here

---

* The tradition may stretch even further if we broaden our definition of *computation* to include substrates beyond silicon.

that the streets of this "new" world are paved with gold and the colonizers have arrived. A large part of this change in scholarly thinking about the digital has been brought about because of the very simple fact that digital objects, digital data stores, and digital libraries in particular have become both large and easily accessible. We have built it, and they are coming. Despite the success of this "thing called digital humanities," as William Deresiewicz derided it in 2008, there remains no general agreement or even general understanding of what the term means or describes. Some, including Matthew Kirschenbaum (2010), think that this ambiguity is a good thing. I am not as certain. Do video-game analysis and stylometry really make good bedfellows? Probably not; these are entirely different threads.* Understanding how we got to this point of free-loving digital humanities is useful not simply as a matter of disciplinary history but as a way of contextualizing and understanding the methods and results presented in this book. So, a few words are in order about the traditions informing my macroanalytic approach to digital literary studies.

· · ·

In 2012 we stand upon the shoulders of giants, and the view from the top is breathtaking. The skies were not always this clear. Susan Hockey summarized the period of the 1980s as one in which "we were still at a stage where academic respectability for computer-based work in the humanities was questionable" (2004, 10). Mark Olsen noted in 1993 that despite advances in text processing, "computerized textual research has not had a significant influence on research in the humanistic disciplines" (309). A decade later, Thomas Rommel argued that "the majority of literary critics still seem reluctant to embrace electronic media as a means of scholarly analysis . . . [and] literary computing has, right from the very beginning, never really made an impact on mainstream scholarship" (2004, 92). Stephen Ramsay wrote in 2007, "The digital revolution, for all its wonders, has not penetrated the core activity of literary studies, which, despite numerous revolutions of a more epistemological nature, remains mostly concerned with the interpretive analysis of written cultural artifacts. Texts are browsed, searched, and disseminated by all but the most hardened Luddites in literary study, but seldom are they transformed algorithmically as a means of gaining entry to the deliberately and self-consciously subjective act of critical interpretation" (478).

---

* Just so it is clear, I am a big fan of the "big tent," or the "big umbrella," if you will. In 2011 Glen Worthey and I cohosted the annual Digital Humanities Conference at Stanford, where our conference theme was "Big Tent Digital Humanities." In the sprit of the Summer of Love, we donned tie-dyed shirts and let a thousand DH flowers bloom. We love our DH colleagues one and all. This book, however, stands at one side of the tent. We do different things in DH; we are vast.

Others from outside the scholarly community of computing humanists, writers such as Sven Birkerts (1994) and Nicholson Baker (2001), have warned of the dangers inherent in the digitization of books, and Emory English professor Mark Bauerlein has offered a sustained, if unspecific, critique of the digital age in general (2008). Even as recently as 2008, the ever-adversarial William Deresiewicz wrote in the *Nation* about the digital humanities, poking fun at something he imagined to be just another fad of scholarship.* But things change.

Despite some early concerns and several contemporary detractors, today— some few years after the most recent lamentations—the scholarly presses and the mainstream media are buzzing with news of this thing called "digital humanities."† Humanities computing, or, more popularly, "digital humanities," is alive and well. The field is healthy: participation in the primary professional organization, the Alliance of Digital Humanities Organizations (ADHO), is vibrant, and attendance at the annual Digital Humanities Conference is at an all-time high.‡ So large have we grown, in fact, that the number of rejected papers now far exceeds the number accepted, and many of the panels and papers that are not rejected draw standing-room crowds and lively discussion. Meanwhile, new degree programs specifically geared toward digital humanities are now offered at universities across the globe.§ Academic jobs for candidates with expertise in the intersection between the humanities and technology are becoming more and

* Wendall Piez offers an interesting response to Deresiewicz's comment in "Something Called 'Digital Humanities'" (2008).

† Matthew Kirschenbaum provides a succinct, six-page overview of the field in his *ADE Bulletin* article titled "What Is Digital Humanities and What's It Doing in English Departments?" (2010). Other examples include Fischman 2008a, 2008b; Goodall 2008; Howard 2008a, 2008b, 2008c; Pannapacker 2011; Parry 2010; Shea 2008; and Young 2009.

‡ The Alliance of Digital Humanities Organizations is a consortium including the Association for Computing and the Humanities, the Association of Literary and Linguistic Computing, the Society for Digital Humanities, and CenterNet.

§ In terms of numbers of institutions per capita and dollars per capita, Canada is the obvious front runner here, but several universities in the UK, Ireland, and the United States have recently begun programs or "tracks" in digital humanities. Stanford began offering an undergraduate emphasis in "digital humanities" through its Interdisciplinary Studies in the Humanities Program back in 2006. In October 2006, Kings College of London announced a Ph.D. in digital humanities. In 2010 the National University of Ireland, Maynooth, began offering a master's of arts in digital humanities (http://www .learndigitalhumanities.ie/), and University College London began offering a master of arts and science in digital humanities (http://www.ucl.ac.uk/dh-blog/2010/07/30/ announcing-the-new-mamsc-in-digital-humanities-at-ucl/). In 2011 Trinity College Dublin began a master of philosophy program in digital humanities under the direction of Susan Schreibman.

more common, and a younger constituent of digital natives is quickly overtaking the aging elders of the tribe.* By one measure, the number of young scholars and graduate students attending the annual digital humanities conference in 2009 was three times the number of those attending one year earlier.† To my 2006 query to the members of the Humanist List about the health of the field, I received a number of encouraging replies that included remarks about the recent "groundswell of research interest" in digitally oriented projects, the development of new "centers" for computing in the humanities, and institutional support for the hiring of computing humanists.‡ Especially impressive has been the news from Canada. Almost all of the "G 10" (that is, the top thirteen research institutions of Canada) have institutionalized digital humanities activities in the form of degrees such as Alberta's master's in digital humanities, programs such as McMaster's in digital media, centers such as the University of Victoria's Humanities Computing Centre, or through institutes such as Victoria's Digital Humanities Summer Institute. Noteworthy too is that the prestigious Canada Research Chair has been appointed to a number of computing humanists.§ Not the least important, the program for the 2011 Modern Language Association conference in Seattle included, by one scholar's count, at least fifty-seven panels in the "digital humanities," up from forty-four the previous year when the panel session titled "The History and Future of the Digital Humanities" had standing-room crowds (Pannapacker 2011).¶ All signs indicate that the digital

* A search, conducted in October 2006, of jobs listed in the *Chronicle of Higher Education* including both the words *digital* and *humanities* resulted in thirty-four hits. Recent searches have contained even more, including opportunities in senior-level posts such as that advertised in July 2010 for a director of Texas A&M's new Digital Humanities Institute. On September 25, 2011, Desmond Schmidt posted the following summary of digital humanities jobs on the Humanist List: "There have been a lot of advertisements for jobs lately on Humanist. So I used the Humanist archive to do a survey of the last 10 years. I counted jobs that had both a digital and a humanities component, were full time, lasted at least 12 months and were at PostDoc level or higher. 2002: 11, 2003: 6, 2004: 15, 2005: 15, 2006: 18, 2007: 24, 2008: 27 (incomplete - 1/2 year), 2009: 36, 2010: 58. 2011: 65 so far."

† In 2009 I was chair of the ADHO Bursary Awards committee. The prize is designed to encourage new scholars in the discipline. From 2008 to 2009, the number of candidates for the Bursary Award jumped from seven to more than thirty.

‡ Humanist, now in its twenty-second year of operation, is, by general consensus, the Listserv of record for all matters related to computing in the humanities.

§ See http://tapor.ualberta.ca/taporwiki/index.php/Canada_Research_Chairs_and _Award_Winners.

¶ See Mark Sample, http://www.samplereality.com/2011/10/04/digital-humanities -sessions-at-the-2012-mla-conference-in-seattle/ and http://www.samplereality .com/2010/11/09/digital-humanities-sessions-at-the-2011-mla/.

humanities have arrived, even while the fields of study sheltering beneath the umbrella remain a somewhat ambiguous and amorphous amalgamation of literary formalists, new media theorists, tool builders, coders, and linguists.

Computational text analysis—by all accounts the foundation of digital humanities and its deepest root—has come a long way since 1949, when Father Roberto Busa began creation of his word index. These days, humanists routinely create word indexes and frequency lists using readily available software. With the spread of broadband and the accessibility of the Internet, many tools that were once platform dependent and command line in nature have been "reinvented" for the web so that scholars may now do small-scale text processing and analysis on remote web servers using any number of web-based applications. Keyword-in-context lists can be quickly generated using TactWeb.* Stéfan Sinclair's HyperPo and Voyant offer self-serve text-analysis tools for traditional concording and co-occurrence alongside more experimental widgets for the processing and deforming of textual data.† There is a growing number of tools specifically geared toward the "visualization" of literary materials.‡ A particularly well-conceived, low-entry project is the "Text Analysis Portal" (TAPoR), which has set itself up as a one-stop shop for basic text analysis. This project, which began life with a six-million-dollar (CAD) grant from the Canadian Foundation for Innovation, is distributed across six universities and provides a centralized and, to some extent, standardized way of accessing a variety of text-analysis applications. TAPoR serves as a model of collaboration and offers a foundational, even seminal, approach to future humanities computing work. Indeed, some in the United States are now attempting to go beyond TAPoR and develop what Chris Mackey, formerly of the Mellon Foundation, once referred to as the "mother of all text-analysis applications."§ These projects, whose names include "Bamboo" and others with such funky acronyms as MONK, SEASR, and DARIAH, are all seeking ways to make leveraging computation as easy for the average literary scholar as finding biblical references in a canonical novel.¶

---

* See http://tactweb.humanities.mcmaster.ca/tactweb/doc/tact.htm.

† See http://tapor1.mcmaster.ca/~sgs/HyperPo/ and http://voyant-tools.org/.

‡ See, for example, Bradford Paley's TextArc application (http://www.textarc.org/) or the word clouds available through Wordle or the Many Eyes project of IBM.

§ The comment was made during a presentation at the Stanford Humanities Center. The project that eventually emerged from these and other discussions is Project Bamboo: http://www.projectbamboo.org.

¶ MONK stands for "Metadata Offers New Knowledge" (http://www.monkproject .org/), SEASR for Software Environment for the Advancement of Scholarly Research (http://seasr.org/), and DARIAH for Digital Research Infrastructure for the Arts and Humanities (http://www.dariah.eu/). See also Project Bamboo at http://www .projectbamboo.org.

Computing humanists have made important contributions to humanities scholarship: thanks to them, we have impressive digital archives and critical editions such as the exemplary Women Writers Project of Brown University and Kevin Kerinan's impressive Electronic Beowulf.* Fellow travelers from linguistics, machine learning, natural language processing, and computer science have developed robust text-analysis programs that can be employed to automatically identify parts of speech, named entities (people, places, and organizations), prominent themes, sentiment, and even poetic meter.† These tools have in turn been deployed for studies in authorship attribution, textual dating, and stylistic analysis.

There are any number of other useful products that have evolved out of collaborations among humanists, linguists, and technologists: the Google search engine performs a type of text analysis when searching for keywords and collocates; using calculations based on vocabulary, sentence length, and syllables, Microsoft Word attempts to determine the grade level of a piece of writing.‡ The XML (extensible markup language) standard that plays such a critical role in data interchange today was heavily influenced by the early work of the Text Encoding Initiative and in particular founding TEI editor Michael Sperberg-McQueen. These have been important and useful contributions, to be sure, and the recent Blackwell publications *A Companion to Digital Humanities* (Schreibman, Siemens, and Unsworth 2004) and *A Companion to Digital Literary Studies* (Siemens and Schreibman 2007) are a testament to the various ways in which technology has established itself in the humanities.

Despite all of this achievement and the overwhelming sense of enthusiasm and collegiality that permeates the DH community, there is much more work to be done. We have in fact only begun to scratch the surface of what is possible. Though the term *digital humanities* has become as omnipresent on our campuses as *multiculturalism* was several years ago, the adoption of "digital" tools and methodologies has been limited, even among those who would self-identify as "digital humanists." To be sure, literary scholars have taken advantage of digitized textual material, but this use has been primarily in the arena of search, retrieval, and access. We have not yet seen the scaling of our scholarly questions in accordance with the massive scaling of digital content that is now

---

* http://www.wwp.brown.edu/ and http://ebeowulf.uky.edu/.

† Examples include the Stanford Natural Language Processing Group's Part of Speech Tagger and Named Entity Recognizer, the University of Massachusetts's Machine Learning for Language Toolkit (MALLET), and many others.

‡ For more on this, just open Microsoft Word's "Help" and search for "Readability Scores." MS Word uses both the Flesch Reading Ease score and the Flesch-Kinkaid Grade Level score.

held in twenty-first-century digital libraries. In this Google Books era, we can take for granted that some digital version of the text we need will be available somewhere online, but we have not yet fully articulated or explored the ways in which these massive corpora offer new avenues for research and new ways of thinking about our literary subject.*

To some extent, our thus-far limited use of digital content is a result of a disciplinary habit of thinking small: the traditionally minded scholar recognizes value in digital texts because they are individually searchable, but this same scholar, as a result of a traditional training, often fails to recognize the potentials for analysis that an electronic processing of texts enables. For others, the limitation is more directly technical and relates to the type and availability of software tools that might be deployed in analysis. The range of what existing computer-based tools have provided for the literary scholar is limited, and these tools have tended to conform to a disciplinary habit of closely studying individual texts: that is, close reading. Such tools are designed with the analysis of single texts in mind and do not offer the typical literary scholar much beyond advanced searching capabilities. Arguably, the existing tools have been a determiner in shaping perceptions about what can and cannot be done with digital texts.† The existing tools have kept our focus firmly on the close reading of individual texts and have undoubtedly prevented some scholars from wandering into the realms of what Franco Moretti has termed "distant reading" (2000). Combine a traditional literary training focused on close reading with the most common text-analysis tools focused on the same thing, and what you end up with is enhanced search—electronic finding aids that replicate and expedite human effort but bring little to the table in terms of new knowledge. I do not intend to demean the use of text-analysis tools at the scale of the single text or at the scale of several texts; quite the contrary, there is an incredibly large body of quantitative work in authorship attribution, gender identification, and what is

---

* My comments here may seem idealistic given the realities of copyright law and contemporary literature in particular. That digital versions of these recent works exist seems a point we can take for granted; that they are or will be readily accessible is a more complicated problem about which I have more to say in chapter 10.

† Duke University historian of science Tim Lenoir has made a similar point in arguing that quarks would not exist were it not for the particle accelerators that were built to discover or produce them. Lenoir has made this comment on multiple occasions, primarily in lectures on pragmatic realism and social construction. He has written about this extensively in his book *Instituting Science* (1997), particularly the chapter on Haber-Bosch, in which he discusses this issue at length. He derived this line of thinking in part from Ian Hacking's argument in *Representing and Intervening*, in which Hacking argues that electrons are real when you can spray them (1983, 23).

more generally referred to as "stylometry" that informs my own work. And even in the less statistically driven realms of computational text analysis, there are tools for visualizing and exploring individual texts that serve as rich platforms for "play," as Stéfan Sinclair has termed it (2003), or what might more formally be termed "discovery" and "exploration." Steven Ramsay's "Algorithmic Criticism" (2007) provides a strong statement regarding the value of text-analysis tools for text "deformation." Such deformations may lead to new and different interpretations and interpretive strategies.*

Our colleagues in linguistics have long understood the value of working with large corpora and have compiled such valuable resources as the British National Corpus and the Standard Corpus of Everyday English Usage. Linguists employ these resources in order to better understand how language is used, is changing, is evolving. The tools employed for this work are not, generally speaking, web-based widgets or text-analysis portals such as the TAPoR project. Instead, our colleagues in linguistics have learned to be comfortable on the command line using programming languages. They have learned to develop applications that run on servers, and they have developed a willingness to wait for their results. Literary scholars, on the other hand, have generally been content to rely upon the web for access to digital material. Even in the text-analysis community, there is a decided bias in favor of developing web-based tools.† Unfortunately, the web is not yet a great platform upon which to build or deliver tools for doing text analysis "at scale." Quick queries of indexed content, yes, but not corpus ingestion or complex analysis.‡

Given the training literary scholars receive, their typical skill set, and the challenges associated with large-scale digitalization and computational analysis, it is easy to understand why literary scholars have not asked and probed with computers the same sorts of questions about "literary language" that linguists

---

* Ramsay's original article has now been extended into a book-length study. See Ramsay 2011.

† Stéfan Sinclair of McGill University is an accomplished text-analysis tool builder, and his recent offering, Voyant, is the best example I have seen of an online tool that can handle a large amount of text. See http://voyant-tools.org/. Even this exceptional tool is still only capable of fairly basic levels of analysis.

‡ Cloud computing and high-performance computing are certainly beginning to change things, and projects such as SEASR may someday provide the web interface to high-performance text analysis. At least in the near term, the success of web-based macroanalysis will depend in large part upon the users of such tools. They will need to abandon the idea that clicking a link returns an immediate result. The web may become a portal into a complex text-analysis platform, but the web is not likely to evolve as a place for instant access to complex data.

have asked about language in general. On the one hand, literary scholars have not had access, until recently, to large amounts of digital literary content, and, on the other, there is a long-standing disciplinary habit of thinking about literature in a limited way: in terms of "close readings." Close reading is a methodological approach that can be applied to individual texts or even small subsets of texts but not, for example, to all British fiction of the nineteenth century. A "close reading" of nineteenth-century British fiction would, in fact, be implausible. Consider, for example, the very real limitations of human reading: Franco Moretti has estimated that of the twenty to thirty thousand English novels published in Britain in the nineteenth century, approximately six thousand are now extant. Assuming that a dedicated scholar could find these novels and read one per day, it would take sixteen and a half years of close reading to get through them all. As a rule, literary scholars are great synthesizers of information, but synthesis here is inconceivable.* A computer-based analysis or synthesis of these same materials is not so difficult to imagine. Though the computer cannot perfectly replicate human synthesis and intuition, it can take us a long way down this road and certainly quite a bit further along than what the human mind can process. It is exactly this kind of macroanalytic approach that is the future of computing in the humanities, and, according to some, the future of literary studies (see, for example, Gottschall 2008 and Martindale 1990).

I am not the first, however, to suggest that a bird's-eye view of literature might prove fruitful. On this point, Franco Moretti has been at the forefront, suggesting "distant reading" as an alternative to "close reading." In *Graphs, Maps, Trees,* Moretti writes of how a study of national bibliographies made him realize "what a minimal fraction of the literary field we all work on: a canon of two hundred novels, for instance, sounds very large for nineteenth-century Britain (and is much larger than the current one), but is still less than one per cent of the novels that were actually published: twenty thousand, thirty, more, no one really knows—and close reading won't help here, a novel a day every day of the year would take a century or so" (2005, 3–4). Moretti's "Graphs" chapter is particularly compelling; it provides a beginning point for the development

---

* In history and in historical economics, there is a recent tradition of thinking big. The Annales school of historiography developed by the French in the early twentieth century has had the goal of applying quantitative and social-scientific methods in order to study history of the "long-term," the *longue durée*. The approach views history in terms of "systems." Lynn Hunt's brief and useful overview of the history of the Annales paradigm argues that "in contrast to earlier forms of historical analysis [namely, exemplar and developmental approaches], the *Annales* school emphasized serial, functional, and structural approaches to understanding society as a total, inter-related organism" (1986, 211).

of a more formal literary time-series analysis methodology. Moretti examines the publication rates for novels (in several countries) over periods of years and decades. Focusing on the peaks and valleys in novel production, he moves from the quantitative facts to speculation and interpretation, posing, for example, that the rise and fall of various novelistic genres in the British corpus can be correlated to twenty-five- to thirty-year cycles or generations of readers. In Moretti's model, the tastes and preferences of one generation are inevitably replaced by those of the next. He suggests that there are connections between literary cycles and political ones, arguing, for example, that the French Revolution was a critical factor in the fall of the French novel. Although such an argument could certainly be made anecdotally, the accompanying data—and the graph showing the sharp decline in novel production in about 1798—leave little room for debate.

Nor am I original in considering the applications of technology to large textual collections. Already noted are the linguists, and there is, of course, an entire community of computer scientists (many of them at Google) who work in the field of text mining and information retrieval. Along with similar agencies in other nations, the National Security Agency is in this business as well: the NSA is reported to have been employing text-mining technologies since the Cold War, and the "classified" ECHELON surveillance system is purported to capture all manner of electronic information, from satellite communications to email correspondences. These captured materials are then analyzed, mined by machines, in order to sniff out threats to national security. The amount of information devoted to ECHELON online is somewhat staggering—a Google search for this supersecret program along with the keywords *text* and *mining* provides 375,000 sites of interest. This figure is trivial next to the Google results for a search for the keyword *Area 51* (154 million hits) but does demonstrate the point that text mining, and ECHELON for that matter, is nothing new. Similar to ECHELON is the technology developed by Palantir Technologies in Palo Alto, California. The company's website describes their software as being "a platform for information analysis . . . designed for environments where the fragments of data that . . . tell a larger story are spread across a vast set of starting material" (Palantir Technologies 2011). Translation: we build technologies for the macroanalysis of large, disparate corpora.

Not quite as spectacular as Palantir and the NSA are projects more specifically aimed at the application of text mining to the humanities. The NORA, MONK, and SEASR projects originally led by John Unsworth at the University of Illinois are three such projects. The expressed goal of the NORA project was to "produce software for discovering, visualizing, and exploring significant patterns across large collections of full-text humanities resources in existing digital libraries" (NORA 2006). Using software developed by the University of Illinois's

National Center for Supercomputing Applications and the "Data to Knowledge" applications of Michael Welge's Automated Learning Group, the NORA team successfully deployed a Java-based application for "sniffing" out preidentified "patterns" in large digital collections. An early version of the software allowed an end user to "tag" or "mark" certain works in a collection, and the system then used those works to build a model—what some biologists who work with DNA and gene expression call a "signal." This signal is then sought throughout the larger collection. The example offered on the NORA website involves marking "erotic" passages in the works of Emily Dickinson. Some 260 individual documents are presented, and the user "marks" or rates a small percentage of these for erotic content.* The human-marked documents constitute a training set, which is used by the software to "predict" which works in the collection are likely to contain erotic content as well. This is essentially an information-retrieval task. MONK and SEASR are more advanced implementations of the NORA technologies. SEASR provides the most deeply abstracted and robust imagining of the early NORA work. SEASR is both a back-end infrastructure and a semifriendly web interface that allows researchers to build text-analysis "flows" that get executed on a server.†

Outside of the humanities, computer scientists working in natural language processing, corpus linguistics, and computational linguistics have developed a wide range of tools that have direct application to work in literary studies. Using a technique called "topic modeling," a group led by David Newman at the University of California–Irvine (UCI) harvested the latent themes, or topics, contained in 330,000 stories published in the *New York Times*. The topic-modeling procedure they employed required no human preprocessing; it was "unsupervised" in its sifting through a corpus of documents and then identifying patterns of words that were frequently collocated.‡ The software categorizes the words in each document into mathematically correlated clusters, which are described as "topics." Not surprisingly, the UCI team first presented their research at the Intelligence and Security Informatics conference in San Diego (Newman, Smyth, and Steyvers 2006). More interesting (for scholars of literature) than the

---

* This process of human intervention is known in data and text mining as "supervised learning."

† From 2011 to 2012, I served as the project lead on "Phase Two" of the SEASR project. The work was generously funded by the Mellon Foundation.

‡ Andrew McCallum and his team at the University of Massachusetts have done exciting work developing a "Machine Learning for Language Toolkit," or "MALLET," which provides functionality for a variety of text-mining applications. The MALLET software includes David Mimno's topic-modeling code, which is used and described at length in chapter 8.

intelligence applications of topic modeling are the applications to humanities research. Historian Sharon Block, for example, teamed up with Newman and employed topic-modeling routines to explore the entire eighteenth-century run of the *Pennsylvania Gazette*. In her essay "Doing More with Digitization: An Introduction to Topic Modeling of Early American Sources" (2006), Block walks readers though a series of examples of how the technique can assist historians and reveal new avenues for research in the form of unanticipated patterns and trends.* Though not designed with literary scholarship in mind, the topic-modeling tools can be applied to literary texts at the level of the corpus or even at the level of the individual book or poem.†

Still another project working to apply the tools and techniques of text mining and corpus linguistics to literature is the WordHoard project at Northwestern University. Ironically, the WordHoard site describes its software as "an application for the close reading and scholarly analysis of deeply tagged texts" but then goes on to say that it "applies to highly canonical literary texts the insights and techniques of corpus linguistics, that is to say, the empirical and computer-assisted study of large bodies of written texts or transcribed speech" (Word-Hoard 2006). The descriptive prose that follows adds that the software allows for a deeply "microscopic" and philological inquiry of the text(s). Although it is true that WordHoard provides access to, or tools for, harvesting richly encoded texts, the results being gleaned from the texts are not so much the results of a close reading–like process as they are the results of a macroscopic text-mining process that aggregates a number of relatively small details into a more global perspective. As such, the process seems to have less in common with close-reading practices and more with Moretti's notion of distant reading. The devil is in the details and in how the details are investigated and aggregated in order to enable a larger perspective. Writing of "detailism" and digital texts, Julia Flanders discusses Randolph Starn's introduction to a special issue of

---

* Cameron Blevins provides another historical example. Blevins uses topic modeling to explore entries in Martha Ballard's eighteenth-century diary. See http://historying. org/2010/04/01/topic-modeling-martha-ballards-diary/.

† David Newman was the first guest speaker in the Beyond Search workshop that I ran at Stanford from 2006 to 2009. Prior to his arrival, I prepared a corpus of texts for Newman to process. Included in those data were the novels of Jane Austen. As part of his presentation, Newman showed how the topic of "sentiment" (composed of words denoting emotion) could be tracked throughout the Austen corpus. Looking at the graphs that he prepared, participants in the workshop could see how Austen employs moments of strong emotion throughout her texts. In some novels, we observed a regular fluctuation, while others showed a steady trend upward: as the novels progressed, the presence of strong emotions increased.

Representations. She notes the effort to connect "detail . . . with a larger historical view." She goes on to emphasize that detail is used "not as 'mere facts' cited as evidence . . . but as the contextually embedded 'trace, clue, sign, shard' that carries a specifiable, signifying linkage to some historical genealogy" to some larger system (2005, 43). WordHoard offers a way of aggregating these signs into a coherent argument. The website offers the word *love*—as it appears in the works of Chaucer, Spenser, and Shakespeare—as an example. Female characters, the data reveal, are "about 50% more likely to speak of love than men." This conclusion is derived not through a computer-based close reading of the texts, but rather via a quantitative zooming out and away from the texts, a zooming out that allows the user to simultaneously "see" all of the separate occurrences of the word throughout the corpus. The end result is that the WordHoard tool takes us quite far away from the actual occurrences of the words in the texts; our attention is drawn to an examination of the bigger picture, the macroview of *love* when used as a noun, of *love* when used as a verb, and in both cases of *love* as it is used by male or female speakers. This is not close reading; this is macroanalysis, and the strength of the approach is that it allows for both zooming in and zooming out.*

* A relatively recent entry into this realm of micro-macro-oriented text-analysis tools is Aditi Muralidharan's WordSeer (http://wordseer.berkeley.edu). Australian digital humanist Tim Sherratt offers another variety of similar tools via his "WraggeLabs Emporium" (http://wraggelabs.com/emporium).

4 MACROANALYSIS

The approach to the study of literature that I am calling "macroanalysis" is in some general ways akin to economics or, more specifically, to macroeconomics. Before the 1930s, before Keynes's *General Theory of Government, Interest, and Money* in 1936, there was no defined field of "macroeconomics." There was, however, neoclassical economics, or "microeconomics," which studies the economic behavior of individual consumers and individual businesses. As such, microeconomics can be seen as analogous to our study of individual texts via "close readings." Macroeconomics, however, is about the study of the entire economy. It tends toward enumeration and quantification and is in this sense similar to bibliographic studies, biographical studies, literary history, philology, and the enumerative, quantitative analysis of text that is the foundation of computing in the humanities. Thinking about macroanalysis in this context, one can see the obvious crossover with WordHoard. Although there is sustained interest in the micro level, individual occurrences of some feature or word, these individual occurrences (of *love,* for example) are either temporarily or permanently de-emphasized in favor of a focus on the larger system: the overall frequencies of *love* as a noun versus *love* as a verb. Indeed, the very object of analysis shifts from looking at the individual occurrences of a feature in context to looking at the trends and patterns of that feature aggregated over an entire corpus. It is here that one makes the move from a study of words in the context of sentences or paragraphs to a study of aggregated word "data" or derivative "information" about word behavior at the scale of an entire corpus.

By way of an analogy, we might think about interpretive close readings as corresponding to microeconomics, whereas quantitative distant reading corresponds to macroeconomics. Consider, then, the study of literary genres or literary periods: are they macroanalytic? Say, for example, a scholar specializes in early-twentieth-century poetry. Presumably, this scholar could be called upon to provide sound generalizations, or "macroreadings," of twentieth-century poetry based on a broad familiarity with the individual works of that period. This would be a type of "macro" or "distant" reading.* But this kind of macroreading falls short of approximating for literature what macroeconomics is to economics, and it is in this context that I prefer the term *analysis* over *reading*. The former term, especially when prefixed with *macro,* places the emphasis on the systematic examination of data, on the quantifiable methodology. It deemphasizes the more interpretive act of "reading." This is no longer reading that we are talking about—even if programmers have come to use the term *read* as a way of naming functions that load a text file into computer memory. Broad attempts to generalize about a period or about a genre by reading and synthesizing a series of texts are just another sort of microanalysis. This is simply close reading, selective sampling, of multiple "cases"; individual texts are digested, and then generalizations are drawn. It remains a largely qualitative approach.† Macroeconomics is a numbers-driven discipline grounded in quantitative analysis, not qualitative assessments. Macroeconomics employs quantitative benchmarks

---

* Ian Watt's impressive study *The Rise of the Novel* (1957) is an example of what I mean in speaking of macro-oriented studies that do not rise far beyond the level of anecdote. Watt's study of the novel is indeed impressive and cannot and should not be dismissed. Having said that, it is ultimately a study of the novel based on an analysis of just a few authors. These authors provide Watt with convenient touchstones for his history, but the choice of these authors cannot be considered representative of the ten to twenty thousand novels that make up the period Watt attempts to cover.

† The human aggregation of multiple case studies could certainly be considered a type of macroanalysis, or assimilation of information, and there are any number of "macro-oriented" studies that take such an approach, studies, for example, that read and interpret economic history by examining various case studies. Alan Liu pointed me to Shoshanna Zuboff's *In the Age of the Smart Machine* (1988) as one exemplary case. Through discussion of eight specific businesses, Zuboff warns readers of the potential downsides (dehumanization) of computer automation. Nevertheless, although eight is better than one, eight is not eight thousand, and, thus, the study is comparatively anecdotal in nature.

for assessing, scrutinizing, and even forecasting the macroeconomy. Although there is an inherent need for understanding the economy at the micro level, in order to contextualize the macro results, macroeconomics does not directly involve itself in the specific cases, choosing instead to see the cases in the aggregate, looking to those elements of the specific cases that can be generalized, aggregated, and quantified.

Just as microeconomics offers important perspectives on the economy, so too does close reading offer fundamentally important insights about literature; I am not suggesting a wholesale shelving of close reading and highly interpretive "readings" of literature. Quite the opposite, I am suggesting a blended approach. In fact, even modern economics is a synthesis—a "neoclassical synthesis," to be exact—of neoclassical economics and Keynesian macroeconomics. It is exactly this sort of unification, of the macro and micro scales, that promises a new, enhanced, and better understanding of the literary record. The two scales of analysis work in tandem and inform each other. Human interpretation of the "data," whether it be mined at the macro or micro scale, remains essential. Although the methods of inquiry, of evidence gathering, are different, they are not antithetical, and they share the same ultimate goal of informing our understanding of the literary record, be it writ large or small. The most fundamental and important difference in the two approaches is that the macroanalytic approach reveals details about texts that are, practically speaking, unavailable to close readers of the texts.

John Burrows was an early innovator in this realm. Burrows's 1987 book-length computational study of Jane Austen's novels provided unprecedented detail into Austen's style by examining the kinds of highly frequent words that most close readers would simply pass over. Writing of Burrows's study of Austen's oeuvre, Julia Flanders points out how Burrows's work brings the most common words, such as *the* and *of,* into our field of view. Flanders writes, "[Burrows's] effort, in other words, is to prove the stylistic and semantic significance of these words, to restore them to our field of view. Their absence from our field of view, their non-existence as facts for us, is precisely because they are so much there, so ubiquitous that they seem to make no difference" (2005, 56–57). More recent is James Pennebaker's book *The Secret Life of Pronouns,* wherein he specifically challenges human instinct and close reading as reliable tools for gathering evidence: "Function words are almost impossible to hear and your stereotypes about how they work may well be wrong" (2011, 28). Reviewing Pennebaker's book for the *New York Times,* Ben Zimmer notes that "mere mortals, as opposed to infallible computers, are woefully bad at keeping track of the ebb and flow of words, especially the tiny, stealthy ones" (2011, n.p.). At its most basic, the macroanalytic approach is simply another method of gathering details, bits of information that may have escaped our attention because of their sheer multitude. At a more sophisticated level, it is about accessing details that are otherwise unavailable, forgotten, ignored, or impossible to extract. The information provided at this scale is different from that derived via close reading, but it is not of lesser or greater value to scholars for being such. Flanders goes on: "Burrows' approach, although it wears its statistics prominently, foreshadows a subtle shift in the way the computer's role *vis-à-vis* the detail is imagined. It foregrounds the computer not as a factual substantiator whose observations are different in kind from our own—because more trustworthy and objective—but as a device that extends the range of our perceptions to phenomena too minutely disseminated for our ordinary reading" (2005, 57). For Burrows, and for Flanders, the corpus being explored is still relatively small—in this case a handful of novels by Jane Austen— compared to the large corpora available today. This increased scale underscores the importance of extending our range of perception beyond ordinary reading practices. Flanders writes specifically of Burrows's use of the computer to help him see more in the texts that he was then reading or studying. The further step, beyond Burrows, is to allow the computer to help us see even more, even deeper, to go beyond what we are capable of reading as solitary scholars.*

The result of such macroscopic investigation is contextualization on an un- precedented scale. The underlying assumption is that by exploring the literary record writ large, we will better understand the context in which individual texts exist and thereby better understand those individual texts. This approach offers specific insights into literary historical questions, including insights into:

- the historical place of individual texts, authors, and genres in relation to a larger literary context
- literary production in terms of growth and decline over time or within re- gions or within demographic groups
- literary patterns and lexicons employed over time, across periods, within regions, or within demographic groups
- the cultural and societal forces that impact literary style and the evolution of style
- the cultural, historical, and societal linkages that bind or do not bind indi- vidual authors, texts, and genres into an aggregate literary culture
- the waxing and waning of literary themes
- the tastes and preferences of the literary establishment and whether those preferences correspond to general tastes and preferences

---

* This approach again resonates with the approaches taken by the Annales historians. Patrick H. Hutton writes that whereas "conventional historians dramatize individual events as landmarks of significant change, the *Annales* historians redirect attention to those vast, anonymous, often unseen structures which shape events by retarding inno- vation" (1981, 240).

Furthermore, macroanalysis provides a practical method for approaching questions such as:

- whether there are stylistic patterns inherent to particular genres
- whether style is nationally determined
- whether and how trends in one nation's literature affect those of another
- the extent to which subgenres reflect the larger genres of which they are a subset
- whether literary trends correlate with historical events
- whether the literature that a nation or region produces is a function of demographics, time, population, degrees of relative freedom, degrees of relative education, and so on
- whether literature is evolutionary
- whether successful works of literature inspire schools or traditions
- whether there are differences between canonical authors and those who have been traditionally marginalized
- whether factors such as gender, ethnicity, and nationality directly influence style and content in literature

A macroanalytic approach helps us not only to see and understand the operations of a larger "literary economy," but, by means of scale, to better see and understand the degree to which literature and the individual authors who manufacture that literature respond to or react against literary and cultural trends. Not the least important, as I explore in chapter 9, the method allows us to chart and understand "anxieties of influence" in concrete, quantitative ways.

For historical and stylistic questions in particular, a macroanalytic approach has distinct advantages over the more traditional practice of studying literary periods and genres by means of a close study of "representative" texts. Franco Moretti has noted how "a field this large cannot be understood by stitching together separate bits of knowledge about individual cases, because it isn't a sum of individual cases: it's a collective system, that should be grasped as a whole" (2005, 4). To generalize about a "period" of literature based on a study of a relatively small number of books is to take a significant leap from the specific to the general. Naturally, it is also problematic to draw conclusions about specific texts based on some general sense of the whole. This, however, is not the aim of macroanalysis. Rather, the macroscale perspective should inform our close readings of the individual texts by providing, if nothing else, a fuller sense of the literary-historical milieu in which a given book exists. It is through the application of both approaches that we reach a new and better-informed understanding of the primary materials.

An early mistake or misconception about what computer-based text analysis could provide scholars of literature was that computers would somehow provide irrefutable conclusions about what a text might mean. The analysis of big corpora being suggested here is not intended for this purpose. Nor is it a strictly scientific practice that will lead us to irrefutable conclusions. Instead, through the study and processing of large amounts of literary data, the method calls our attention to general trends and missed patterns that we must explore in detail and account for with new theories. If we consider that this macroanalytic approach simply provides an alternative method for accessing texts and simply another way of harvesting facts from and around texts, then it may seem less threatening to those who worry that a quantification of the humanities is tantamount to the destruction of the humanities.

In literary studies, we are drawn to and impressed by grand theories, by deep and extended interpretations, and by complex speculations about what a text—or even a part of a text—might mean: the indeterminacies of deconstruction, the ramifications of postcolonialism, or how, for example, the manifold allusions in Joyce's *Ulysses* extend the meaning of the core text. These are all compelling. Small findings, on the other hand, are frequently relegated to the pages of journals that specialize in the publication of "notes." Craig Smith and M. C. Bisch's small note in the *Explicator* (1990), for example, provides a definitive statement on Joyce's obscure allusion to the *Illiad* in *Ulysses*, but who reads it and who remembers it?* Larger findings of fact, more objective studies of form, or even literary biography or literary history have, at least for a time, been "out of style." Perhaps they have been out of style because these less interpretive, less speculative studies seem to close a discussion rather than to invite further speculation. John Burrows's fine computational analysis of common words in the fiction of Jane Austen is an example of a more objectively determined exploration of facts, in this case lexical and stylistic facts. There is no doubt that the work helps us to better understand Austen's corpus, but it does so in a way that leaves few doors open for further speculation (at least within the domain of common word usage, or "idiolects," as Burrows defines them). A typical criticism levied against Burrows's work is that "most of the conclusions which he reaches are not far from the ordinary reader's natural assumptions" (Wiltshire 1988, 380). Despite its complexity, the result of the work is an extended statement of the facts regarding Austen's use of pronouns and function words. This final statement, regardless of how interesting it is to this reader, has about it a simplicity that inspires only a lukewarm reaction among contemporary literary scholars who are evidently more passionate about and accustomed to deeper theoreti-

---

* Smith and Bisch note how Joyce's use of "bronze b[u]y[s] gold" in Sirens mirrors a "minor encounter in the Illiad . . . [in which] Diomedes trades his bronze armor for the gold armor of Glaucos" (1990, 206). See Joyce's *Ulysses* 11.1–4.

cal maneuverings. To Burrows's credit, Wiltshire acknowledges that the value of Burrows's study is "not that it produces novel or startling conclusions—still less 'readings'—as that it allows us to say that such 'impressions' are soundly based on verifiable facts" (ibid.).

Arguments like those made by Burrows have been, and perhaps remain, underappreciated in contemporary literary discourse precisely because they are, or appear to be, definitive statements. As "findings," not "interpretations," they have about them a deceptive simplicity, a simplicity or finality that appears to render them "uninteresting" to scholars conditioned to reject the idea of a closed argument. Some years ago, my colleague Steven Ramsay warned a group of computing humanists against "present[ing] ourselves as the people who go after the facts."* He is right, of course, in the sense that we ought to avoid contracting that unpleasant disease of quantitative arrogance. It is not the facts themselves we want to avoid; however, we certainly still want and need "the facts."

Among the branches of literary study, there are many in which access to and apprehension of "the facts" about literature are exactly what is sought. Most obvious here are biographical studies and literary history, where determining what the facts are has a great deal of relevance not simply in terms of explaining context but also in terms of determining how we understand and interpret the literary works within that context: the works of a given author or the works of a given historical period. Then there is the matter of stylistics and of close reading, which are both concerned with ascertaining, by means of analysis, certain distinguishing features or facts about a text.

Clearly, literary scholars do not have problems with the facts about texts per se. Yet there remains a hesitation—or in some cases a flat-out rejection— when it comes to the usefulness of quantification. This hesitation is more than likely the result of a mistaken impression that the conclusions following from a computational or quantitative analysis are somehow to be preferred to conclusions that are arrived at by other means. A computational approach need not be viewed as an alternative to interpretation—though there are some, such as Gottschall (2008), who suggest as much. Instead, and much less controversially, computational analysis may be seen as an alternative methodology for the discovery and the gathering of facts. Whether derived by machine or through hours in the archive, the data through which our literary arguments are built will always require the careful and imaginative scrutiny of the scholar. There will always be a movement from facts to interpretation of facts. The computer is a tool that assists in the identification and compilation of evidence. We must, in turn, interpret and explain that derivative data. Importantly, though, the

* Ramsay made these comments at the "Face of Text" conference hosted by McMaster University in November 2004. See http://tapor1.mcmaster.ca/~faceoftext/index.htm.

computer is not a mere tool, nor is it simply a tool of expedience. Later chapters will demonstrate how certain types of research exist only because of the tools that make them possible.

Few would object to a comparative study of Joyce and Hemingway that concludes that Hemingway's style is more minimalist or more "journalistic" than Joyce's. One approach to making this argument would be to pull representative sentences, phrases, and paragraphs from the works of both authors and from some sampling of journalistic prose in order to compare them and highlight the differences and similarities. An alternative approach would involve "processing" the entire corpus of both authors, as well as the journalistic samples, and then to compute the differences and similarities using features that computers can recognize or calculate, features such as average sentence length, frequent syntactical patterns, lexical richness, and so on. If the patterns common to Hemingway match more closely the patterns of the journalistic sample, then new evidence and new knowledge would have been generated. And the latter, computational, approach would be all the more convincing for being both comprehensive and definitive, whereas the former approach was anecdotal and speculative. The conclusions reached by the first approach are not necessarily wrong, only less certain and less convincing. Likewise, the second approach may be wrong, but that possibility is less likely, given the method.* Far more controversial and objectionable would be an argument along the lines of "Moby Dick is God, and I have the numbers to prove it." The issue, as this intentionally silly example makes clear, is not so much about the gathering of facts but rather what it is that we are doing with the facts once we have them.

It is this business of new knowledge, distant reading, and the potentials of a computer-based macroanalysis of large literary corpora that I take up in this book. The chapters that follow explore methods of large-scale corpus analysis

---

* There are those who object to this sort of research on the grounds that these methods succeed only in telling us what we already know. In a *New York Times* article, for example, Kathryn Schulz (2011) responded to some similar research with a resounding "Duh." I think Schulz misses the point here and misreads the work she is discussing (my blog post explaining why can be found at http://www.matthewjockers.net/2011/07/01/on-distant-reading-and-macroanalysis/). To me, at least, her response indicates a lack of seriousness about literature as a field of study. Why should further confirmation of a point of speculation engender a negative response? If the matter at hand were not literary, if it were global warming, for example, and new evidence confirmed a particular "interpretation" or thesis, surely this would not cause a thousand scientists to collectively sigh and say, "Duh." A resounding "I told you so," perhaps, but not "Duh." But then Schulz bears down on the straw man and thus avoids the real revelations of the research being reviewed.

and are unified by a recurring theme of probing the quirks of literary influence that push and pull against the creative freedom of writers. Unlike Harold Bloom's anecdotal, and for me too frequently impenetrable, study of influence, the work presented here is primarily quantitative, primarily empirical, and almost entirely dependent upon computation—something that Bloom himself anticipated in writing *Anxiety of Influence* back in 1973. Bloom, with some degree of derision, wrote of "an industry of source-hunting, of allusion-counting, an industry that will soon touch apocalypse anyway when it passes from scholars to computers" (31). Though my book ends up being largely about literary influence—or, if you prefer, influences upon literary creativity—and to a lesser extent about the place of Irish and Irish American writers in the macro system of British and American literature, it is meant fundamentally to be a book about method and how a new method of studying large collections of digital material can help us to better understand and contextualize the individual works within those collections. The larger argument I wish to make is that the study of literature should be approached not simply as an examination of seminal works but as an examination of an aggregated ecosystem or "economy" of texts. Some may wish to classify my research as "exploratory" or as "experimental" because the work I present here does more to open doors than it does to close them. I hope that this is true, that I open some doors. I hope that this work is also provocative in the sense of provoking more work, more exploration, and more experimentation.

I am also conscious that work classified under the umbrella of "digital humanities" is frequently criticized for failing to bring new knowledge to our study of literature. Be assured, then, that this work of mine is not simply provocative. There are conclusions, some small and a few grand. This work shows, sometimes in dramatic ways, how individual creativity—the individual agency of authors and the ability of authors to invent fiction that is stylistically and thematically original—is highly constrained, even determined, by factors outside of what we consider to be a writer's conscious control. Alongside minor revelations about, for example, Irish American writing in the early 1900s and the nature of the novelistic genre in the nineteenth century, I continually engage this matter of "influence" and the grander notions of literary history and creativity that so concerned Elliot, Bloom, and the more or less forgotten Russian formalists whose bold work in literary evolution was so far ahead of its time.

The chapters that follow share a common theme: they are not about individual texts or even individual authors. The methods described and the results reported represent a generational shift away from traditional literary scholarship, and away even from traditional text analysis and computational authorship attribution. The macroanalysis I describe represents a new approach to the study of the literary record, an approach designed for probing the digital-textual world as it exists today, in digital form and in large quantities.

PART II ANALYSIS

5 METADATA

To answer those questions you need good metadata.

—Geoff Nunberg

This chapter offers a first example of how the macroanalytic approach brings new knowledge to our understanding of literary history. This chapter also begins the larger exploration of influence that forms a unifying thread in this book. The evidence presented here is primarily quantitative; it was gathered from a large literary bibliography using ad hoc computational tools. To an extent, this chapter is about harvesting some of the lowest hanging fruit of literary history. Many decades before mass-digitization efforts, libraries were digitizing an important component of their collections in the form of online, electronic catalogs. These searchable bibliographies contain a wealth of information in the form of metadata. Consider, for example, Library of Congress call numbers and the Library of Congress subject headings, which they represent. Call numbers are a type of metadata that indicate something special about a book. Literary researchers understand that the "P" series is especially relevant to their work and that works classed as PR or PS have relevance at an even finer level of granularity—that is, English language and literature. This is an abundant, if somewhat general, form of literary data that can be processed and mined. Subject headings are an even richer source. Headings are added by human coders who take the time to check the text they are cataloging in order to determine, for example, whether it is fiction or nonfiction, whether it is folk literature or from the English Renaissance, and in the case of American literature whether it is a regional text from the northern, southern, central, or western region.

This type of catalog metadata has been largely untapped as a means of exploring literary history. Even literary bibliographers have tended to focus more on developing comprehensive bibliographies than on how the data contained within them might be leveraged to bring new knowledge to our understanding of the literary record. In the absence of full text, this bibliographic metadata can reveal useful information about literary trends. In 2003 Franco Moretti and I began a series of investigations involving two bibliographic data sets. Moretti's data set was a bibliography of nineteenth-century novels: titles, authors, and publication dates, not rich metadata, but a lot of records, around 7,000 citations. Moretti's work eventually led to a study of nineteenth-century novel titles published in *Critical Inquiry* (2009). My data set was a much smaller collection of about 800 works by Irish American authors.* The Irish American bibliography, however, was carefully curated and manually enriched with metadata indicating the geographic settings of the works, as well as the author gender, birthplace, age, and place of residence. Geospatial coordinates—longitudes and latitudes—indicating where each author was from and where each text was set were also added to the records.

The Irish American database began as research in support of my dissertation, which explored Irish American literature in the western United States (Jockers 1997). In 2001 the original bibliography of primary materials was transformed into a searchable relational database, which allowed for quick and easy querying and sorting. The selection criteria for a work's inclusion in the database were borrowed, with some minor variation, from those that Charles Fanning had established in his seminal history of Irish American literature, *The Irish Voice in America: 250 Years of Irish-American Fiction* (2000). To qualify for inclusion in the database, a writer must have some verifiable Irish ethnic ancestry, and the writer's work must address or engage the matter of being Irish in America. Because of this second criterion, certain obviously Irish authors, such as F. Scott Fitzgerald and John O'Hara, are not represented in the collection. Both of these writers, as Fanning and others have explained, generally wanted to distance themselves from their Irish roots, so they avoided writing along ethnic lines. Thus, the database ultimately focused not simply on writers of Irish roots, but on writers of Irish roots who specifically chose to explore Irish identity in their prose.

Determining how and whether a work got included in the database was sometimes a subjective process. Some of the decisions made could, and perhaps should, be challenged. A perfect example is the classification of Kathleen Norris as a Californian. Norris was raised and began her writing career in and among the Irish community of San Francisco. After marrying, though, she moved to

---

* The results of Moretti's project were first delivered as the keynote address at the 2007 digital humanities conference in Champaign-Urbana and then published in *Critical Inquiry* (Moretti 2009). The results of my analysis of the Irish American data set were presented in two different formats: first in 2007 as an invited lecture titled "Metadata Mining the Irish-American Literary Corpus," at the University of St. Louis, and then again at the 2007 meeting of the Modern Language Association in a paper titled "Beyond Boston: Georeferencing Irish-American Literature."

New York, where she continued to write, sometimes setting her fiction in California and sometimes in New York. In the database, she is consistently classed as a Californian and not a New Yorker. Norris strongly identified with her San Francisco Irish American heritage, stating in her autobiography that she was part of the San Francisco "Irishocracy" (1959). Even though she lived and wrote for a time on the East Coast, she never lost her California Irish identity. She ultimately returned to California and died at her home in Palo Alto.

Constructed over the course of ten years, this database includes bibliographic records for 758 works of Irish American prose literature spanning 250 years.* Given the great time span, this is not a huge corpus. Nevertheless, it is a corpus that approaches being comprehensive in terms of its selection criteria. Each record in the database includes a full bibliographic citation, a short abstract, and additional metadata indicating the setting of the book: geographic coordinates and information such as state or region, as well as more subjectively derived information such as whether the setting of the text is primarily urban or rural. The records also include information about the books' authors: their genders and in many cases short biographical excerpts.†

In the absence of this data, our understanding of Irish American literature as a unique ethnic subgenre of American literature has been dependent upon critical studies of individual authors in the canon and upon Fanning's study of the subject.‡ In *The Irish Voice in America,* Fanning explores the history and evolution of the canon using a "generational" approach. He begins with the watershed moment in Irish history, the Irish Famine of the 1840s, and then explores the generations of writers who came before, during, and after the

---

* The database includes other types of works in addition to prose fiction, but my analysis excludes these works. I began collecting these data as part of my doctoral dissertation and continued expanding it through 2005. During that time, I was assisted by students enrolled in my Irish American literature courses at Stanford and by graduate students employed as part of a grant I received from the Stanford Humanities Lab to fund the "Irish-American West" project. In 2004 I cofounded the Western Institute of Irish Studies with then Irish consul Dónal Denham and gave the database to the institute to make it available to the public. I turned over directorship of the institute in 2009, and some years later the project folded and the database is no longer available online.

† This process of human "coding" of data for analysis has been used with interesting results in Gottschall 2008.

‡ There are other works that have attempted to encapsulate large segments of Irish American literary history. My own published work on Irish American authors in the San Francisco Bay Area, in Montana, and in the Midwest are fairly recent examples (Jockers 2004, 2005, 2009). Ron Ebest's *Private Histories* (2005), profiling several writers who were active between 1900 and 1930, is another.

famine. When he reaches the turn of the twentieth century, Fanning moves to an examination of the literature in the context of key events in American and world history: the world wars and then the social movements of the 1960s and 1970s. Fanning's is a far-reaching study that manages to provide astonishing insight into the works of several dozen individual authors while at the same time providing readers with a broad perspective of the canon's 250-year evo-lution. It is a remarkable work. A rough count of primary works in Fanning's bibliography comes in at nearly 300.*

In the course of his research, Fanning discovered an apparent dearth of writ-ers active in the period from 1900 to 1930, and as an explanation for this literary "recession," Fanning proposes that 1900 to 1930 represents a "lost generation," a period he defines as one "of wholesale cultural amnesia" (2000, 3). Fanning hy-pothesizes that a variety of social forces led Irish Americans away from writing about the Irish experience, and he notes how "with the approach of World War I, Irish-American ethnic assertiveness became positively unsavory in the eyes of many non-Irish Americans. When the war began in August of 1914, anti-British feeling surfaced again strongly in Irish-American nationalist circles. . . . [T]he War effort as England's ally, and the negative perception of Irish nationalism after the Easter Rising all contributed to a significant dampening of the fires of Irish-American ethnic self-assertion during these years" (ibid., 238). The num-bers, however, tell a different story. Figure 5.1 shows a chronological plotting of 758 works of Irish American fiction published between the years 1800 and 2005.† The solid black line presents the data as a five-year moving average; the noisier dotted line shows the actual, year-to-year, publications. This graph shows nothing more elaborate than the publication history. Noteworthy, however, is that the literary depression, or lost generation, that Fanning hypothesizes appears to be much more short-lived than he imagines. A first peak in Irish American publication occurs just at the turn of the twentieth century. This is followed by a short period of decline until 1910. Then, however, the trend shifts upward, and the number of publications increases in the latter half of the exact

---

* As both a reader and a former student of Charles Fanning, I am indebted to and deeply influenced by his work. My research has been aided by modern technology, and the number and variety of works that Fanning unearthed, without the aid of such tech-nology, serve as a model of scholarly perseverance.

† I began collecting works for this database in 1993 as part of a study of Irish Ameri-can writing in the West. The database has grown significantly over the years, and in my Irish American literature courses at Stanford, students conducted research in order to help fill out missing metadata in the records. Note that in all charts, data for the decade from 2000 to 2010 are incomplete.

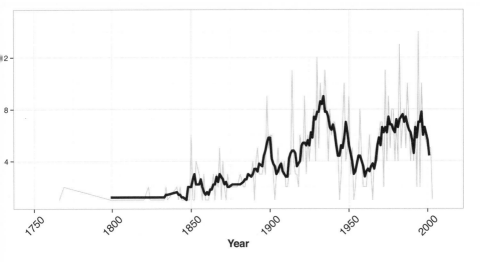

Figure 5.1. Chronological plotting of Irish American fiction

period that Fanning identifies as one when Irish Americans were supposed to have been silenced by cultural and social forces. Where is the lost generation that Fanning postulates?

When the results are regraphed, as shown in figure 5.2, so as to differentiate between Irish American authors from east and west of the Mississippi, we begin to see how Fanning may have been led to his conclusion: publication of works by eastern Irish American writers does indeed begin to decline in 1900, reaching a nadir in 1920. Eastern writing does not begin to recover from this "recession" until the decade of the 1930s, and full recovery is not achieved until the late 1960s and early 1970s.

If we look only to the dotted (eastern) line, then figure 5.2 confirms Fanning's further observation that Irish American fiction flourished at the turn of the century and then again in the 1960s and '70s, when cultural changes made writing along ethnic lines more popular and appealing. The western line, however, tells a different story. Western writers make a somewhat sudden appearance in 1900 and then begin a forty-year period of ascendancy that reaches an apex in 1941. Western writers clearly dominated the early part of the twentieth century.

A further separation of texts based on author gender reveals even more about what was happening in this period. To begin, figure 5.3 shows all texts separated by gender. With the exception of the 1850s, male productivity is consistently greater than female productivity. Aside from this somewhat curious situation

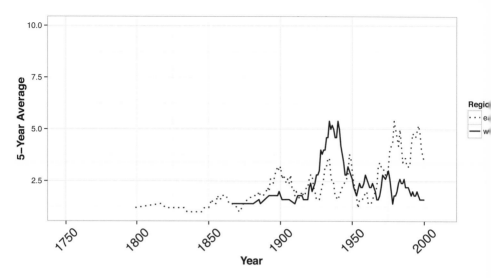

Figure 5.2. Chronological plotting of Irish American fiction by region

in the 1850s, the male and female lines tend to follow a similar course, suggesting that the general trends in Irish American literary production are driven by forces external to gender.*

Figure 5.4, however, presents a view of only *eastern* Irish American texts separated by gender. Here, in the East, publications by male authors are seen to suffer a much more precipitous drop after the turn of the century, declining from an average of 2.3 publications per year to 1.3 by 1916. Females are seen to have a slight increase in productivity around 1906, a surge lasting for about ten years.

More striking than this graph of eastern publications, however, is figure 5.5, which charts western publications separated according to gender. Whereas western male authors are increasing their production of texts beginning in the 1860s to an apex in the late 1930s, Irish American women in the West first appear in the late 1890s and then rise rapidly in the 1920s to a point at which they are producing an equal number of books per year to their male counterparts in the West. Given the overall tendency for women to produce at a rate lower than males, this is especially noteworthy. It suggests either that the West offered

* The limited amount of data here makes correlating the lines unproductive, even while there are some noticeable similarities. When linear trend lines are calculated, it is seen that production is slowly increasing over time, and the two trend lines are almost parallel, indicating a similar rate of overall increase.

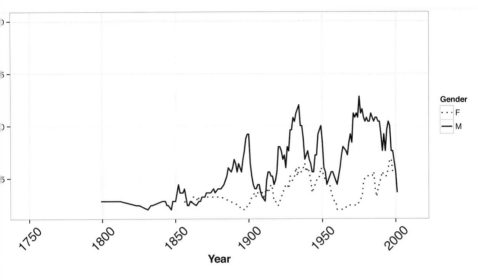

Figure 5.3. Chronological plotting of Irish American fiction by gender

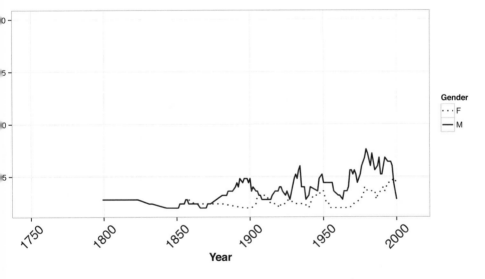

Figure 5.4. Chronological plotting of Irish American fiction by gender and eastern region

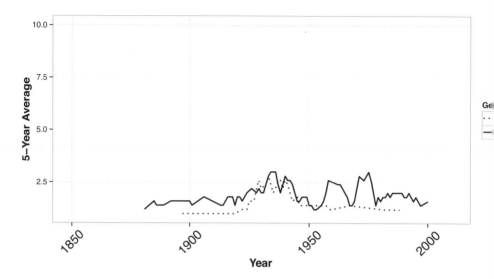

Figure 5.5. Chronological plotting of Irish American fiction by gender and western region

something special for Irish American women or that there was something special about the Irish women who went west, or, still more likely, that it was some
combination of both.*

Western authors, both male and female, certainly appear to have countered
any literary recession of the East. That they succeeded in doing so despite (or
perhaps directly because of) a significantly smaller Irish ethnic population in
the West is fascinating. Figure 5.6 incorporates census figures to explore Irish
American literary output in the context of eastern and western demographics.
The chart plots Irish American books published per ten thousand Irish-born
immigrants in the region. A natural assumption here is that there should be a
positive correlation between the size of a population and the number of potential writers within it. What the data reveal, however, is quite the opposite: the
more sparsely populated West produced more books per capita.

In addition to further dramatizing the problems with Fanning's argument
about Irish American authors being stifled in the early part of the twentieth
century, these data reveal a counterintuitive trend in literary productivity. Geo-
graphically removed from the heart of the publishing industry in the East, Irish
Americans in the West were also further removed from the primary hubs of Irish

* Elsewhere I have argued that it is most likely a combination of both factors (Jockers
2005).

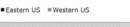

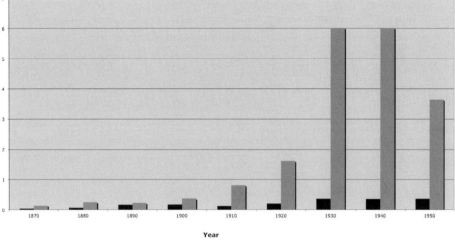

Figure 5.6. Irish American fiction per capita

culture in cities such as Boston, New York, and Chicago. Given a lack of access to the steady influences of the home culture, we might expect Irish immigrants in the West to more quickly adopt the practices and tendencies of the host culture. One might even imagine that in the absence of a supportive Irish American culture, American writers of Irish extraction would tend to drift away from ethnic identifications and write less ethnically oriented fictions. Quite to the contrary, though, Irish Americans in the West wrote about being Irish in America at a per capita rate exponentially greater than their countrymen in the East.

The bar graph in figure 5.6 shows book publications per ten thousand Irish immigrants. The gray bar shows productivity of western authors and the black bar that of eastern. In the 1930s, as an example, western writers were producing 6 works for every ten thousand Irish immigrants. East of the Mississippi, in the same year, Irish American authors managed just 0.3 books per ten thousand, or 1 book for every thirty thousand Irish immigrants.* Even in the years outside of

---

* Census figures provide information relative only to first-generation Irish immigrants, whereas the publication data do not discriminate based on generational status. Thus, the authors of these books may be first-generation Irish immigrants or second- or third-generation American descendants of Irish immigrants. One assumption that is debunked by this data is that a steady influx of new immigrants would tend to perpetuate an interest in ethnic and cultural matters; the more new immigrants, the more

the period, from 1900 to 1940, Irish American authors in the West consistently outpublished their eastern counterparts in terms of books per Irish immigrants.* Although it is true that 758 texts spread over 250 years does not amount to very many data, the aggregation of the data into decades and the visualization of the data in terms of ten-year moving averages do provide a useful way of considering what are in essence "latent" macro trends. Given the sparsity of the data, this analysis is inconclusive if still suggestive.† It suggests that geography, or some manifestation of culture correlated to geography, exerted an influence on Irish American literary productivity.

A similar avenue of investigation can be traveled by studying the distribution of texts based on their fictional settings. In addition to metadata pertinent to author gender, state of residence, and geographic region, works in this database are coded with information about their fictional settings. Each record is marked as being either "rural," "urban," or "mixed." Graphing only those works that fall clearly into the category of being either rural or urban provides additional information for understanding the distribution and makeup of Irish American literature. Figure 5.7 shows the publication of fictional works with either rural or urban settings that were published between 1760 and 2010. Looking specifically at the period from 1900 to 1940, a trend toward the dominance of urban works begins in 1930s and peaks around 1940. What is not revealed here is that western authors were in fact writing the majority of the works with urban settings. From 1900 to 1930, it was western Irish Americans who put urban America on the map, and this leads us to further interrogate Fanning's observations of a lost generation. It appears that this lost generation is in fact a lost generation of eastern, and probably male, Irish Americans with a penchant for writing about urban themes.

---

one would expect to see a literary manifestation of Irish themes. On the contrary, the evidence suggests no correlation between immigrant population and the production of ethnically oriented fiction. Census figures are from the historical Census Browser, retrieved January 29, 2007, from the University of Virginia, Geospatial and Statistical Data Center, http://fisher.lib.virginia.edu/collections/stats/histcensus/index.html.

* My working assumption here is that there should be a connection between a writer's proclivity to write about the Irish experience in America and the strength of the Irish community in which the writer lives. More Irish-born citizens should mean more Irish-oriented books. Obviously, there are many other factors that could be at play here. Take, for example, economics. Would Irish writers in more vibrant local economies be more inclined to write? It is entirely possible. What is compelling and unquestionable here is the sheer number of Irish American books in the West—whatever the demographics.

† A total of 758 texts spread over 250 years is only about 3 texts per year on average, and in reality the number of texts from the earlier years is much fewer. To be conclusive, I think we would need a larger and more evenly distributed corpus of texts. Nevertheless, I suspect that this corpus approaches being comprehensive in terms of the "actual" population of texts that may exist in this category. In that sense, the results are convincing.

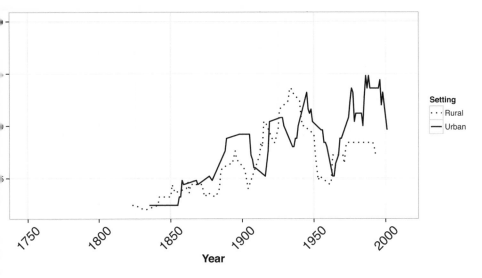

Figure 5.7. Chronological plotting of Irish American fiction by setting

It is hard not to draw this conclusion, especially when we consider that the history of the Irish in America, and to a much greater extent the history of Irish American literature, has had a decidedly eastern bias. Just how prevalent this eastern bias is can be read in the preface to Casey and Rhodes's 1979 collection, *Irish-American Fiction: Essays in Criticism.* William V. Shannon writes in the preface that the essay collection examines the "whole ground of American-Irish writing [and] demonstrates the scope and variety of the Irish community's experience in the United States" (ix). Although Shannon's enthusiasm is in keeping with the significance of this seminal collection, his remarks about its breadth are incredibly misleading. An examination of the essays in the collection reveals not a comprehensive study but rather a study of Irish American authors centered almost exclusively in eastern, urban locations. Writers from the Great Plains and farther west are absent, and thus the collection misses the "whole ground" of the Irish American literary experience by about 1,806,692 square miles.*

Such neglect is surprising given the critical attention that the Irish in the West have received from American and Irish historians. Although it is true that a majority of historical studies have tended to focus on Irish communities in eastern, urban locations such as Boston and New York, since the 1970s, at least, there has been a serious effort made to chronicle the Irish experience beyond the Mississippi. By 1977 Patrick Blessing had pointed out that the current view of Irish America had "been painted rather gloomily" by historians focusing too much on cities like Boston (2). At that time, he noted that "studies of the Irish

---

* An estimate of the area west of the Mississippi.

in the United States [had] been confined to the urban industrial centers on the East coast" (ibid.). Scholarly opinion of the Irish in America was also still very eastern centric and largely fixated on the struggles faced by famine-era immigrants. Blessing's study of Irish migration to California, however, forced reconsideration of the existing views. The census figures that Blessing cites from the late nineteenth century reveal what few had been willing to recognize: not only were there large numbers of Irish in the West, but in many cases they were the dominant ethnic group. From 1850 to 1880, for example, the Irish were the largest immigrant group in Minnesota, Colorado, New Mexico, Wyoming, Montana, Arizona, Nevada, and Washington, and they were the second largest in Utah, Idaho, Oregon, and the Dakota Territory (ibid., 169). Using these figures along with other qualitative evidence, Blessing argued that the long-held opinion that "Irish immigrants were reluctant to move out of the urban Northeast" needed serious reconsideration (ibid., 162). More important, he dispelled the idea that the Irish were "strongly averse to going West" by pointing to figures showing how by 1850, "200,000 Irish labored in regions outside of the eastern states." By 1880 the number had risen to "almost 700,000, fully 36 percent of the entire group in the United States" (ibid., 163). Of this eastern bias, Blessing writes, "That historians should attend to the Irish clustered in Eastern cities is understandable, for the majority could be found in or around their port of arrival for decades after debarkation in the United States. . . . To emphasize Irish reluctance to depart the urban Northeast, however, is to neglect the considerable proportion of newcomers from the Emerald Isle who did leave the region" (ibid.).

If neglecting the West is one problem, another is most certainly the neglect of Irish American women. Writing of this neglect, Caledonia Kearns notes that the "history of Irish American women in this country has been little recognized, with the exception of Hasia Diner's groundbreaking book *Erin's Daughters in America*" (1997, xvii). When it comes to studies of Irish American literature by women, the record is even worse. Kearns goes on to point out that there are, to begin with, very "few studies of Irish-American fiction . . . and when [Irish American fiction is] considered, the focus tends to be on male writers" (ibid., xviii). Assuming that scholars, the reading public, and book reviewers have been guilty of exactly what Blessing and Kearns suggest, it is instructive to consider what is available to counter these biases within the Irish American literary canon. A reader, reviewer, or scholar with this sort of male, urban, and eastern bias finds very little in the Irish American corpus between 1900 and 1940. Indeed, only 5 percent of the texts published in that forty-year period meet the criteria of being male, eastern, and urban. When the biases are completely reversed (female, western, and rural), we find almost twice as many books. In retrospect it is clear that even Fanning's sweeping study of Irish American literature is fundamentally canonical and anecdotal. Nevertheless, he cannot be faulted on this point, as he had neither the data nor the methodology for doing otherwise. There is only so much material that can be accounted for using traditional methods of close reading and scholarly synthesis.*

The macroanalytic perspective applied here provides a useful, albeit incomplete, corrective. The approach identifies larger trends and provides critical insights into the periods of growth and decline in the corpus. The graphs and figures are generated from a corpus of 758 works of fiction, and although it is not unreasonable or even impossible to expect that an individual scholar might read and digest this many texts, it is a task that would take considerable time and would push the limits of the human capacity for synthesis. Moreover, it would be a nontrivial task for even the most competent of traditional scholars to assemble the varied impressions resulting from a close reading of more than 750 texts into a coherent and manageable literary history. Not impossible, for sure, but surely impractical on many counts. Cherry-picking of evidence in support of a broad hypothesis seems inevitable in the close-reading scholarly tradition.

Given the impracticalities of reading everything, the tendency among traditional literary historians has been to draw conclusions about literary periods from a limited sample of texts. This practice of generalization from the specific can be particularly dangerous when the texts examined are not representative of the whole. It is worth repeating here what was cited earlier. Speaking of the nineteenth-century British novel, Moretti writes, "A minimal fraction of the literary field we all work on: a canon of two hundred novels, for instance, sounds very large for nineteenth-century Britain . . . but is still less than one per cent of the novels that were actually published. . . . [A] field this large cannot be understood by stitching together separate bits of knowledge about individual cases" (2005, 4). Comments such as these have moved some to charge that Moretti's enterprise runs counter to, and perhaps even threatens, the very study of literature. William Deresiewicz (2006) uses his review of Moretti's edited collection *The Novel* as a platform on which to cast Moretti as some sort

---

* It is important to point out that a primary aim of Fanning's work in the *Irish Voice in America* was to call attention to the works that best represent the Irish experience in the United States. Fanning sought to highlight not simply those works that most accurately depict Irishness in America but, more important, those works that depict the Irish experience with the greatest degree of craft and literary style. Fanning's success in identifying and calling our attention to many of the very finest authors in the tradition is decisive, and the matter of whether these new western writers are aesthetically comparable to their eastern counterparts remains an open question that I am taking up in another project. The lost generation Fanning discusses may indeed be a lost generation of high-quality writers. It is not my purpose here to further separate the books into classes based upon my perceptions of their aesthetic merit.

of literary "conquistador." He depicts Moretti as a warrior in a literary-critical "campaign." Deresiewicz draws a line in the sand; he sets up an opposition and sees no room in literary criticism for both macro (distant) and micro (close) approaches to the study of literature. In his combat zone of criticism, scholars must choose one methodology or the other. But Deresiewicz is wrong. Moretti's intent is not to vanquish traditional literary scholarship by employing the how-itzer of distant reading, and macroanalysis is not a competitor pitted against close reading. Both the theory and the methodology are aimed at the discovery and delivery of evidence. This evidence is different from what is derived through close reading, but it is evidence, important evidence. At times the new evidence will confirm what we have already gathered through anecdotal study (such as Fanning's observation of the flourishing of Irish American fiction in the 1960 and 1970s). At other times, the evidence will alter our sense of what we thought we knew. Either way the result is a more accurate picture of our subject. This is not the stuff of radical campaigns or individual efforts to "conquer" and lay waste to traditional modes of scholarship.

• • •

Simple counting and sorting of texts based on metadata inform the analysis of Irish American fiction provided above but by no means provide material for an exhaustive study. Any number of measures might be brought to bear on an attempt to better understand a literary period or canon. We might be interested in looking at sheer literary output, or we might be interested in output as it relates to population. A "books per capita" analysis, such as that seen in figure 5.6, may prove useful in assessing the validity of claims that are frequently made for literary "renaissances." Was the flowering of black American drama during the 1930s and 1940s attributable to the creative genius of a few key writers, or was the production of so much writing simply a probability given the number of potential writers?

    In order to assess this question reliably, it would be appropriate to explore first the sheer number of plays produced per year. We might then calculate the average number of plays per decade, or in some other time span. It might also be appropriate to compare the production of black drama against or within the context of the larger canon of American drama in general. Was the output of black dramatists in these years significantly greater than their Caucasian counterparts? Was there a similar burgeoning of drama outside of the Afri-can American community during this time period? Obviously, the answers to these questions could have a profound influence on the way that we understand American drama in general and African American literature in particular. An-swering these questions is dependent not just upon the availability of the plays themselves but also upon the added information that is provided in the form

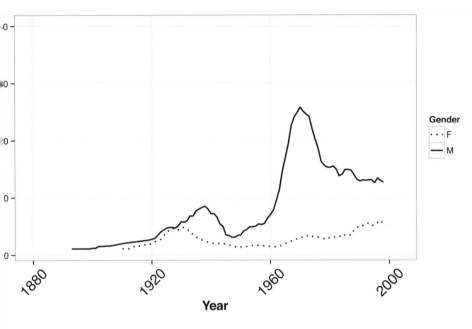

Figure 5.8. Chronological plotting of black drama by gender

of metadata about the plays. For readers eager to investigate this question, such metadata (and much more) are part of the wonderfully conceived Alexander Street Press collection *Black Drama*. The current (second) edition of the collection includes 1,450 plays written from the mid-1800s to the present by more than 250 playwrights from North America, English-speaking Africa, the Caribbean, and other African diaspora countries.* Figure 5.8, showing a chronological plotting of plays in the *Black Drama* collection separated by gender, probably tells us more about the collection practices of the Alexander Street Press editors than it does about black dramatic history.

Whatever the case, the chart is revealing all the same. It may suggest, for example, that black males are far more likely dramatists, or maybe there was something special about the 1970s that led male authors and not female authors to write drama. It may also reveal that the Harlem Renaissance of the 1920s and '30s was a period when female dramatists were either more active or more appreciated by posterity. Needless to say, these are the kind of questions that should be taken up by those with domain expertise in African American literature. Collections such as this one from Alexander Street Press are fertile

* See http://bld2.alexanderstreet.com (subscription required).

ground for even deeper macroanalytic research because the collection has both rich metadata and full text.

We have seen what appears to be a strong connection between geography and Irish American productivity. In addition to informing our understanding of raw productivity, metadata such as those contained in the Irish American database can also provide some limited insight into the content and style of novels. In the United States, it is common to explore literature in terms of region, to separate, distinguish, and categorize genres based on geographical distinctions: the New England poets, the southern regionalists, western American fiction, and so on. The Irish American database is limited; it is ultimately no more than an enhanced bibliography. Given a full-text database with similarly rich metadata, however, we can construct queries that allow for exploration of how literary style and the choices that authors make in linguistic expression vary across disparate regions. Much in the way that linguists study dialects or "registers" in the context of geography, a study of "literary" style in connection with geographic context has the potential to reveal that western writers are given to certain habits of style that do not find similar expression in the East. Where linguists are interested in the general evolution of language, scholars of literary style are interested in the ways in which a writer's technique, or method of delivery, is unique. Do the southern regionalists have a distinct literary style or dialect that marks them as different from their northern counterparts? Is the "pace" of prose by southern writers slower? Are southern writers more prone to metaphorical expression? Do northerners use a larger working lexicon? Obviously, we would expect certain lexical differences between southern and northern writers—by definition these works are influenced by geography; regional writers inevitably reference local places and customs. An intriguing question, though, is whether there exists a detectable stylistic difference beyond these toponyms or regional distinctions. An even thornier question might investigate the extent to which novelistic genre determines novelistic style or the degree to which literature operates as a system composed of predictable stylistic expressions. These are bigger questions reserved for the later chapters of this book. A less ambitious question is useful for further introducing the macroanalytic methodology: to what extent does geography influence content in Irish American literature? Without a full-text corpus, a slightly more focused question is necessary: are Irish American writers from the West more or less likely to identify their ethnic backgrounds than writers from the East? Not only is this a tractable question in its practicality, but it is also an important question, because a good number of Irish American authors, particularly some very prominent writers, including Fitzgerald and O'Hara, have intentionally avoided the use of ethic markers that would brand their work as "Irish." Not until the election of John F. Kennedy did Irish Americans fully transcend (whether in actuality or just symbolically) the anti-Catholic and anti-Irish prejudice that typified the late 1800s, when poor Irish Catholic immigrants flooded American shores. Arguably, some of the same stigma and stereotyping remain today, but by and large the typecasting of Irish Americans is no longer of a particularly disparaging sort. Nevertheless, for those Irish Americans who wrote and wished to succeed as writers in the wake of the Great Famine, having an Irish surname was not necessarily a marketable asset. Unless a writer was willing to play up all the usual stereotypes of the so-called stage Irishman, that writer would do best to avoid Irish themes and characters altogether. If we accept this premise, then those who do engage ethnic elements in their fiction are worthy of study as a distinct subset of American authors.

Claude Duchet has written that the titles of novels are "a coded message—in a market situation" (quoted in Moretti 2009, 134). In fact, the titles of novels are an incredibly useful and important, if undertheorized, aspect of the literary record. As Moretti has demonstrated, in the absence of a full-text archive, the titles of works may serve as a useful, if imperfect, proxy for the novels themselves. In the case of Irish American fiction, where there is a historical or cultural background of intolerance for Irish themes, the titles of works carry a special weight, for it is in the title that an author first meets his readers. To what extent, then, do Irish American authors identify themselves as Irish in the titles of their books? By comparing the frequency and distribution of specific word types—ethnic and religious markers in this case—over time and by region, the analysis of publication history presented above can be further demystified.* The use of ethnic and religious markers in the titles of works of Irish American literature first surges in the decades between 1850 and 1870: ethnic or Catholic markers (or both) appear in 30 percent of the titles in the 1850s, 33 percent in the 1860s, and 43 percent in the 1870s. These are the years just after the Great Famine in Ireland. Many of the authors employing these terms are immigrants: first-generation Irish Americans writing about what they know best—their homeland and their people. These are mostly educated authors who may have, as a result of their class or wealth, avoided direct discrimination upon arrival in America. In the decade of the 1880s, however, we find exactly zero occurrences of ethnic markers in titles of Irish American texts, and from 1890 through 2000, the usage of marker words reaches only 11 percent in the 1890s and then never exceeds 6 percent. This naturally raises a question: what happens in or around 1880 to cause the precipitous decrease? Here we must move from our newly found facts to interpretation.

* I define "ethnic markers" to include words that a typical reader would identify or associate with Irish ethnicity. These markers include such obvious words as *Irish, Ireland, Erin, Dublin, Shamrock,* and *Donegal* as well as less obvious but equally loaded words and surnames such as *priest, Patrick, parish, diocese, Catholic, Lonigan, Murphy, O'Phelan, O'Regan, O'Neill, O'Mahony, O'Donnells, O'Flarrity, O'Halloran, O'Shaughnessy,* and so on.

The most obvious answer is postimmigration discrimination. By 1880 the greatest movement of immigrants escaping the famine had occurred, and by 1880 there is likely to have been enough anti-Irish, anti-Catholic sentiment in the United States to make identifying one's Irishness a rather uncomfortable and unprofitable idea.* A closer inspection of these data, however, reveals that after 1880, the use of these markers decreases only in the titles of books written by and about Irish people east of the Mississippi. Irish writers west of the Mississippi continue to employ these "markers" in the titles of their fictional works, especially so in the decade between 1890 and 1900, when every single text employing one of these ethnic identifiers, and accounting for 11 percent of all the Irish American texts published that decade, comes from a writer who lived west of the Mississippi.

Writers employing ethnic markers are also predominantly writers of rural fiction. After 1900 all but a few instances of these markers occur in titles of works that take place in rural settings, as in Charles Driscoll's book *Kansas Irish*, for example.† As we see in table 5.1, in the decade from 1900 to 1909, 7 percent of rural works included an obviously ethnic identifier, 22 percent in the decade from 1910 to 1919. Urban texts using ethnic identifiers during the same decades appeared only in 1940–49 at 7 percent, 1970–79 at 4 percent, and 1980–89 at 2 percent. The pattern here is fairly straightforward: western writers and writers of rural fiction are more likely to depict Irishness and more likely to declare that interest to would-be readers in the titles of their books.‡ Western Irish American writers are evidently more comfortable, or at least more interested in, declaring the Irishness of their subject.

In obvious ways, titles serve as advertisements or marketing tools for the book as a whole, but they frequently also serve to convey authors' condensed impressions of their works. Consider, for example, the following two titles: *The Irish Emigrant: An Historical Tale Founded on Fact* and *The Aliens*. Both of these texts deal with Irish immigration to the United States. The first, a book published in 1817, clearly identifies the subject of Irish immigration. The later book, from 1886, deals with the same subject, but provides nothing to identify

---

* This is a point somewhat similar to the one made by Fanning in the context of the early 1900s.

† My critical introduction to Driscoll's novel can be found in the recent republication of *Kansas Irish* by Rowfant Press, of Wichita, Kansas, in 2011.

‡ The possibility that these titling patterns are publisher driven and not author driven has occurred to me. Publisher and publication place are also recorded in the metadata, and there was nothing found in those data to suggest that the trends were driven by anything other than authorial choice.

Table 5.1. Percentage of rural and urban texts using ethnic markers

Decade	Rural texts (%)	Urban texts (%)
1900–1909	7	0
1910–19	22	0
1920–29	0	0
1930–39	4	0
1940–49	0	7
1950–59	0	0
1960–69	0	0
1970–79	18	4
1980–89	29	2
1990–99	0	0
2000–2005	9	0

itself in ethnic terms. Might it be the case that the author of the former text felt comfortable (prior to the famine and prior to the significant anti-Irish prejudice that permeated American society in the postfamine years) identifying the Irishness of his subject? Pure conjecture, to be sure, but such a hypothesis makes intuitive sense.

To scholars of Irish American literature and culture, the geographic and chronological analysis explored here confirms an important suspicion about the role that culture and geography play in determining not only a writer's proclivity to write but also the content and sentiment that the writing contains. Historians including James Walsh (1978), David Emmons (1989, 2010), Patrick Blessing (1977), and Patrick Dowling (1988, 1998) have documented how Irish immigrants to the American West faced a different set of challenges from that of their countrymen who settled in the East. The foremost challenges that these western immigrants endured were natural challenges associated with frontier living. With minor variations, these historians all attribute the comparative success of the Irish in the West to the fact that these Irish did not face the same kinds of religious and ethnic intolerance that was common fare among the established Anglo-Protestant enclaves of the East. Quite the opposite, the Irish who ventured west to the states of New Mexico, Texas, and California found in the existing Catholic population a community that welcomed rather than rejected them. Those who went to Colorado and Montana found plentiful jobs in the mines and an environment in which a man was judged primarily upon the amount of rock he could put in the box.* These conditions laid the groundwork not simply for greater material success but, as these data confirm, greater literary productivity

---

* Immigration here was male dominated.

and a body of literature that is characterized by a willingness to record specifically Irish perspectives and to do so with an atypical degree of optimism.*

A still closer analysis of all these data is warranted, but even this preliminary investigation reveals a regular and predictable pattern to the way that Irish American authors title their works. This pattern corresponds to the authors' chronological and geographic position in the overall history of Irish immigration to the United States. This type of analysis is ripe for comparative approaches; an exploration of titles produced by other ethnic immigrants to the United States would provide fruitful context. Might a similar pattern be found in Jewish American fiction? Surely, there are a number of similarities between the two groups in terms of their fiction and their experiences as immigrants to the United States. An interested researcher need only identify and code the bibliographic data for the Jewish American tradition to make such an analysis possible.

In addition to various forms of comparative analysis that might be made by compiling and comparing parallel bibliographies, it is possible to take these data still further, to go beyond the mere counting of title words, and to analyze the actual use of words within those titles. Figure 5.9, for example, provides a graphical representation of lexical richness, one of several ways of measuring linguistic variety. Lexical richness, also called a Type Token Ratio, or TTR, is a measure of the ratio of unique words to total word tokens in a given text. Lexical richness may be used to compare the lexicon of two authors. Herman Melville's *Moby Dick,* for example, has a TTR of 7.8 and draws on a large vocabulary of 16,872 unique word types. Jane Austen's *Sense and Sensibility* has a TTR of 5.2 and a much smaller vocabulary of 6,325 unique word types. Austen uses each word type an average of nineteen times, whereas Melville uses each word an average of thirteen times. The experience of reading *Moby Dick,* therefore, appears to be one in which a reader encounters many more unique words and fewer repeated words, on average. However, into this equation, we must also consider novel length. Although Melville's working vocabulary in *Moby Dick* is considerably larger than Austen's in *Sense and Sensibility,* Melville's novel, at 214,889 total words, is almost double the length of Austen's novel, at 120,766. We can compensate for this difference in length by taking multiple random samples of 10,000 words from both novels, calculating the lexical richness for each sample, and then averaging the results. In the case of Austen, 100 random samples of 10,000 words returned an average lexical richness of 0.19. A similar test for Melville returned an average of 0.29. In other words, in any given sample of 10,000 words from *Moby Dick,* there are an average of 2,903 unique word types, whereas a similar sample from Austen

---

* For more on optimism and the general success of the Irish in the western states, see Jockers 1997, 2004, 2005, 2009.

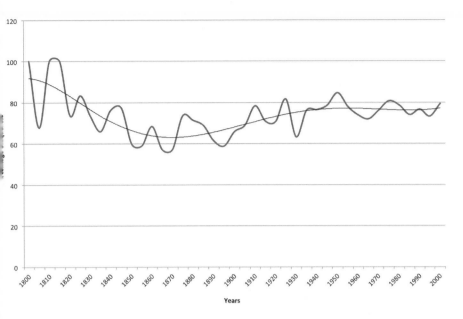

Years

Figure 5.9. Chronological plotting of lexical richness in Irish American fiction titles

returns an average of just 1,935. In terms of vocabulary, Melville's *Moby Dick* is a far richer work than *Sense and Sensibility*.

Applying a lexical-richness measure to the titles of works, it is possible to examine the degree to which the "title lexicon" of a given period is or is not homogeneous. Using title data, we can approximate the lexical variety of titles in the marketplace at any given time. Figure 5.9 charts lexical richness in Irish American titles over time and makes immediately obvious a movement toward lexical equilibrium. The smoother line in the graph shows the overall trend (that is, the mean) in lexical richness of titles; the other, wavier, line allows us to visualize the movement toward less variation. Deviation from the mean decreases over time. The fluctuations, the deviations from the mean, become smaller and smaller and reach a steadier state in the 1930s.* In the early years of the corpus, there is greater heterogeneity among the titles; that is, there is a higher percentage of unique words than in later periods. In practical terms, what this means is that a potential reader browsing titles in the 1820s would have

---

* Title length almost certainly plays a role here. As we move from past to present, the ten-year moving average for title length drops from roughly seventy-five characters before 1840 to fifty characters in the latter half of the nineteenth century and then to twenty to twenty-five characters after 1900.

found them very diverse (in terms of their vocabularies—and, by extension, their presumed subjects), whereas a reader of more recently published texts would find greater similarity among the titles available on this hypothetical bookshelf. More interesting than the general movement toward equilibrium, at least for readers interested in Irish American literature, is the "richness recession" that bottoms out in a period roughly concomitant to the Great Famine. Fanning, who has read more of this literature than any other scholar, has characterized this period of Irish American fiction as one that is generally lacking imagination. The low lexical richness of titles from this period serves as a useful quantitative complement to his qualitative observation. Still, given the relatively small size of this corpus, hard conclusions remain difficult to substantiate statistically.

With a larger collection, such as Moretti's bibliography of British novels published from 1740 to 1850, a measure of lexical richness over time can be much more informative. Moretti's bibliography includes 7,304 titles spanning 110 years, an average of 66 titles per year. Figure 5.10 provides a graphical representation of the lexical richness of these titles over time. In the year 1800, to pick a somewhat arbitrary example, there are 81 novels. Only one of these novel titles contains the word *Rackrent*: Maria Edgeworth's *Castle Rackrent*. Castles, on the other hand, were quite popular in 1800. The word *castle* appears in 10 percent of the 81 titles for 1800. After filtering out the most common function words (*the, of, on, a, in, or, and, to, at, an, from*) and the genre markers (*novel, tale, romance*), *castle* is, in fact, the most frequently occurring word. This is not entirely surprising, given the prominence of the Gothic genre between 1790 and 1830 and the fact that the prototype novel of the genre, Walpole's *Castle of Otranto*, establishes the locale and sets the stage for many years of imitation.

Figure 5.10 charts the year-to-year Type Token Ratio. In 1800 there were 275 word types and 659 total tokens, a richness of 42 percent. Titles in that year averaged 8 words in length and contained an average of 3.4 unique words each. The richness figure provides one measure of the relative homogeneity of titles available to readers of British novels in 1800. Looking at the bigger picture, we see that as time progresses, from 1740 to 1840, titles are becoming less unique, and the working vocabulary of title words is shrinking, and all this is happening at a time when the overall number of titles published is increasing dramatically. Figure 5.11 plots the number of titles in the corpus in every year, dramatizing the extent to which the corpus expands over time.

Put another way, the lexicon of words that authors are using to title their works is becoming more homogeneous even while the number of books and the number of authors in the marketplace are increasing. If we accept, with Duchet and Moretti, that titles are an important signal or code in a crowded market, then this is a sobering trend, at least for authors wishing to stand out at the bookseller's. Instead of titles that distinguish one book from another, what

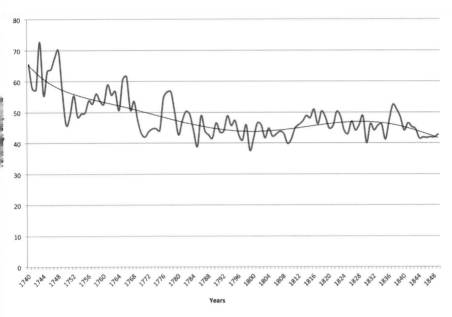

Figure 5.10. Chronological plotting of lexical richness in British novel titles

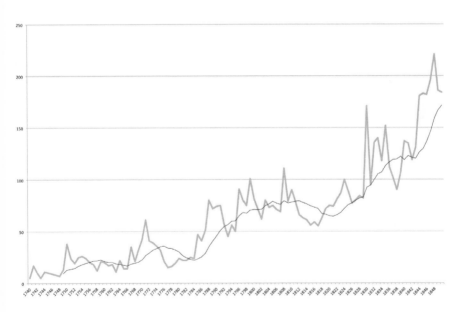

Figure 5.11. The number of British novel titles per year

is found is a homogenization in which more and more book titles look more and more the same. Moretti has commented on a similar trend in the length of the titles, but not on the specific vocabulary that is deployed.*

The word *romance,* for example, is a popular word in this corpus of titles. After removing function words, it is, in fact, the sixteenth most frequently occurring title word overall. It is also a word that goes through a distinct period of popularity, peaking around 1810 and then going out of fashion for thirty years before resurfacing in the 1840s (see figure 5.12). There are any number of explanations for the trend seen here, but my purpose is not to explain the uptick in *romance,* but to instead show the larger context in which titles bearing the word *romance* appear, or, put more crassly, to show what the competition looks like. A writer using the word *romance* in the 1810s is far less original than those writers employing the term in the mid- to late 1700s. Those early, smaller, "blips" in the *romance* timeline, seen around the 1740s and 1760s, are early adopters, outliers to the main trend; they are pioneers in the usage of the term, and anyone wishing to understand the massive use of *romance* at the turn of the century should most certainly contextualize that analysis by a closer look at the forerunners to the trend.

In comparison, the word *love* is a relative nonstarter, a title word that maintains a fairly steady usage across the corpus (figure 5.13) and never experiences the sort of heyday that is witnessed with *romance.*

Castle (figure 5.14), on the other hand, behaves much more like *romance,* whereas *London* (figure 5.15) is similar to *love.* The behavior of the word *century* (figure 5.16) is unsurprising—it begins a rise toward prominence just before the turn of the century, peaks just after the turn, around 1808, and then hangs on until about 1840, when it apparently became old news, passé, cliché. Scholars of the Irish will find food for thought in figure 5.17, which plots the frequency of the word *Irish* in this corpus of titles. It is never a particularly popular term, just sixty-second overall, but as we can see, it experiences a slight rise in the third quarter of the eighteenth century and then a stronger surge in the first quarter of the nineteenth. Most thought provoking, though, is the silence seen in the last quarter of the eighteenth century and first decade of the nineteenth. Talk about a lost generation! Why Ireland and the Irish were unpopular subjects for novel titles in this period is uncertain; that they utterly disappear from the library and bookstore shelves is clear.

• • •

---

* Obviously, some authors may not wish to stand out in the market at all. Quite the contrary, they may wish to capitalize upon the success of prior works and to follow the most lucrative titling trends.

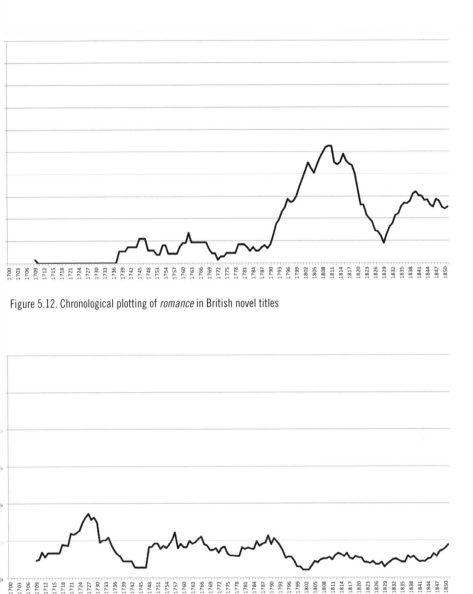

Figure 5.12. Chronological plotting of *romance* in British novel titles

Figure 5.13. Chronological plotting of *love* in British novel titles

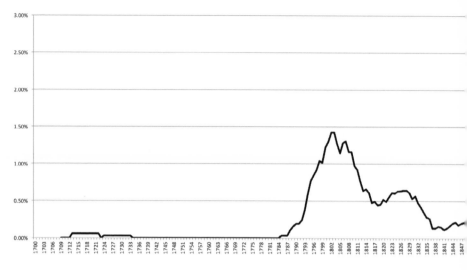

Figure 5.14. Chronological plotting of *castle* in British novel titles

Figure 5.15. Chronological plotting of *London* in British novel titles

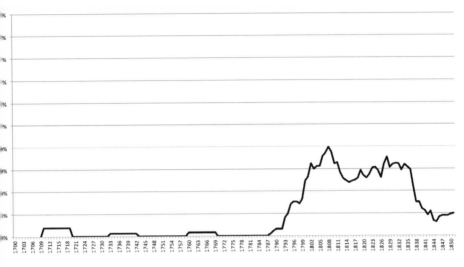

Figure 5.16. Chronological plotting of *century* in British novel titles

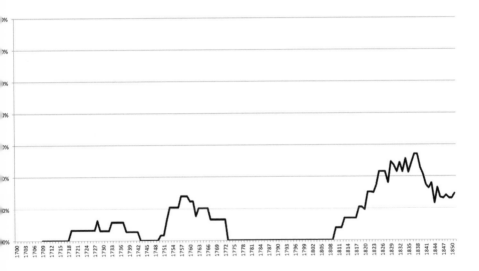

Figure 5.17. Chronological plotting of *Irish* in British novel titles

The data discussed in this chapter raise more questions than they answer. Such a fact should come as some relief to those who worry that the quantification of literature will ring the death knell for further study. At least one intriguing thread to arise from this explorative analysis, however, involves the matter of external influence and the extent to which factors such as gender, ethnicity, time, and geography play a role in determining the choices that authors make about what they write and how their works get titled. It does appear that gender, geography, and time are influential factors in novel production, novel titles, and even the subjects that authors decide to write about. But titles and rich metadata take us only so far. The next chapter investigates these questions by exploring linguistic style in the full text of 106 novels from twelve popular genres of nineteenth-century prose fiction.

6 STYLE

All art is collaboration, and there is little doubt
that in the happy ages of literature, striking and
beautiful phrases were as ready to the story-teller's
hand as the rich cloaks and dresses of his time.

—J. M. Synge, preface to *Playboy of the Western World*

In statistical or quantitative authorship attribution, a researcher attempts to classify a work of unknown or disputed authorship in order to assign it to a known author based on a training set of works of known authorship. Unlike more general document classification, in authorship attribution we do not want to classify documents based on shared or similar document *content.* Instead, the researcher performs classification based upon an author's unique *signal,* or "style." The working assumption of all such investigation is that writers have distinct and detectable stylistic habits, or "tics." A consistent problem for authorship researchers, however, is the possibility that other external factors (for example, linguistic register, genre, nationality, gender, ethnicity, and so on) may influence or even overpower the latent authorial signal. Accounting for the influence of external factors on authorial style is an important task for authorship researchers, but the study of influence is also a concern to literary scholars who wish to understand the creative impulse and the degree to which authors are the products of their times and environments. After all, in the quarry of great literature, it is style, or "technique," that ultimately separates the ore from the tailings.* To greater and lesser extents, individual authors agonize over their craft. After a day spent working on two sentences of *Ulysses,* James Joyce is reported to have said in response to a question from Frank Budgen: "I have the words already. What I am seeking is the perfect order of words in the sentence" (Budgen 1934, 20).† Some readers will prefer Stephanie Meyer to Anne Rice

---

* Even if the difference between the two finally boils down to a simple matter of opinion. One man's ore is another man's silt.

† How long Joyce spent picking the right words remains a mystery.

or Bram Stoker, but when the plots, themes, and genre are essentially similar, reader preference is, in the end, largely a matter of style.

No computation is necessary for readers to distinguish between the writings of Jane Austen and Herman Melville; they write about different subjects, and they each have distinct styles of expression. An obvious point of comparison can be found in the two writers' use of personal pronouns. As a simple example, consider how Austen, who writes more widely about women than Melville, is far more likely to use feminine pronouns. In *Sense and Sensibility*, for example, Austen uses the female pronoun *she* 136 times per 10,000 words. In *Moby Dick*, Melville uses *she* only 5 times per 10,000.* This is a huge difference but one that is not immediately obvious, or conscious, to readers of the two books. What is obvious is that there are not many women in *Moby Dick*. Readers are much more likely to notice the absence of women in the book than they are to notice the absence of feminine pronouns; even the most careful close reader is unlikely to pay much attention to the frequency of common pronouns.† It is exactly these subtle "features" (pronouns, articles, conjunctions, and the like), however, that authorship and stylometry researchers have discovered to be the most telling when it comes to revealing an author's individual style.‡ There are, of course, other stylistic differences that are quite obvious, things that leap out to readers. These are not primarily differences in subject matter but differences in the manner of expression, in the way authors tell their stories. One writer may use an inordinate number of sentence fragments; another may have a fondness for the dash. When these kinds of obvious difference are abundant, and when we simply wish to identify their presence in one author, the use of computation may be unnecessary. Joyce has the habit of introducing dialogue with a dash, whereas D. H. Lawrence does not. The differences between these two writers with regard to the dash are rather striking. Often, however, the differences are not so striking: attributing an unsigned manuscript to one or the other of the Brontë sisters would be a far more challenging problem; their linguistic signatures are quite similar to each other.

* These frequencies were derived from the plain text files archived at Project Gutenberg. File metadata were removed prior to processing.

† On the stealthy nature of pronouns, James W. Pennebaker's *Secret Life of Pronouns* offers an enlightening and entertaining perspective (2011).

‡ There are many ways in which a feature set may be derived, but the growing consensus is that the analysis of high-frequency words (mostly function, or closed-class, words) or n-grams, or both, provides the most consistently reliable results in authorship-attribution problems. See Burrows 2002; Diederich et al. 2000; Grieve 2007; Hoover 2003a, 2003b; Koppel, Argamon, and Shimoni 2002; Martindale and McKenzie 1995; Uzuner and Katz 2005; Yu 2008.

For the sake of illustration, let's imagine a researcher has discovered an anonymous, unpublished manuscript. External evidence shows that either Melville or Austen wrote it. For simplicity, assume that Melville and Austen published only the two aforementioned books, *Sense and Sensibility* and *Moby Dick*. After calculating the relative frequency of *she* in the anonymous text at 86 occurrences per 10,000 words, we might be fairly confident in asserting that Austen, with an average of 94, is the likely author—Melville, remember, uses *she* just 4–5 times per 10,000. However unlikely, it remains possible that the unknown text is in fact a story by Melville with a female protagonist and thus has many more feminine pronouns than what one finds in *Moby Dick*. Were authorship-attribution problems as simple as comparing the use of a single feature, then they would not be problems at all!

Real problems in computational authorship attribution are far more complicated and subtle than the above, one-feature, example. In fact, these problems involve processing "high-dimensional" data. To explain this concept requires expansion of our current example to include a second word; we add the male pronoun *he*. When it comes to *Sense and Sensibility* and *Moby Dick,* the results are almost identical: 63 occurrences per 10,000 for *Sense and Sensibility* and 64 for *Moby Dick*. Plotting these pronoun measurements on a two-dimensional grid, in which the *y* axis is the measure of *he* and the *x* axis the measure of *she,* results in the two-dimensional graph seen in figure 6.1. On the *y* axis, both authors are close to each other, but they are quite far apart on the *she x* axis. Were we to calculate the relative frequency of *he* for the anonymous text at 54 occurrences per 10,000 and plot it alongside Melville and Austen, we would see that in terms of these two dimensions, the anonymous text is much "closer" to Austen, where *she* occurred 86 times per 10,000 words (figure 6.2). Still, this would not be very convincing evidence in support of an attribution to Austen. To be convincing, the researcher must account for many more features, and since the number of dimensions corresponds to the number of features examined, any charting of distances quickly goes beyond what can be represented on a two-dimensional *x-y* grid. Imagine adding a third word feature, the word *it*, for example. By extending a *z* axis back in space, the relative frequencies of *it* in Melville, Austen, and the anonymous text could be plotted, as in figure 6.3. The task would now be to identify which author is closest to the anonymous text in a three-dimensional space. Add a fourth or fifth feature, and things get complicated. Whereas the human mind is incapable of visualizing this problem much further than three dimensions, mathematics is not so hobbled, and there are a variety of statistical methods for plotting and calculating distances between objects in multidimensional space.

Principal component analysis was one of the earliest statistical techniques applied to this multidimensional problem (see, for example, Burrows 1989).

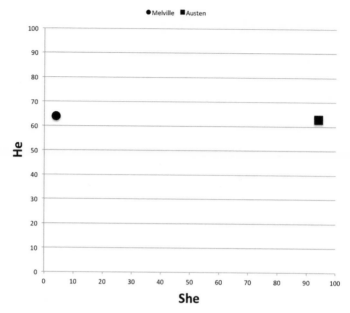

Figure 6.1. Two-dimensional feature plot with two books

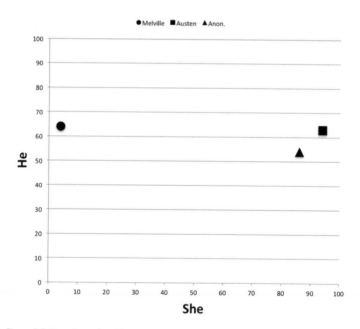

Figure 6.2. Two-dimensional feature plot with three books

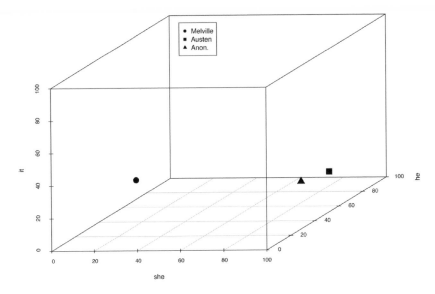

Figure 6.3. Three-dimensional feature plot with three books

PCA is a method of condensing multiple features into "principal components," components that represent, somewhat closely, but not perfectly, the amount of variance in the data.* More recently, authorship researchers have adopted statistical methods from the machine-learning literature.† Generally speaking, these methods involve some form of supervised classification: a process that involves "training" a machine to recognize a particular author's feature-usage patterns and then allowing the machine to classify a new text according to how well it "matches" or is similar to the training data. Unlike PCA, these methods are designed to grapple with all of the features in a high-dimensional space. As such, these classification results are often more interpretable.‡ Whereas PCA condenses features into components, these techniques keep the features as distinct dimensions.

* Mick Alt provides an excellent, nontechnical, discussion of how PCA works in *Exploring Hyperspace* (1990).

† Jockers and Witten (2010) offer a benchmarking analysis of five high-dimensional, machine-learning algorithms for authorship attribution. See also Jockers, Witten, and Criddle 2008; Yu 2008; and a more extensive analysis in Zhao and Zobel 2005.

‡ Machine classification is employed extensively in what follows here and in subsequent chapters. A more extensive overview of the benefits will become apparent.

Even with a suitable statistical method and an appropriate feature set, there are still outstanding problems that challenge authorship-attribution researchers. In particular, there is the challenge associated with not knowing exactly what is responsible for the usage patterns measured in the feature set. For example, if the training samples include nonfiction texts and the text to be identified is fictional, it may be that the different usage patterns detected are better attributed to genre differences than to authorial differences. In an ideal authorship case, the training data and the test data are as homogenous as possible. The *Federalist Papers,* studied extensively by Mosteller and Wallace (1964) in their landmark work, serves as an ideal case. Of the eighty-five *Federalist Papers,* fifteen are considered to be of unclear authorship. But each of the fifteen disputed papers is known to have been written by at least one of three men: James Madison, Alexander Hamilton, and John Jay.* The undisputed papers offer an ample collection of works by Madison, Hamilton, and Jay for use in training a classifier. Because all the papers deal with the same subject and are of fairly uniform length, the *Federalist Papers* is considered by many to be an ideal corpus for authorship-attribution research, and, as R. S. Forsyth noted some years ago, the *Federalist Papers* problem "is possibly the best candidate for an accepted benchmark in stylometry" (1997). But researchers rarely find such well-defined and well-controlled problems. They must inevitably grapple with the possibility of unknown external factors influencing their attribution results and offer caveats when it comes to the role that nonauthorial factors such as genre may or may not play in the determination of style. Because each problem is unique, there is no simple way of defining or accounting for the extent to which factors external to an author's personal style may influence a given composition.

In recent work analyzing the degree to which novelistic genres express a distinguishable stylistic signal, my colleagues and I were faced with a problem of having to assess how much of a detected "genre" signal could be reasonably attributed to the conventions of the genre and how much of the signal was likely to be attributable to other factors, such as author, time period, or author gender. The work began as a collaboration with Mike Witmore of the University of Wisconsin. Witmore and his colleague Jonathan Hope had published a series of papers that used a software package called Docuscope to extract features from Shakespeare's plays. These features are called Language Action Types, or LATs (Hope 2004; Witmore 2007). Using these LATs, Witmore and Hope machine-clustered Shakespeare's plays into categories that aligned extremely well with our human-defined genre classes of "history," "tragedy," and "comedy." After learning of Witmore's results, Franco Moretti was interested to see whether

---

* This is a bit of a simplification; some of the papers are thought to have been coauthored. Details can be found in Mosteller and Wallace 1964.

the same technique could be employed to classify nineteenth-century novels into their novelistic subgenres (for example, "Bildungsroman," "national tale," "Gothic," and so on). If the techniques were successful, then there would be evidence to support the hypothesis that genre operates at a lexical, linguistic, and stylistic level. Through analysis of the features used in the clustering, a variety of assertions about how the different genres are "expressed" might be made. The research team at the Stanford Literary Lab compiled a corpus of 106 nineteenth-century novels, and Moretti identified each according to novelistic genre. Each novel was then segmented into tenths, for a total of 1,060 segments. Witmore was given these data without any identifying information—title pages were stripped out—and his task was to work over the data with his methods and then report his findings at Stanford in February 2009. The results of Witmore's experiment were impressive, and the entire experiment was later documented in "Quantitative Formalism: An Experiment," published in *Pamphlet One* of the Stanford Literary Lab (Allison et al. 2012).

At the same time that Witmore was preparing his results, I began a series of parallel experiments. Witmore's work used Docuscope to convert lexical information into LATs, which were then counted, normalized, and used as features in his clustering procedures. For the parallel experiments, frequently occurring words and punctuation tokens were extracted and used as the basis for a feature set. Any word or mark of punctuation with a mean relative frequency across the corpus of above 0.03 percent was selected.* This resulted in a feature set of 42 high-frequency word and punctuation types: a matrix of 1,060 texts by 42 features with measurements of relative frequency for each.† Using these features, an unsupervised clustering of the data was performed: first a distance matrix computation was applied and then a hierarchical clustering analysis.‡ The procedure calculates the Euclidian distance between the texts and then groups them according to the "closeness" of their individual signals. The results were

---

* The decision to use 0.03 percent was arbitrary. The number was selected in order to ensure that the features were not context-specific words but function words that are used at a high rate. Zipf's law has demonstrated empirically that the frequency of any word in a corpus is inversely proportional to its rank in the frequency table. In other words, the frequency of the words drops off steeply.

† The forty-two words and punctuation features are as follows: *a, all, an, and, as, at, be, but, by, for, from, had, have, he, her, his, I, in, is, it, me, my, not, of, on, p_apos, p_comma, p_exlam, p_hyphen, p_period, p_quote, p_semi, she, that, the, this, to, was, were, which, with, you.*

‡ The mathematical details may be found by consulting the help files for the "dist" and "hclust" functions of the R statistical software package (http://www.R-project.org). Euclidean distance ("dist" in R) is explained in greater detail in chapter 9.

startling: using just 42 features, the routine not only grouped chunks from the same texts together (an unsurprising result in itself), but also grouped works from the same genres in close proximity. The results suggested that there were grounds for believing that genres have a distinct linguistic signal; at the same time, however, a close analysis of the data tended to confirm the general consensus among authorship-attribution researchers, namely, that the individual usage of high-frequency words and punctuation serves as an excellent discriminator between authors. In other words, though genre signals were observed, there was also the presence of author signals and no obvious way of determining which feature-usage patterns were most clearly "authorial" and which "generic."

Although the results were encouraging, they forced us to more carefully consider our claims about genre. If genres, like authors, appear to have distinguishable linguistic expressions that can be detected at the level of common function words, then a way was needed for disambiguating the "author" effects from those of genre and for determining whether such effects were diluting or otherwise obscuring the genre signals we observed. If there were author effects as well as genre effects, then one must consider the further possibility that there are generational effects (that is, time-based factors) in the usage of language: perhaps the genre signals being observed were in fact just characteristic of a particular generation's habits of style. In other words, although it was clear that the novels were clustering together in genre groups, it was not clear that these groupings could be attributed to signals expressed by unique genres. Although the results looked compelling, they were not satisfying. A way of separating and controlling for author, gender, and generation was required.

In the initial experiment, unsupervised machine clustering was used to "sift" the texts based on similarities in common-word and punctuation usage. In machine clustering, the objective is to group similar items into clusters. We get an algorithm and feed it a lot of information about our novels and ask it to group the novels into clusters based on how similar they are to each other. We measure similarity in this case based on a set of variables or features. If we were clustering shapes, for example, we might have a feature called "number of sides." The computer would cluster three-sided objects into one pile and four-sided objects into another; the machine would not know in advance that these shapes were examples of what we call "triangles" and "squares." In machine clustering, an algorithm assesses all the data at once with no prior information about potential groupings. The process clusters novels with similar data patterns together, and these data can be plotted in a treelike structure that links the genres based on similarity across the 42 features (figure 6.4). It is up to the researcher to then assess the outcome and determine the extent to which the clusters make human sense. The clusters of genres in figure 6.4 do make sense.

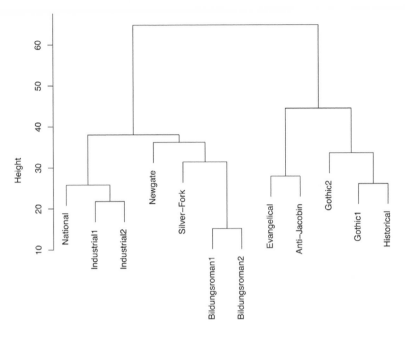

Figure 6.4. Cluster dendrogram of genres

Industrial novels grouped together, as did the Bildungsroman novels. Gothics clustered with historical novels and so on. The results conform to our human expectations, which are, of course, based on our human "definitions" of what constitutes these genres in the first place.

In a *supervised* experiment, however, the goal is not to cluster similar objects, but to classify an unknown text, or texts, into any one of a set of predefined categories or classes. The researcher groups and labels a set of "training texts" in advance, and the machine uses this information to build a "model." The machine assesses a new text and places it into the most similar of the previously defined categories that the model has learned. Once the model is constructed, a new text can be analyzed and "classified" into one of the existing categories. This is an approach frequently used in authorship attribution: the process assigns an anonymous text to a known author within a closed set of candidates. In the case of this genre experiment, however, there are no texts of unknown origin; we already know "the answers." Instead of trying to classify some unseen text into a known category, the goal here is to use the machine to assess the relative strength of the genre signal against the other potential signals. Because we already know the "correct" answers, the accuracy of the classification can be known with absolute certainty, and the accuracies can then be compared across different tests. In other words, it is possible to apply the techniques of author-ship attribution as a way to investigate factors other than author.

To investigate this matter thoroughly, a process of iterative sampling is re-quired. Using scripts written in R, an iterative experiment was conducted in which with each iteration two-thirds of the texts in the data set were selected at random for training a model, and the remaining one-third were held out as "test" data for classification. After each iteration of sampling and classification, the rate of classification error was recorded. The rates of error were then aver-aged over the number of runs of the process to arrive at an average or expected rate of error. When conducting this experiment using novelistic genre as the predefined class, an error rate of 33 percent was observed.* In other words, given this closed set of 1,060 text segments from 106 nineteenth-century nov-els, the algorithm could correctly guess the segment's genre 67 percent of the time. Considering the fairly high number of available classes (twelve genres) and the relatively small number of samples, 67 percent was a decent average.† Nevertheless, this figure, which represents the mean number of cases in which a correct result was returned, tells only part of the story. To fully understand the results requires analysis of the resulting confusion matrix, which measures the "precision" and "recall" of the classification.

Precision is a measurement of the number of "true positives" for any given class divided by the sum of the true positives and false positives. In other words, we divide the number of times that the machine correctly guessed "Gothic" by how many times it guessed "Gothic" overall (including the incorrect guesses). *Precision* is, therefore, a measure of correct Gothic guesses (true positives) ver-sus incorrect Gothic guesses (false positives).‡ *Recall*, on the other hand, is a measurement of the number of true positives divided by the actual number of items in the class; or, to put it another way, *recall* is the number of correctly

---

* The Nearest Shrunken Centroid classification algorithm (Tibshirani et al. 2003) was used in this experiment. A more detailed description of NSC follows below. The figure 33 percent represents the F-measure, or "F-score," which is an aggregate measure of model accuracy.

† For example, there were only four evangelical novels, thus only forty fragment samples in the corpus upon which to train and test the model. The complete data set is available online at http://www.stanford.edu/group/litlab/cgi-bin/pamphletData/index .php?data_requested=one.

‡ Naturally, these human-assigned genres are not perfect. Scholars may in fact argue over whether any single novel is more appropriately placed in one genre or another, or perhaps, as is often the case, more than one. For this work, however, the selection of novels was done in a conservative fashion and in order to avoid novels that might be deemed too ambiguous.

guessed Gothic texts divided by the sum of correctly guessed Gothic texts and texts that should have been identified as Gothic but were classified as something else. Table 6.1 shows the full confusion matrix for the genre test.

In this experiment, the classifier achieved the highest degree of precision (88 percent) when classifying the sensation novels. Of the thirty-four sensation ("Sens") assignments, only four were incorrect. For sensation novels, recall was also fairly good, at 75 percent. The classifier correctly identified "Sens" in 75 percent of the novel fragments that were in fact sensation novels. National ("Natl") novels present a different case. Precision for national novels was just 48 percent, meaning that only 48 percent of the "national" guesses that the classifier made were in fact true positives. In other words, the national "genre signal" that the machine established during training was relatively weak and was frequently "misdetected" in novels of other genres. Recall, however, was exceptional, meaning that when the actual genre class was national, the classifier rarely misclassified it as something else. This does not necessarily mean that the national model was especially good at classifying national novels; it could mean that the signals the model constructed for the other genres were comparatively better, and the national signal became a kind of default assignment when none of the other genre signals offered a strong match.

In fact, every assignment that the model makes is based on a probability of one class versus another, and in some cases the most probable choice is only slightly better than the second most probable choice. Take the case of a randomly selected text sample from the data: a sample with the unique ID 642. This text sample is from an anti-Jacobin novel, and the classifier correctly classified it as anti-Jacobin with 99.3 percent probability over the other genre classes in this closed set of genres. The next closest genre assignment was evangelical with 0.04 percent. In this case, the classifier is very confident about its selection of anti-Jacobin. Less certain is the machine's classification of sample ID 990, which is a segment from a Gothic novel. The machine misclassified sample 990 as anti-Jacobin with 52 percent probability. The second-place candidate, however, was Gothic, the correct genre, to which the machine assigned a probability of 47 percent. The choice the machine made between Gothic and anti-Jacobin for this particular segment was based on a very small probability margin. Were we not dealing with a computer and statistics, one might even say that the choice was "not an easy one to make." Text sample 990 had much about it that seemed anti-Jacobin and much about it that seemed Gothic. Given the reality of these "close-call" situations, it is useful to consider both the first- and the second-place assignments when assessing the overall performance and value of the model, especially so when we consider that the classes that we are dealing with here, genres, are human inventions that are not always clearly delineated and

Table 6.1. Twelve novelistic subgenres

	Hist	Newg	Jaco	Goth	Silv	Sens	Bild	Indu	Evan	Natl	Anti	Precision (%)
Hist	117	16	1	25	4	2	0	9	1	0	3	65.7
Newg	5	31	1	1	1	1	1	6	0	0	0	66.0
Jaco	1	1	42	9	0	1	1	3	2	1	3	65.6
Goth	7	2	16	51	1	0	0	0	0	0	8	60.0
Silv	7	12	5	7	20	0	2	2	2	1	5	31.7
Sens	0	0	0	0	1	30	1	2	0	0	0	88.2
Bild	1	2	0	1	2	5	44	2	0	0	1	67.7
Indu	1	3	0	1	0	1	10	38	1	0	0	69.1
Evan	0	0	3	3	0	0	0	0	20	0	0	76.9
Natl	13	0	3	1	4	0	0	7	0	26	0	48.1
Anti	0	0	1	2	2	0	0	0	1	0	29	82.9
Recall (%)	77.0	46.3	58.3	50.5	57.1	75.0	74.6	50.0	74.1	92.9	59.2	

Note: The categories are as follows: historical, Newgate, Jacobin, Gothic, silver-fork, sensation, Bildungsroman, industrial, evangelical, national, and anti-Jacobin.

can "bleed" into each other. We might, for example, find a novel that is in our human estimation composed of equal parts Bildungsroman and silver-fork.*

If we consider either a first- or a second-place assignment as an "accurate" or useful assignment, then overall model quality looks quite a lot better. Figure 6.5 shows the percentage of correct assignments for each genre when "accuracy" is defined as a true positive in either the first or the second place. The genres in figure 6.5 are sorted from left to right based on the accuracy of the first, or primary, assignment. So, while sensation and industrial novels have the highest percentage of correct first-place assignments, 100 percent of Newgate and evangelical novels are assigned as either first or second most probable.

In order to contextualize these data, it is instructive to examine the places where the classifier went wrong, the misclassifications. When a novel segment is assigned to the wrong class, it is useful to know what that wrong class is. It is particularly useful to know if a specific type of incorrect class assignment occurs frequently. For example, when Bildungsroman segments are misclassified, they are most often (50 percent of all the misclassifications) classified as industrial novels, a fact that suggests that there may be some linguistic or stylistic affinity between the Bildungsroman and industrial novels in these test data. Figure 6.6 shows a breakdown of the misclassified Bildungsroman novel segments.

An examination of figure 6.5 and figure 6.6 provides us with a way of better understanding not only the stylistic signal of genres but also the extent to which genres share stylistic affinity. For example, every one of the Bildungsroman novels that was misclassified in first place as industrial was correctly identified in the second-place position as Bildungsroman. In other words, there appears to be a special affinity between Bildungsroman and industrial novels when it comes to the usage of these high-frequency words and marks of punctuation. What exactly this stylistic affinity is requires a still deeper analysis of the data returned by the algorithm; however, it is interesting to note here that the Bildungsroman segments that were misclassified as industrial novels were also all from novels roughly within the time period that we typically associate with the industrial. The segments misidentified as industrial came from Thackeray's *Pendennis* (1849) and from two novels by George Eliot, *Middlemarch* (1872) and *Daniel Deronda* (1876). Given that Eliot's 1866 industrial novel *Felix Holt* is also in the data set, it is natural to wonder whether the misassignments here could be attributed to a latent author signal overpowering the forces of genre. Alternatively, it may be that the pull toward industrial is in fact a "generational" force. Is it perhaps not genre style at all but some other factor that is influencing

---

* Remember too, that the texts have been segmented, so a particular segment could quite possibly be more "silver-forkey" than the novel as a whole.

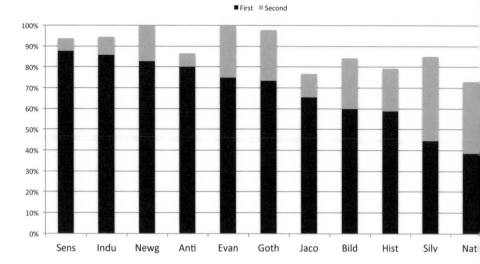

Figure 6.5. First- and second-place genre assignments

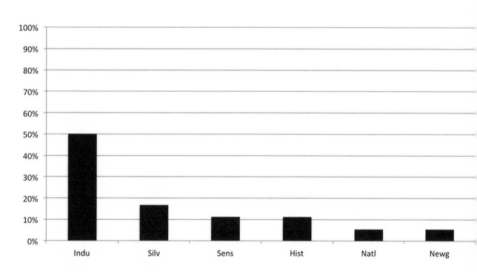

Figure 6.6. Incorrect assignment of Bildungsroman novels

these misclassifications? Before exploring this possibility, a few final observations are in order, so that we might fully understand the scope and diversity of evidence made available to us for analysis.

· · ·

In addition to the data already discussed, the machine also provides information about the features used in the analysis and which among these features proved most useful in separating between the different classes. For example, three features that are positively correlated with the Bildungsroman are the word features *like, young,* and *little,* which is to say that these three words are overrepresented in Bildungsroman novels compared to the other genres in the test data. Alternatively, the words *upon, by,* and *this* are underutilized in the Bildungsroman compared to other genres. The comma finds greatest expression in the national tale but is comparatively absent from sensation novels, where there is a preference for the period. Like the national tale, historical novels also overutilize the comma at the expense of the period. The exclamation mark appears prominently in Newgate novels, unsurprising given the nature of the genre, but is relatively absent from evangelical novels. This is by no means an exhaustive analysis of the available features or their relative weights within each class; such an analysis would amount to a discussion of 1,932 unique data points. Instead, these features represent a sampling of the richness of data available for interpretation. In other words, although it is clear that there is stylistic separation between the genres, it is not obvious why that separation exists or how that separation is embodied in the texts. The answer to the question of why undoubtedly lies in the details of the relative feature weights and requires careful analysis and interpretation in order to be able to move from the individual features toward a larger-scale description of how these features constitute a particular genre.

In prior work (Allison et al. 2012), my colleagues and I speculated that a high incidence of locative prepositions in the Gothic novel is a direct result of the genre's being heavily "place oriented." As such, this genre demands a relatively greater frequency of locative prepositions in order to situate the novel's settings in space. This current investigation reveals strong evidence that there are even deeper subtleties of style, of linguistic usage, lurking beneath the surface of our long-established, noncomputational taxonomy of genre. Though not necessarily obvious or apparent to readers, these linguistic nuances are detectable by machine and lead us not only to a deeper understanding of the genres, which they define, but also to clearer definitions of genre itself.

Like the earlier experiments with clustering described in "Quantitative Formalism" (Allison et al. 2011), the supervised classification tests conducted here have added support to the hypothesis that genres indeed have a distinct stylistic signature, and they demonstrate that a genre signal exists and can be detected at the level of high-frequency word and punctuation features. The possible presence of other influential factors—factors such as time period, nationality, author, and author gender, for example—requires deeper investigation. Before we can argue that genres have measurable linguistic fingerprints, we must be able to isolate those feature fluctuations that are attributable only to genre and are not simply artifacts of some other external factor.

A further experiment was constructed using the same set of 106 novels but expanding the feature set from the 42 most frequent features to include all lexical and typographical elements exceeding a mean relative frequency threshold of 0.005. The idea was to expand the feature set in such a way that more features were included but context-sensitive features were still excluded. As noted previously, this feature winnowing, or "culling," is designed to exclude context-sensitive words that might bias a classifier in favor of texts that share a common subject and not simply a similar style. A visual inspection of the word list suggested that .005 was an effective frequency threshold, one that selected few context-sensitive words.* Novel segmentation remained the same: each book was divided into 10 equal-size sample fragments. The result of this preprocessing and feature extraction was a data matrix of 1,060 segment "rows" by 161 feature "columns." A unique ID further identified each sample, and to each row five additional metadata fields were added, indicating the gender of the author, the genre of the sample, the decade of publication, the author, and the title of the novel from which the sample was extracted.† The objective was to then analyze and rank each of the five metadata categories in terms of their effectiveness in accurately predicting the classes of the test data. Or, put another way, the goal was to assess which of these five categories "secretes" the strongest linguistic signal as measured by overall classification accuracy and by precision and recall. Complicating matters, however, each of the five categories has a dif-

---

* The 161 features selected were as follows: *a, about, after, again, all, am, an, and, any, are, as, at, be, been, before, being, but, by, can, come, could, day, did, do, down, even, ever, every, eyes, father, first, for, from, go, good, great, had, hand, has, have, he, heart, her, here, him, himself, his, house, how, I, if, in, into, is, it, its, know, lady, last, life, like, little, long, lord, love, made, make, man, may, me, might, mind, miss, more, most, Mr., Mrs., much, must, my, myself, never, no, not, now, of, old, on, one, only, or, other, our, out, over, own, p_apos, p_colon, p_comma, p_exclam, p_hyphen, p_period, p_ques, p_quot, p_semi, room, said, say, see, seemed, shall, she, should, sir, so, some, still, such, take, than, that, the, their, them, then, there, these, they, think, this, those, though, thought, time, to, too, two, up, upon, us, very, was, way, we, well, were, what, when, where, which, while, who, whom, will, with, without, would, yet, you, young, your.*

† A complete list of all the texts and their novelistic genres can be found in Allison et al. 2012.

ferent number of classes and thus presents a different degree of difficulty for the classifier. This in turn makes the simple comparison of accuracies problematic. With gender, for example, there are only two possible classes, male or female, whereas there are 47 different authors and 106 different titles in this data set. Thus, any comparison of relative strengths must take into consideration both the difficulty of the specific classification problem and the overall classification accuracy result. Ultimately, the relative strength of the five categories—calculated in terms of their predictive power—must be determined. Only then does it become possible to construct a hierarchy of signal strengths and thereby rank the stylistic pull associated with each category of metadata.

Unlike a real classification problem, in which there is some hitherto unclassified text of unknown origins, in this experiment all of the true classes are already known in advance. Because the classes are known in advance, the effectiveness of the classification process can be measured with perfect accuracy. Instead of using the classifier to guess the most likely source of a particular signal, the classifier's output is used as a way of gauging the signal strength of the sources. The classifier becomes a means for better understanding the interrelationships of the five categories with the linguistic data—the assumption being that the stronger the linguistic signal, the more accurate the classification accuracy. In other words, the classifier can be used to help understand which of the five different categories exerts the most influence on the resulting patterns found in the linguistic data. By way of analogy, we might imagine a clinical trial in which we wish to understand the factors influencing the effectiveness of a new blood-pressure drug. In this hypothetical trial, we begin by evaluating a patient's weight, age, gender, height, and beginning blood pressure. We then administer the drug. At the end of the trial, we measure the blood pressure and assess the degree to which the drug was effective. However, we also must look for any correlation between overall effectiveness and any one or more patient features that we evaluated at the beginning of the trial. For example, it may be discovered that the age of a patient influences the efficacy of the drug; for example, patients over fifty do not respond to treatment.*

To test the predictive power of each metadata category, the Nearest Shrunken Centroid (Tibshirani et al. 2003) classification algorithm was employed.† The NSC is a subtype of "nearest centroid" algorithms that begin by computing a

---

* The analysis of style undertaken here is very similar if in fact a bit more complicated than this analogy might suggest.

† The NSC algorithms are available as part of the Prediction Analysis of Microarrays (pamr) package in the open-source R statistics software (R Development Core Team 2011).

standard centroid* for each class, calculating the average frequency for a feature in each class, and then dividing by the in-class standard deviation for that feature. The NSC takes an additional step of shrinking the centroids in a way that has the end result of eliminating features that contribute "noise" to the model.† Although the NSC was developed to aid in the diagnosis of cancer types through the analysis of gene-expression data, it has been shown to perform well in stylistic analysis, especially so in authorship attribution (Jockers, Witten, and Criddle 2008; Jockers and Witten 2010).‡ From a statistical perspective, the two types of problems (genetic and stylistic) are similar: both are composed of high-dimensional data, and the linguistic features are roughly analogous to the individual genes.

For each metadata category (gender, genre, decade, author, text), the model is run, and a tenfold cross-validation provides the resulting rates of error. These errors are averaged to generate an overall estimate of accuracy for each category.§ The average rates of error and accuracy are recorded in table 6.2. The cross-validation results indicated that "decade" was the weakest influence and "author" the strongest. However, as noted previously, each rate of error must be understood in the context of the number of potential classes within the category and in terms of both precision and recall. For example, "gender" involves classifying samples into one of two possible classes (male or female). A classifier guessing purely at random could be expected to guess correctly 50 percent of the time (at least in cases where there were equal numbers of male and female test samples).¶ Thus, with an overall error rate of 20 percent, the gender-based model is 1.6 times better than chance. Thought of another way, the addition of the linguistic data improves classification accuracy from 50 percent to 80 percent.# For "decade" there are ten potential classes, so a classifier guessing at random could be expected to guess correctly 10 percent of the time. In this

* A centroid is the geometric center of a cluster of points.

† A layman's overview of how NSC works is available at http://www-stat.stanford.edu/~tibs/PAM/Rdist/howwork.html.

‡ Other classifiers could have been selected as well, but there was no reason to believe that one or another would be better suited to this problem than NSC. In separate research (Jockers and Witten 2010), it has been shown that five machine-learning algorithms performed well on this type of problem and that NSC was marginally better than the four other techniques tested.

§ A uniform prior was assumed on all classes during cross-validation.

¶ A 50 percent baseline for accuracy in binary classification is in fact true only in cases where there are an equal number of both classes in the test data. In the case of this experiment, it was very close to even: 52 percent of the test segments were from male authors and 48 percent from females.

An examination of the confusion matrix, which is discussed below, indicates that the classifier does slightly better in classifying males versus females: 80 percent and 76

Table 6.2. Classification accuracy across metadata types

Category	Rate of error (%)	Accuracy (%)	Improvement over chance (number of times)
Author	7	93	44
Text	15	85	90
Gender	20	80	1.6
Genre	33	67	8.0
Decade	47	53	5.3

experiment, we observe 53 percent correct classifications, 5.3 times better than chance. In the case of "genre" where there are twelve potential classes and an expected rate of accuracy of 8.3 percent, a classification accuracy rate of 67 percent was observed. This result is eight times better than chance. For "text" there were 106 potential classes. This is clearly the most challenging of the five problems. Based on chance alone, less than 1 percent (0.94) could be expected to be classed correctly. However, 85 percent of the classifications are correct for a result that is 90 times better than chance alone. Finally, for "author" there are 47 potential classes. We should expect 2.1 percent correct assignments by chance; nevertheless, 93 percent of the samples were classed correctly for a result that is 44 times better than chance! This is an impressive result, indicating the strength of the author signal. In fact, the author signal overpowers even the signal associated with a particular text written by that same author. Which is to say that when using only high-frequency linguistic word and punctuation features, we are more likely to capture who wrote a given segment of text than we are to guess which text the segment was selected from. Although particular segments of a single text do appear to have quantifiable "signatures," even those signatures do not overpower the strong linguistic fingerprints left by authorship alone. This result supports the conventional wisdom favoring the use of high-frequency, context-insensitive features in authorship-attribution problems.*

---

percent precision, respectively. Recall is slightly better for females, 79 percent versus 77 percent for males.

* In the above analysis, it was convenient to assume uniform prior probabilities for each class—if there are ten possible classes, then each class has a 10 percent likelihood of being selected by chance. In reality, the classes were never evenly distributed in this manner, and, thus, each class has a different baseline for accuracy. To fully explicate the results would require discussion of each class within each experiment. The confusion matrices (found online at http://www.matthewjockers.net/macroanalysisbook/confusion-matrices/) provide all the detail necessary for the reader to evaluate the results of these classification tests.

The primary aim of the experiment, however, was not to classify the samples but instead to use the classification methodology as a way of measuring the extent to which factors beyond an individual author's personal style may play a role in determining the linguistic usage and style of the resulting text. There is no simple process for making such a determination; nevertheless, these figures offer a beginning point for assessing the relative "pull" or strength of each category. Prior to running this experiment, my colleagues and I in the Literary Lab hypothesized that the authorial signal would be strongest, followed, we suspected, by a generational signal, as determined by date of publication.

Franco Moretti's earlier work in *Graphs, Maps, Trees* (2005) had suggested the possibility of literary generations, periods of generic homogeneity, that lasted roughly thirty years. The most surprising result of the classification tests is that the time signal appears to be comparatively weak. When asked to assign texts based on their decade of publication, an error rate of 47 percent was observed. In other words, whereas the algorithm could correctly assign 67 percent of the text segments to their proper genre, it could correctly assign only 47 percent to their proper decade of publication. This result appears to show, at least when it comes to the most frequently occurring words and marks of punctuation, that genre produces a more reliable and detectable signal than decade. A closer analysis of these data, however, reveals that decades and time periods are far more complicated and influential than we might expect.

The trouble with using decades as described above is that as a delimiter of time, they impose arbitrary and artificial boundaries. If novelistic style changes over time, it is not likely to change according to a ten-year window that begins and ends at the turn of a new decade—or any other span of time, for that matter.* In a study of forty-four genres covering a 160-year period, Moretti describes finding six "generations" or "bursts of creativity" in which certain genres appear, are expressed for twenty-five to thirty years, and then disappear, replaced by new genres, in what he calls a "regular changing of the guard" (ibid., 18). Moretti argues that what we see in genre over the course of the nineteenth century are periods of relative "stillness" followed by brief "punctuating" moments of more extreme generic change.† A close examination of the classification results for decade revealed that when the classifications were incorrect—when a text segment was assigned to a decade from which it did not originate—the erroneous assignments in classification tended to cluster near to the target decade. In other words, when a classification was wrong, it tended to be just missing

---

* Chronological stylistic change is explored in greater detail in chapter 9.

† We are reminded here of Harold Bloom's (1973) notion of "anxiety" as a motivation for change, of Colin Martindale's (1990) "law of novelty," and of the Russian formalist Tynjanov's generational model of "archaists and innovators" in literary history.

the mark, assigned to the decade just before or just after the "correct" decade. In essence, what is seen in these data is a shifting of style somewhat analogous to what Moretti observed in terms of shifting genres. This observation raised a new question: are the two trends, stylistic and generic, independent? Before tackling that question, it is instructive to examine table 6.3, showing the classifier's assignments and highlighting these latent thirty-year generations of style. The percentages in the cells indicate the proportion of all of the assignments to a given decade signal (row) that appears in a given decade (column). The gray shading highlights the target decade and the decades immediately to either side of the target where the greatest number of assignments was made. This reveals what are, in essence, thirty-year clusters of stylistic similarity.

Without exception the majority of assignments for each decade's signal are found in the correct decade. To take the 1790s as an example: 60 percent of all assignments the classifier made based on its modeling of a 1790s signal were correctly assigned to the 1790s. When the classifier does make an incorrect assignment, with only a few exceptions, the erroneous classification is assigned to a decade just before or just after the correct decade. In the case of the 1790s, 14 percent of the works classified as being from the 1790s were in fact published in the 1780s. Studying the attribution patterns reveals that the majority of incorrect assignments occur in the adjacent decades, leading to a slightly artificial plotting of thirty-year generations of style. The generations are not, of course, perfect; nor would we expect them to be. But the presence of these roughly thirty-year clusters is undeniable. Take, for example, the signal that most typifies the 1790s. It begins in the 1780s and then tapers off in the four decades following the 1790s. The signal most strongly associated with the 1840s first appears

Table 6.3. Classification accuracy and thirty-year generations

	1780 (%)	1790 (%)	1800 (%)	1810 (%)	1820 (%)	1830 (%)	1840 (%)	1850 (%)	1860 (%)	1870 (%)
1780s signal	92	8								
1790s signal	14	60	8	7	2	1	4		3	
1800s signal	14	16	39	13	5	2	5	8		
1810s signal	9	8	8	53	5	3	6	8		
1820s signal	9	1	7	29	32	11	7	2		1
1830s signal	11	4	10	7	7	31	13	4	11	
1840s signal			5	5	9	7	28	34	7	4
1850s signal					2		4	58	36	
1860s signal								16	71	14
1870s signal										100

Note: Columns represent the actual decades of composition, and rows represent the computed "signal" associated with the decade in the row label. Percentages in the cells show the proportion of attributions to the row signal in the column decade.

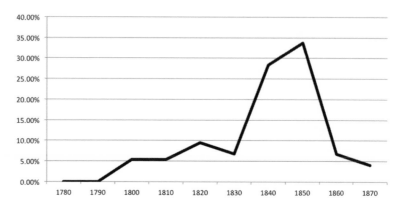

Figure 6.7. The 1840s signal over time

in the 1800s and then builds steadily in the 1830s before peaking in the 1850s. Also noteworthy is how the signals experience a period of strength and then taper off over time in what appears to be some sort of residual effect. A good example of this is seen in figure 6.7, showing the 1840s signal. Trace elements of material constituting the 1840s signal are detected in works from the 1800s to 1830s. Much more of the signal is detected in the 1840s and 1850s. Then the signal more or less disappears.

This phenomenon of successive generations, or waves, of style is visualized further in figure 6.8, where time is represented on the x axis, and the assignments are plotted as a percentage of all assignments in the given class on the y axis. Each shaded area represents a single decade's signal as it is detected across the entire one hundred years of the data set. The signals, like ripples in a pond of prose, peak chronologically from left to right. Ninety percent of the 1780s assignments appear in the 1780s. The remaining 10 percent (not visible behind the other areas in the chart) are assigned to text segments from the 1790s. The second-to-last signal in the chart, the 1860s signal, is first seen in the 1850s, with 16 percent of all the assignments to this signal, followed by 71 percent in the 1860s and then 14 percent in the 1870s. The data appear to confirm Moretti's observation that literary genres evolve and disappear over roughly thirty-year generations. Remember, however, that Moretti is speaking specifically of genre. Here we are not tracking genre signals at all; we are tracking decade signals. Or are we?

If we look at the distribution of novels in the corpus based on their genres and decades of publication, we see something similar to the generations discovered in the plotting of the stylistic "decade" signals. Table 6.4 shows the composition of the full corpus of 106 novels in terms of genre and decade: percentages are calculated by row and represent the proportion of texts from a genre (noted in the row label) that was published in a specific decade column. For example,

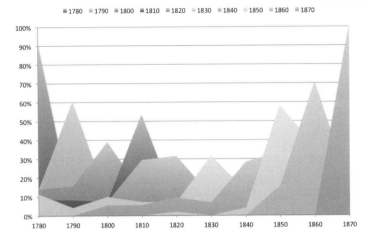

Figure 6.8. Generational waves of genre

Table 6.4. Distribution of novel genres over time

	1780s (%)	1790s (%)	1800s (%)	1810s (%)	1820s (%)	1830s (%)	1840s (%)	1850s (%)	1860s (%)	1870s (%)
Goth	15	54	8	15	8					
Jaco		100								
Anti		40	60							
Evan			33	67						
Natl			38	63						
Hist			4	44	33	7	11			
Silv				11	56	22	11			
Newg						86	14			
Indu							44	44	11	
Bild							27	36	18	18
Sens								20	80	

the first row tells us that 15 percent of the Gothic novels in the corpus were published in the 1780s.

Table 6.4 is thus similar to Moretti's representation of genre in figure 9 of *Graphs, Maps, Trees* (2005), but with the addition here of percentages to represent the distributions of texts in our particular test corpus. No statistics are required to see that there is an obvious linear correlation between time and genre.* Nor is it too surprising to discover this given that the genre designations

* At least in this corpus of 106 novels, which was not constructed in order to be representative of novelistic variety or genre but rather as a way of exploring genre.

were probably assigned, at least in part, to help delineate the texts by period. The open question remains unanswered: are the "signals" that the model constructed to identify decades in fact stylistic manifestations of genre? The answer turns out to be no, but no with enough caveats and qualifications that in the absence of further data, one might argue the contrary.

Notice in table 6.4 how in every decade, except for the 1780s and 1870s, at least two genres are represented. In the 1800s column, for example, there are five genres. The same is true for the 1840s. Excepting the 1780s and 1870s, the stylistic signal of each decade in the model is constructed from a sampling of texts covering at least two and up to five different genres. It cannot, therefore, be asserted that the decade model the algorithm produced is really just a genre model in disguise—each decade signal is constructed from a sample of more than one genre. It is a complicating factor that genres are not confined to single decades; they bleed into subsequent and prior decades.

To better understand how the decade model in this experiment is generated, it is instructive to see the distribution of texts in each decade broken down by genre. Table 6.5 provides such a breakdown. Unlike table 6.4, where percentages are calculated to show distributions of each genre across all of the decades, table 6.5 shows the distribution of genres within each decade as a percentage of all works in a given decade. In other words, the percentages in table 6.5 are calculated according to the decade columns (adding up to 100 percent), whereas in table 6.4 it was the rows that totaled 100 percent. Table 6.5 allows us to see the raw, generic material upon which the model builds its "picture" of a given decade. The decade signal the model builds for the 1790s, for example, is composed of five parts Jacobin texts, four parts Gothic, and one part anti-Jacobin. Only the signals created for the 1780s and 1870s are "pure" in terms of being constructed of material from a single genre: the former composed entirely of Gothic texts and the latter of Bildungsroman.

To probe this evolving and complex chicken-versus-egg phenomenon, it is necessary to chart the presence (and absence) of the various genre signals over the course of time as a form of comparison. In other words, we must build a model sensitive to generic differences and then chart the resulting genre assignments over time. Regardless of whether the classifier's assignment is correct, we assume that the "signal" it has constructed is correct. Doing so allows us to track the signals that are characteristic of each novel's genre style and then to plot the manifestations of these signals over the course of the century.

Figure 6.9 provides an adequate if somewhat impoverished way of visualizing the presence of genre signals over time. Keep in mind that the data being plotted here come not from the actual human-identified genres of the novel but rather from the genre signals that the model has detected, regardless of whether the model is "correct." To make the chart easier to read, I have ordered the genres

Table 6.5. Genre composition by decade

	1780s (%)	1790s (%)	1800s (%)	1810s (%)	1820s (%)	1830s (%)	1840s (%)	1850s (%)	1860s (%)	1870s (%)
Goth	100	39	11	9	7					
Jaco		50								
Anti		11	33							
Evan			11	9						
Natl			33	23						
Hist			11	55	60	20	25			
Silv				5	33	20	8			
Newg						60	8			
Indu							33	44	14	
Bild							25	44	29	100
Sens								11	57	

in a way that maximizes the visibility of each data series. From this graphic, we may conclude that at least some genre signals exist as generations, and at least in these data the genres that exhibit the thirty-year generations that Moretti hypothesized tend to be what we might call the "minor" genres. The anti-Jacobin signal, for example, is clearly operative for just three decades, 1780–1810. So too with the Jacobin signal, which is expressed from 1790 to 1820. Less generational are the industrial, historical, and Gothic signals. The industrial signal spans nine decades, with a brief hiatus from 1800 to 1810. The historical signal begins in the 1780s and then persists for seven decades. The Gothic signal operates for six decades, beginning in the 1780s. The most befuddling signal is that derived from the silver-fork novels. The silver-fork signal, though never very strong, covers the entire period from 1790 to 1859, seven decades. The silver-fork novels in this corpus derive primarily from the 1820s (five novels) and 1830s (two novels). There is one each from the 1810s and 1840s. The signal is, however, more widely and more evenly (in terms of variance) distributed across the century than any of the other signals.*

* The matter of finding atypical texts, or outliers within a given genre, is a problem worth probing. Students in my 2009 seminar discovered, for example, that Sir Walter Scott was a historical outlier in terms of the use of concrete diction versus abstractions. Scott, they argued, can thus be seen as a forerunner of a lexical tradition that is seen to develop in writers of later periods. The extent to which Scott can be viewed as the originator of this pattern is unclear, but it does seem that there are "evolutionary" forces at work. Scott may have been the first to develop this stylistic "mutation." Whether the style that then persisted afterward was a result of a marketplace that preferred this style or whether later writers were consciously or unconsciously emulating Scott is a matter for future consideration. These questions are probed more deeply in chapter 9.

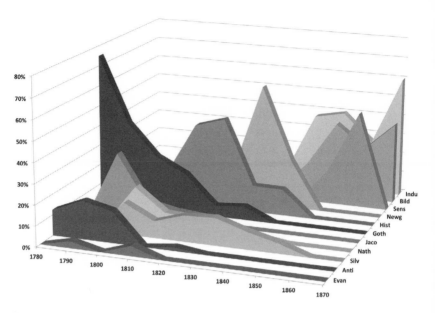

Figure 6.9. Genre signals over time

Returning to the probability data for the assignments reveals that of all the genre signals, the silver-fork signal is the weakest in terms of distinguishing itself. In other words, because so few features truly define the silver-fork class and set it apart from the other genres, it rarely manages to score very high in terms of probability over the other classes. In short, the silver-fork signal just is not distinctive; it is, compared to the other eleven genres, relatively bland and average. As a result of its weak signal, those cases where silver-fork is selected as the most likely class are often cases with only a slight edge over another competing genre. In one classification test, for example, 27 of 354 test segments were assigned to the silver-fork genre, yet, of those 27, only 5 (19 percent) were considered to have a probability greater than 90 percent. In the same test, 46 out of 55 (84 percent) Gothic novels were considered to have a probability above 90 percent. That the Gothic is more easily detected than the silver-fork is clear, but why?

Put to the side, for a moment at least, what we know about the silver-fork as a genre (that is, that it was a genre of novels about the fashionable life of the upper class typically penned by writers of the middle class who—at least according to William Hazlitt—knew not of what they wrote) and consider simply the linguistic features that distinguish the Gothic and silver-fork novels. In the top-ten words most important to distinguishing the Gothic from the other eleven genres, we find *upon, from, by,* and *where* all frequently used. Least important to the Gothic is the apostrophe followed by quotation marks, which are, naturally, indicative of dialogue. In total, there are forty-eight features that clearly identify the Gothic novel by either their presence or their absence.* The silver-fork, on the other hand, offers only six such distinguishing features. Standout features in the silver-fork genre include an above-average use of the semicolon; the words *even, too, how,* and *ever;* and the single underutilized word *father.* Obviously, the classifier uses more than these six (or even forty-eight) words in its calculations, but drawing attention to these "highly indicative" features gives some insight into the comparative difficulty the learning algorithm will have in building a signal for each class.

Although the classifier has no knowledge of genre, or even of the meanings of words themselves, it is instructive to use our human knowledge to understand or even interpret the classifier's discoveries. Among the words that best define the Bildungsroman, the top three are the words *like, young,* and *little.*† The significance of *young* to the Bildungsroman genre seems obvious enough: these are novels about development into adulthood. And *little,* an adjective describing youth and size, is an unsurprising term to find prominently in a novelistic genre that deals with maturation and growth from childhood. *Like,* on the other hand, is a word expressing resemblance or comparison. Here a move in the direction of close reading is warranted and informative. A closer look at several Bildungsroman texts in the corpus reveals that *like* frequently occurs in scenes in which a protagonist is seen discovering a new adult world and is using *like* as a means of comparison to the more familiar child's world. Young David Copperfield, for example, frequently employs *like* to bring the larger world around him into terms that his child's sensibility is able to comprehend: for example, "As the elms bent to one another, *like* giants who were whispering secrets . . ." (Dickens 1850, 4). *Like* also appears frequently in places where Copperfield seeks to make sense of the adult world around him, as in the following examples: "Mr. Chillip laid his head a little more on one side, and looked at my aunt *like* an amiable bird" (ibid., 9). "She vanished *like* a discontented fairy; or *like* one of those supernatural beings, whom it was popularly supposed I was entitled to see" (ibid.). "If she were employed to lose me *like* the boy in the fairy tale, I should be able to track my way home again by the buttons she would

---

* Features that are overrepresented in Gothic novels include the words *upon, eyes, still, from, by, now, were, these, where, had, himself,* and *he.* Underutilized features include the apostrophe, the quotation mark, and the following words: *lady, one, is, are, have, can, has, very, like, see, or, say, young, sir, little, know, good, own, as, think, well, make, us, two, must, house, made, do, take, man, come, Mr., if,* and *out.*

† Other overutilized features of the Bildungsroman include the colon and the words *made, when, thought, over, a, did, seemed, life, said, there, was,* and *then.* Underutilized features include the words *upon, by, your, may, the,* and *this.*

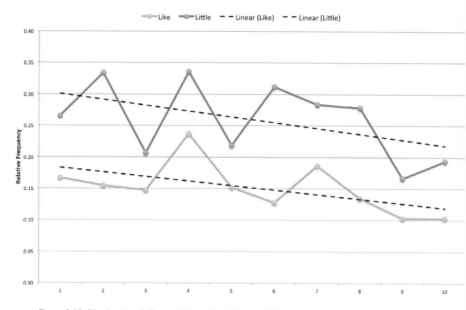

Figure 6.10. Distribution of *like* and *little* in *David Copperfield*

shed" (ibid., 20). "Opposite me was an elderly lady in a great fur cloak, who looked in the dark more *like* a haystack than a lady" (ibid., 52). Not surprisingly, as the narrative progresses, and Copperfield ages, the usage of *like* diminishes. Figure 6.10 shows the distributions of *like* and *little* over ten equal-size chunks of the novel. The *y* axis is the relative frequency of the terms and the *x* axis the course of the novel from beginning to end. Linear trend lines (dashed) have been added to each data series. Similar patterns for different word types can be found among the other genres as well. Newgate novels, which glamorize the lives of criminals, show a disproportionate fondness for the exclamation point and a disproportionately low usage of the female pronouns and honorifics *she, her,* and *miss.* Both Jacobin and anti-Jacobin novels tend to favor first-person pronouns with a high incidence of *my, me, myself,* and *I,* but in anti-Jacobin novels more feminine words are found, words such as *her, lady,* and *Mrs.,* which are all negatively indicated for the Jacobin novel.

Industrial novels, more than any other genre in the collection, favor the use of the possessive. These are novels about possessions: what is "mine" versus "yours," that which belongs to the rich and that which the poor aspire to have. But the industrial novel also favors the use of the conditional *if:* a word representing both possibility and contingency, a word that can effectively express juxtaposition and call attention to antithesis. Describing Coketown, Dickens writes in *Hard Times,* "It was a town of red brick, or of brick that would have been red *if* the smoke and ashes had allowed it" (1854, 26). Here *if* serves to overturn expectation with reality, first to set up and then to undermine. The overall effect is one that highlights and calls attention to the less than ideal realities of the working class. At first the narrator sees redbrick—that is, after all, what buildings are made of. So commonplace is this sight that at first the narrator fails to see what the bricks have become in the realities of Coketown. Some pages later, writing more specifically about the Coketown working class, Dickens again employs *if* to dramatic effect: "among the multitude of Coketown, generically called 'the Hands,'—a race who would have found more favour with some people, *if* Providence had seen fit to make them only hands, or, like the lower creatures of the sea-shore, only hands and stomachs" (ibid., 75). Unlike the former example in which *if* is used as a corrective to a reader's (and the narrator's) expectations, here *if* dramatizes the helplessness of the workers who would have been better liked *if* only they had been been not people, but mere "hands," some form of primitive organism capable only of fulfilling some simple task.

In *Mary Barton,* Elizabeth Gaskell allows John Barton to address similar matters in an even more direct way. Here *if* is employed repeatedly and dramatically to contrast the differences between the rich and the poor:

> "And what good have they ever done me that I should like them?" asked Barton, the latent fire lighting up his eye: and bursting forth, he continued, "*If* I am sick, do they come and nurse me? *If* my child lies dying (as poor Tom lay, with his white wan lips quivering, for want of better food than I could give him), does the rich man bring the wine or broth that might save his life? If I am out of work for weeks in the bad times, and winter comes, with black frost, and keen east wind, and there is no coal for the grate, and no clothes for the bed, and the thin bones are seen through the ragged clothes, does the rich man share his plenty with me, as he ought to do, *if* his religion wasn't a humbug? When I lie on my death-bed, and Mary (bless her) stands fretting, as I know she will fret," and here his voice faltered a little, "will a rich lady come and take her to her own home *if* need be, till she can look round, and see what best to do? No, I tell you, it's the poor, and the poor only, as does such things for the poor. Don't think to come over me with th' old tale, that the rich know nothing of the trials of the poor, I say, *if* they don't know, they ought to know. We're their slaves as long as we can work; we pile up their fortunes with the sweat of our brows; and yet we are to live as separate as *if* we were in two worlds." (1849, 10–11)

These examples underscore how the micro scale (that is, close reading) must be contextualized by the macro scale: genres do have distinct ways of employing linguistic features, and unless we bring these distinctions to consciousness, we risk misinterpretation. So genres can be detected algorithmically with a fair degree of precision. In and of itself, this is not especially useful. Although with a good genre detector in place we could imagine mining the "great unread" in search of new texts that possess a specific, or even "preferred," signal, it is more interesting to consider what this discovery means in terms of authorial freedom and how novels actually get written, to draw the inevitable connections between content, form, and style. A writer wishing to produce a novel of a certain genre, of a certain type, is bound, either consciously or unconsciously—and I believe it to be more of the latter than the former—by the conventions of linguistic usage that are endemic to that form.

Previously, we have thought of these conventions in terms of plot: a Bildungsroman involves the protagonist's maturation; a Newgate novel involves a criminal's exploits. But with these plot conventions come stylistic constraints, constraints that determine the very vocabulary an author has to work with. These constraints exist at the level of the most common linguistic features. The "feel" of a piece of writing, its "style," is made manifest through the type and variety of common words and marks of punctuation that a writer deploys. But it is the "big" words writers agonize over, not the little ones. Should the sunset be described as beautiful or magnificent? *Beautiful* and *magnificent,* these are the class of words that we use with care and reservation. The little words—*the, of, it*—are engaged automatically, spontaneously. These little words fall outside of deliberate, conscious control, much like the tics of a poker player who gives away his hand by a telling twitch or sigh. We know this to be true: authors have these idiosyncrasies. An analysis of the *Federalist Papers*—a corpus in which context, genre, gender, and historical time are all held constant—reveals that Hamilton prefers using *a* more than Madison and Jay, but he uses the conjunction *and* less often than Madison and far less often than Jay. And Hamilton prefers the infinitive *to be* over Jay and Madison, whose preference swings toward *is.* Subtle peculiarities of word usage offer telling signals of genre, but are even more telling of their makers. These subtle habits give authors away, but they do so in ways that only a machine is likely to detect.

At least under normal circumstances, we can assume that the author of *Hard Times* really is Charles Dickens, that Charles Dickens really is a male author, and that any randomly selected chunk of text from *Hard Times* really is a chunk of text from the novel *Hard Times* by the male author Charles Dickens. Unsurprisingly, the classification data show quite clearly that the better a category is defined, the better the classifier can detect and build a signal upon it. In other words, classifications based on loosely defined genres produce comparatively poor results when viewed next to the results for a more objectively defined category such as gender or author. Despite the presence of forty-seven different authors in this test corpus, the model was able to detect enough variation between author signals to correctly identify the authors of a random set of samples with 93 percent accuracy. This may feel uncomfortable, even controversial, to those reared in the "there is no author" school of literary criticism. The data are undeniable. Ultimately, it does not matter if Dickens is really Dickens or some amalgamation of voices driven to paper by the hand of Dickens. The signal derived from 161 linguistic features and extracted from books bearing the name "Charles Dickens" on the cover is consistent.

The strength of the author signals in this experiment in fact trumps the signals of individual texts—something intuition does not prepare us for.* The classifier is more likely to identify the author of a given text segment than it is to correctly assign that same text segment to its novel of origin. What ultimately separates one Jane Austen novel from another is not linguistic style but subject matter. Austen, in fact, has one of the most consistent and unvaried styles of all the writers in this corpus. No offense to Austen fans intended, but Jane is easy to detect—her style is, as it were, an open book. Prose by a writer such as Mark Twain or James Joyce, on the other hand, is extremely hard to quantify and then detect because the works of these two writers demonstrate a much greater stylistic range. Their range makes the development of a stable signal far more difficult.

Before coming to that analysis, however, it is worth unpacking what happens with author gender. A gender signal was evident, and at 80 percent accuracy it is a strong signal, if still comparatively weak next to the author signal. This overall rate of accuracy is consistent with the conclusions of Moshe Koppel, Shlomo Argamon, and Anat Rachel Shimoni, who demonstrate that "automated text categorization techniques can exploit combinations of simple lexical and syntactic features to infer the gender of the author of an unseen formal written document with approximately 80 per cent accuracy" (2002, 401). The feature data from my gender classification experiment show that female authors are far more likely to write about women, and they use the pronouns *her* and *she* far more often than their male counterparts.† In fact, these are the two features that most distinguish the male and female authors in this corpus. The females in this data set also show a preference for the colon and the semicolon, which are the third and fourth most distinguishing features. Not surprisingly, it is also seen that women authors show higher usage of the words *heart* and *love*—not surprising in the sense that this fact is consistent with our stereotypes of "feminine" prose. Nevertheless, there are the features that contradict our stereotypes: male authors in this corpus are far more likely to use marks of exclamation, and women are not the primary users of *we* and *us,* despite what some may think

---

* Most people, I think, would assume that it would be easier to assign a text segment to its originating text than to its author.

† Koppel's analysis also reveals the importance of gendered pronouns. Women tend to use feminine pronouns at a significantly higher rate than males.

about which is the more conciliatory gender. Table 6.6 provides an ordered list of the features most influential in distinguishing between the male and female authors in this corpus. The parenthetical *M/F* indicates which gender has a higher use pattern for the given term, and the *P* indicates a punctuation feature.

Faced with this evidence and the prior work of Koppel, it is hard to argue against the influence of gender on an author's style. Although there may be some genres of prose in which these signals become muted—in legal writing, for example—when it comes to the nineteenth-century novel, it is not terribly

Table 6.6. Features best distinguishing male and female authors

the (M)	did (F)	been (M)	much (F)
heart (F)	here (M)	way (M)	upon (M)
would (F)	life (F)	down (M)	after (M)
we (M)	out (M)	you (M)	own (F)
lady (F)	still (F)	shall (M)	made (M)
love (F)	my (F)	is (M)	than (M)
every (F)	a (M)	what (M)	any (F)
from (F)	your (M)	up (M)	over (F)
have (M)	other (M)	in. (M)	last (F)
had (F)	mrs. (F)	where (F)	should (F)
yet (F)	exclamation (M-P)	house (M)	into (F)
not (F)	may (M)	can (M)	on (M)
only (F)	himself (M)	were (M)	without (M)
now (F)	and (M)	has (M)	me (F)
quote (M-P)	like (M)	he (F)	those (M)
as (M)	at (M)	be (M)	before (F)
when (F)	little (F)	are (M)	more (F)
man (M)	do (M)	hyphen (M-P)	period (F-P)
our (M)	how (F)	his (M)	one (M)
could (F)	was (F)	sir (M)	most (M)
us (M)	though (F)	that (M)	make (F)
eyes (F)	about (M)	mr. (M)	know (F)
two (M)	will (M)	i (M)	these (F)
apostrophe (M-P)	miss (F)	by (F)	
never (F)	room (F)	father (F)	
even (F)	all (F)	hand (M)	
while. (F)	seemed (F)	who (F)	
question (M-P)	it (M)	lord (F)	
for. (F)	them (M)	am (M)	
old (M)	come (M)	then (F)	
but (F)	again (F)	good (M)	
ever (F)	an (F)	their (M)	
thought (F)	they (M)	day (F)	
well (M)	think (M)	or (M)	

Table 6.7. Misattribution of gender

Author	Percentage error
Mary Elizabeth Braddon	50.00
William Beckford	40.00
George Eliot	33.33
M. G. Lewis	30.00
John Moore	30.00
Robert Bage	20.00
William Godwin	20.00
Ann Thomas	20.00
Maria Edgeworth	17.50
Catherine Gore	15.00
Lady Caroline Lamb	10.00
Edward Lytton	10.00
Lady Morgan	10.00
Anthony Trollope	10.00
Anna Marie Porter	5.00
Ann Radcliffe	5.00
Benjamin Disraeli	3.33
John Galt	3.33
Walter Scott	3.33
Charlotte Brontë	2.50

difficult to separate the men from the women. Far more interesting than this revelation, however, is an examination of which authors get misclassified as being of the other gender. Table 6.7 provides a list of all the authors who received misattributions and how often.

Mary Elizabeth Braddon has the distinction of being the most androgynous writer in the corpus, with 50 percent of her segments being classed as male. William Beckford is next, with 40 percent of his segments being labeled as female. The greatest number of raw misclassifications goes to George Eliot, an interesting distinction for a female author who wrote under a male pseudonym. Ten out of thirty samples from Eliot are incorrectly attributed to the male signal. Of the ten, six are from *Middlemarch,* three from *Felix Holt,* and one from *Daniel Deronda.* The remaining authors were "outed" fairly easily—convincing evidence, to be sure, that authors are not above the influences of their gender.

Where author and gender were easy to detect, detecting genres and time periods presented an especially challenging situation. These two are challenging because they are deeply interconnected but also because they are constructed upon arbitrary distinctions. Genres are a subjectively derived and human-defined classification system in which boundaries are primarily drawn in terms of subject matter. Genre boundaries are notoriously porous, and genres bleed into each other.* Decade is even more arbitrary. Decades are simple chunks of time in an infinite continuum. Even years are arbitrary—if a bit less arbitrary than decades since books happen to be published in years, but arbitrary all the same since books get written and then published in different years.† Nevertheless, some interesting facts about genres and time periods are made manifest by this analysis. It turns out that to write a Gothic novel, an author inevitably ends up using more positional prepositions than if writing a Bildungsroman. If a writer is employing a few too many exclamation points, it is more likely that either *she* is a *he* or that *he/she* is writing a Newgate novel rather than a more comma-heavy historical novel. Even though context-sensitive words have been intentionally excluded from this analysis, there is most certainly some correlation between subject and frequent word usage. That said, there is evidence too that subject matter is only part of the equation; the author, gender, and text-based signals are incredibly strong. At least some genres are, or appear to be, generational in nature. This is especially true of the "minor" genres. Where genre signals break down, time-oriented signals step in, revealing cycles of style that, though at times appearing to connect with genre, also transcend genre and suggest the presence of a larger stylistic system.

· · ·

Despite strong evidence derived from this classification analysis, further verification of these tendencies was warranted. To take the analysis one step further, I constructed a second test using linear regression to model and measure the extent to which each of the five "external" variables (text, author, genre, decade, and gender) accurately predicts the dependent variables (that is, the usage of frequent words and marks of punctuation). Linear regression is a statistical technique that is used to "fit" a predictive model to an observed data set. Given any one of the five categories, linear regression can be employed to quantify the strength of the relationship between the category and the individual linguistic features in the data set. Once the models are constructed, the statistical "F-test" may then be employed to compare the models in order to ascertain which of

---

* If you doubt this fact, spend a few hours trying to parse out the meaning in the publishing industry's BISAC codes.

† Serialized fiction presents an interesting case, and several students in the Stanford Literary Lab have been pursuing the question of whether serialization leads to any detectable differences in style. Students Ellen Truxaw and Connie Zhu hypothesize that the need to keep readers from one serial to the next puts stylistic demands upon writers and that these stylistic aberrations would be most apparent at the beginning and end of chapters and serial breaks. Truxaw and Zhu presented this work as "'The Start of a New Chapter': Serialization and the 19th-Century Novel" at the 2010 meeting of the International Conference on Narrative.

the models best fit the overall data. The F-test provides a measure of statistical probability in a "p-value," and the p-value shows how strongly the features in the model predict the outcome. A small p-value indicates a feature that is strongly predictive of the outcome.

In this experiment, 5 by 161 linear models were fit, and p-values for each were calculated. The resultant p-values for each of the 161 variables within each of the five categories were then tabulated such that each column represented one of the five categories (author, genre, and so on) and each row one of the 161 linguistic features. The resulting cells contained the corresponding p-value for a given dependent variable in a category. For each of the 161 dependent variables, the smallest of the five corresponding p-values reveals which of the five external variables is most predictive of the dependent variable. In other words, it is possible to determine whether it is the author, the text, the genre, the decade, or the gender that best explains or predicts the behavior of each one of the 161 linguistic variables. The p-values can then be tabulated and ranked for each column so as to arrive at a single value representing the estimated percentage of "influence" that each category exerts on the final linguistic product.

With minor exceptions, the results of this linear regression analysis confirmed what was seen in the machine-classification experiment described above. The only difference is that in this secondary analysis, the strengths of the "author" and "text" signals were reversed: here the text was seen to be the strongest predictor of the linguistic features. Figure 6.11 provides a percentage-based view of the relative influence of each factor in the overall linguistic signal captured by the 161 variables.

For all but 17 of the 161 variables, text was the strongest predictor of usage. Next strongest was author, followed by genre, then decade, and finally gender. Plotting all five categories on a stacked bar chart (figure 6.12) allows for visualization of the relative strength of each feature within each category. Working from the bottom of the chart upward, the text (black) and author (dark gray) signals dominate the chart, followed by genre, decade, and gender (in very light gray).

Even more interesting than these overall trends, however, are the ways in which specific features appear to be tied to specific categories. The gender signal is by far the least important, but gender does have greater influence on some variables than others. Confirming the results from the classification tests explored above, the linear regression test identified the two variables most determined by gender as *her* and *she*. *Heart* and *love* follow closely behind.* Again,

---

* A separate analysis of the usage of these terms in a larger corpus of 250 nineteenth-century British novels made available through Chadwyck-Healey shows that female authors use these terms at much higher rates than their male counterparts. See also Koppel, Argamon, and Shimoni 2002.

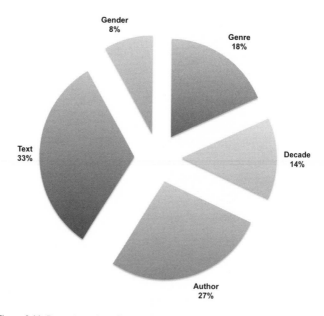

Figure 6.11. Percentage view of category influence

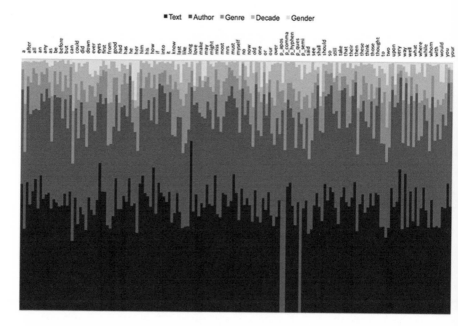

Figure 6.12. Relative view of category influence

as was seen in the classification tests, when it comes to the author signal, the linguistic features that have the greatest importance are not words, but marks of punctuation. In the linear regression test, six of the top eight variables that are most easily predicted by author are marks of punctuation: the comma is first, followed by the period in fourth place, the colon in fifth, semicolon in sixth, and hyphen in eighth. With genre, we find an overwhelming presence of prepositions as top predictors, particularly locative prepositions including, in order, *to, about,* and *up.* Also in the top ten are *come* and *there,* two more words indicative of location or "scene-setting" language and two words that showed up as important in the other method as well. Also found are the previously discussed words *like* and *little,* which we know to be of particular importance in distinguishing the Bildungsroman from other genres.

• • •

Some micro thoughts . . . Claudi Guillén writes in *Literature as a System* that "genre is an invitation to form" (1971, 109). To "form" we must certainly now add "style," or if style is too broad a term for some tastes, then at the very least we must add "language usage." The data presented here provide strong evidence for existing notions of individual authorial "fingerprints," but show further that author signal alone does not account for the variance in the linguistic data. No doubt, a good share of the variance may be attributed to the particular text that the author is writing, and since the text belongs to, is the creation of, an author, it may be right to conflate the author and text signals into one piece of the pie. Having done so, however, we still have another half pie to account for. Both the classification tests and the linear regression tests showed gender to be a bit player. This was especially evident in the linear regression, where gender rises to only 8 percent of the influence. Even when the classifier showed strong accuracy (at 80 percent), it was still magnitudes below the other categories in terms of improvement over chance. Time and genre are clearly the most complicated factors to understand and thus the most interesting to pursue. It is clear that an author's choice of genre plays a role in determining the subject and form that a novel takes, but genre also plays a role in determining the linguistic material from which the content is derived. Some genre forms clearly move writers to employ more prepositions; other genres demand more articles, or more pronouns, and so on. Given the powerful influence of the author signal and the less powerful but still important factors of time and gender, it is difficult to go much further at the macroanalytic scale. What is required to probe the strength of genre further is an environment in which we can control for gender, author, and time and thus truly isolate the genre signal. In short, we need Charles Dickens, Edward Lytton, and Benjamin Disraeli.

These authors are useful because they are all represented in the test corpus, and they share the distinction of each having authored novels in at least three different genres. From Dickens, the test corpus includes one Bildungsroman, one industrial novel, and one Newgate novel; from Lytton, there is one historical novel, one Newgate novel, and one silver-fork novel; from Disraeli, there is one Bildungsroman, one industrial novel, and one silver-fork novel. Before analyzing the contributions from these three authors and five genres, I will begin by exploring a larger subset of my original corpus that includes just the authors of novels in the Bildungsroman and industrial genres. This allows for a rough approximation of how well the data separate according to genre. Using the same linguistic feature set employed previously, all of the text segments of Bildungsroman and industrial novels (two hundred segments from ten different authors) were isolated and compared. First, an unsupervised clustering of the data was used in order to determine whether the two genres would naturally cluster into two distinct categories. The results of the clustering (table 6.8) were inconclusive: ninety (81 percent) Bildungsroman segments clustered with forty (44 percent) industrial segments into one group and twenty (18 percent) Bildungsroman with fifty (56 percent) industrial into another.* In other words, though there was some separation, neither cluster was dramatically dominated by one genre or another. When the same data were grouped into ten clusters (there are ten authors in the data set who authored novels in either the Bildungsroman or the industrial genre), however, author clustering was quite apparent. Only one (Elizabeth Gaskell) of the ten authors had text segments assigned to more than two clusters. Table 6.9 shows the distribution of segment assignments by author and cluster.

In addition to the clustering analysis, principal component analysis was used to explore the data. In this test, the first two principal components accounted for 31 percent of the variance in the data, and like the clustering test, PCA revealed a good deal of overlap between the two genres (figure 6.13). Closer inspection of the PCA data, however, showed significant internal subclustering based on author (figure 6.14), confirming what was seen in the clustering analysis. In other words, in both tests, the author signal continued to overpower the genre signal.

Narrowing the field to include only data from the novels of Dickens, Disraeli, and Lytton continued to produce results in which the author signal dominated the clustering (figure 6.15). In this test, four novels from Dickens were isolated on the east side of the plot, away from the other two novelists, who are located

---

* Clustering was performed in R using the Distance Matrix Computation function (dist) and the Euclidean distance method. Hierarchical cluster analysis (hclust) was performed on the resulting distance object using the complete linkage method to determine similar clusters.

Table 6.8. Clustering results for Bildungsroman and industrial

Cluster	1	2
Bildungsroman	90	20
Industrial	40	50

le 6.9. Distribution of segment assignments by author and cluster

	Cluster 1	Cluster 2	Cluster 3	Cluster 4	Cluster 5	Cluster 6	Cluster 7	Cluster 8	Cluster 9	Cluster 10
ntë	24	16								
ik			5	5						
kens				23	7					
raeli					20					
ot					18	12				
skell						19	9	2		
gsley								10		
redith								10		
ackeray									1	9
llope										10

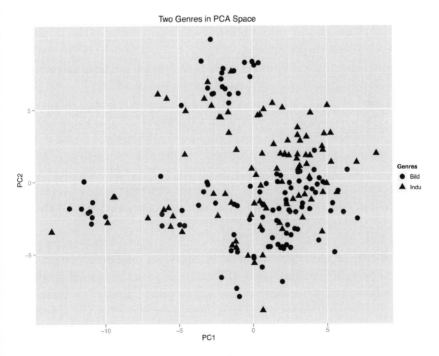

Figure 6.13. Bildungsroman and industrial novels in PCA space

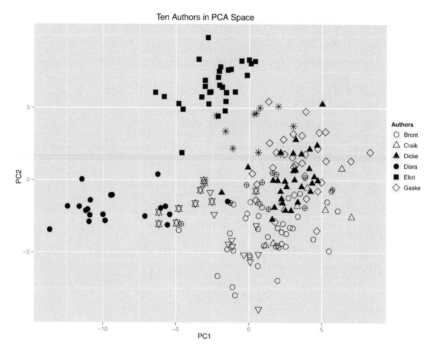

Figure 6.14. Ten authors in PCA space

to the west side of PC1. The three novels from Disraeli are separate from the four novels by Lytton on the north-south dividing axis of PC2.

What then of genre? What is not evident in figure 6.15 is that within each author cluster, there is further separation to be found and that the separation is largely attributable to genre. Figure 6.16 shows just the three novels of Disraeli: *Coningsby, or, The New Generation* (Bildungsroman); *Sybil, or, The Two Nations* (industrial); and *Vivian Grey* (silver-fork). PC1 and PC2 account for 53 percent of the variation in the data. Though the clustering here is not perfect, it is very close—one segment from *Sybil* appears in the *Coningsby* cluster and vice versa—and the misalignment of this one segment makes sense given the themes of the two books. Nevertheless, it could be argued that the separation seen here is just as easily attributable to the text signal, and perhaps more correctly so. We must therefore turn to Dickens, from whom we have four novels.

With Dickens a similar separation is seen by genre (figure 6.17), but in this case we see the two Bildungsroman novels (ten segments each from *Copperfield* and *Great Expectations*) cluster together in the northwest, all of the Newgate segments from *Oliver Twist* in the northeast, and *Hard Times* almost entirely in the south-central regions. In other words, the linguistic signals associated with

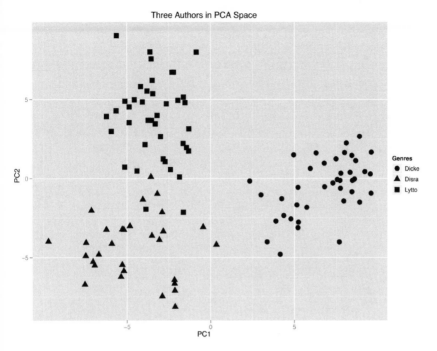

Figure 6.15. Three authors in PCA space

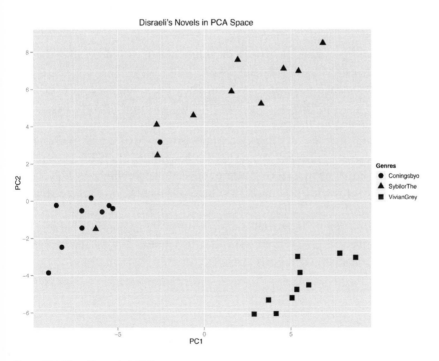

Figure 6.16. Disraeli's novels in PCA space

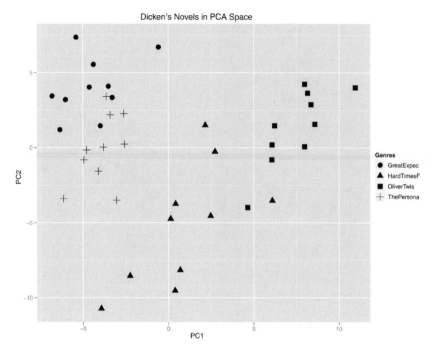

Figure 6.17. Dicken's novels in PCA space

the two Bildungsromans have more in common with each other than they do with the other non-Bildungsroman novels.

Once we control for author, the full force of genre in this corpus can be seen. The linguistic choices that authors make are, in some notable ways, dependent upon, or entailed by, their genre choices. Having said that, additional experimentation has revealed—quite as we would expect—that not all genres exert equal force; some genres pull at style harder than others. Thought of in another way, some genres are more formal, more conventional. In this collection of data from twelve genres, the Bildungsroman holds the distinction of possessing the strongest signal, while Newgate novels contain a much more amorphous mixture of signals. The Bildungsroman has a stronger signal precisely because it is more formulaic, its conventions more clearly delineated. If form ever follows function, then style ever follows form.

7 NATIONALITY

The historical sense compels a man to write not
merely with his own generation in his bones, but
with a feeling that the whole of the literature of
Europe from Homer and within it the whole of the
literature of his own country has a simultaneous
existence and composes a simultaneous order.

—T. S. Eliot, *Tradition and the Individual Talent* (1917)

The previous chapter demonstrated how stylistic signals could be derived from high-frequency features and how the usage, or nonusage, of those features was susceptible to influences that are external to what might we might call "authorial style," external influences such as genre, time, and gender. These aspects of style were explored using a controlled corpus of 106 British texts where genre was a key point of analysis. The potential influences or entailments of nationality have not yet been examined. Clearly, nations have habits of style that can be identified and traced. Consider, for example, the British habit of dropping the word *the* in front of certain nouns for which American speakers and writers always deploy the article: "I have to go to hospital," says the British speaker. The American speaker says, "I have to go to *the* hospital."* Given a linguistic habit such as this, it is no surprise to find that the mean relative frequency of the word *the* is lower in British and Irish novels than in American novels. In a larger corpus of 3,346 nineteenth-century novels that is explored in this and the following chapters, British novelists use the word *the* at a rate of 5 percent. For the American texts in this corpus, the rate is 6 percent. By itself, usage of the word *the* is a strong indicator of nationality, at least when trying to differentiate between British and American texts. In fact, using just the word *the*, the NSC classifier reported a cross-validation accuracy of 64 percent. That is, 64 percent of the time, the classifier can tell if a novel is British or American simply by

---

* Irish and Australian speakers and writers are similar to the British in using *the* less frequently.

examining the novel's usage of the word *the*. What is puzzling about the word *the,* however, is not that it is used almost a full percentage point more by the Americans than by the British but rather that the minor fluctuations in usage between the two nations are closely correlated over time. In other words, when in the course of the century British usage drops, American usage drops almost simultaneously. The fluctuations are not perfectly aligned to years, but they are close. When the data are smoothed, as in figure 7.1, using a five-year rolling average, the remarkably parallel nature of the two trends becomes apparent.*

Over a period of one hundred years, it is as if the writers in these two nations—two nations separated by several thousand miles of water in an age before mass communication—made a concerted effort to modulate their usage of this most common of common words. However, *the* is not the kind of word that authors would consciously agonize over; quite the contrary, *the* is a trivial word, a function word, a word used automatically and by necessity. Whereas the use of the word *beautiful,* for example, may come and go with the fads of culture, the word *the* is a whole different animal. For comparison, consider figure 7.2, which charts the relative frequency of the word *beautiful* in the same corpus. Whereas *the* is nearly parallel, *beautiful* is erratic and unpredictable.

The degree of correlation between the British and American patterns can be calculated statistically using a "correlation coefficient." A correlation coefficient measures the strength of a linear relationship between two variables: for example, we may wish to know the correlation between Montana's average winter temperature and the use of heating oil. To calculate this relationship, we can use the Pearson correlation coefficient formula, which takes the covariance of two variables and divides by the product of their standard deviations. The resulting value is a number on an "R" scale ranging from –1 to 1, where 0 corresponds to no correlation. The correlation coefficient for the year-to-year fluctuations between British and American usage of *the* is 0.382. For the word *beautiful,* on the other hand, the correlation coefficient is just –0.08.† The correlation coefficient of 0.382 for the word *the* is certainly not what would be considered an exceptionally "high" correlation. Nevertheless, when seen in the context of the irregular behavior of *beautiful, the* is comparatively stable. When we consider

---

* It is possible, perhaps even likely, that a larger corpus would show a similar level of smoothness on a year-to-year basis without the need to use a moving average. Some of the more dramatic year-to-year fluctuations seen in this corpus occur in years when there is only one text from one country and several texts from the other.

† A coefficient of 1 would indicate perfectly positive correlation: the two lines in the chart would be perfectly matched, or parallel. As one increased, the other would increase to the same extent and at the same time. Alternatively, a coefficient of –1 would represent a negative correlation: as one decreases, the other increases proportionally.

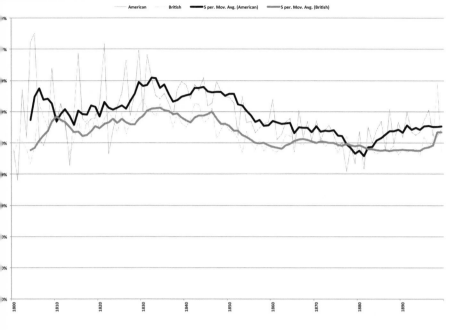

Figure 7.1. Usage of the word *the* in British and American novels

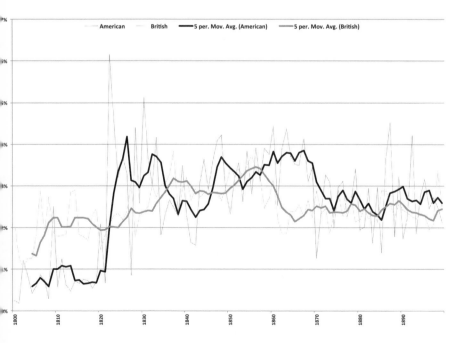

Figure 7.2. Usage of the word *beautiful* in British and American novels

that the coefficient for *the* was calculated based on the year-to-year fluctuations, not upon the smoothed moving average seen in figure 7.1, its observed stability is even more remarkable. This coefficient of 0.382 is derived from tracking the year-to-year fluctuations and not the larger macro behavior. If, instead of taking the year-to-year means, we calculate the correlation coefficient based upon decade-to-decade averages, the coefficient rises to 0.92! By removing the year-to-year "noise" in the data, we observe the larger macro pattern more clearly, and the macro pattern of British and American usage of the word *the* is highly correlated. The decade results are charted in figure 7.3.

So as to be clear about the calculations here, for each nation I begin by counting all of the occurrences of *the* in each decade and then divide by the total number of words in each decade. This returns the "relative frequency" of *the* usage in each given decade. The relative frequencies are then plotted chronologically from 1800 to 1900 to produce the trends seen in figure 7.3. When the fluctuations in the use of *beautiful* are similarly calculated, the correlation coefficient increases from −0.08 to 0.36 (figure 7.4).

The pattern of tandem fluctuation seen with the word *the* defies easy explanation. My conclusion regarding this phenomenon is quite literally "to be determined." Unless one is willing to entertain Rupert Sheldrake's notion of "morphic resonance," then the behavior of *the* is downright mysterious.* I first observed this behavior of *the* in 2005 in a much smaller corpus of one thousand novels. After six years of contemplation, and twenty-five hundred more books, plausible explanations remain few and far between.† Perhaps these trends are brought about by publishers, or by editors, or by industry pressures, or by reader demand? None of these seems likely, given that the word in question is *the*. Surely, ten decades of American writers were not consciously adjusting their

* Which is not to say that Sheldrake's observations are not likewise mysterious. Sheldrake's idea, which is in some ways similar to the notion of a Jungian collective unconscious, describes a telepathy-like interconnection between organisms within a species. In Sheldrake's conception, there are "morphogenetic fields" through which information is transmitted, as if by magic. Sheldrake's "theory" is designed to explain how change is wrought in subsequent generations, how successive generations of day-old chicks, for example, might become reluctant to perform some behavior because they "remember" the experiences of prior generations (Rose 1992; Sheldrake 1992). But even Sheldrake's questionable theory of morphic resonance fails to explain the fluctuations seen in these data. Unlike the chicks that are conditioned to behave in a certain way, there is no apparent stimulus here, either positive or negative. Given our formalist, even materialist, approach, Sheldrake's idea seems far too immaterial, too immeasurable, to put much stock in it.

† At one point, I believed the behavior was an aberration of the data, a result of having too small of a corpus. Thirty-five hundred more texts later, and the trend is the same.

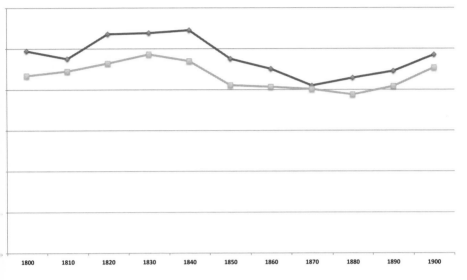

Figure 7.3. Usage of the word *the* in British and American novels by decade

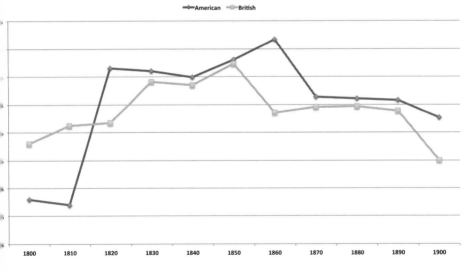

Figure 7.4. Usage of the word *beautiful* in British and American novels by decade

usage of this common function word in order to match British fluctuations—or visa versa—even though they were perhaps reading, editing, and discussing each other. Perhaps the distribution of these data is simply the result of chance, an anomaly of the data? To test the possibility that this correlation coefficient could have been derived simply by chance, I shuffled the year-to-year data for American usage of *the* one thousand times, such that with each shuffling, the values were randomized and no longer in chronological order. After each shuffling, a new correlation coefficient was calculated against the year-to-year chronologically arranged British data. The resulting coefficients, a thousand of them, were examined and plotted in a histogram. They followed a normal distribution centered around a coefficient of 0. The test confirmed that the 0.382 correlation coefficient was not likely to have been a result of chance (see figure 7.5).

The mean correlation coefficient of these one thousand random iterations was just 0.005; the observed correlation coefficient, 0.382, is, therefore, nearly four standard deviations from the mean; that is, 99.7 percent of the distribution lies within +/– three standard deviations from the mean. In short, the probability of getting 0.382 correlation for the word *the* by chance is less than 0.01 percent.* For whatever reason(s), the behavior of *the* in these two national literatures is correlated in time. The important point is not that the two nations' usage patterns mirror each other but, rather, that they do so in the context of this most unimaginative of words. Few would be willing to argue that these authors were consciously modulating their usage of *the*. A far more plausible explanation may be that the usage of *the* is secondary to some other unknown and shifting feature, a covariation in which changes in some unknown variable lead to the shifts seen in the known variable. The identity of the unknown variable remains an enigma, but the overall behavior surely indicates that there are forces beyond authorial creativity.

The behavior of the word *the* is, indeed, unusual. I found no other common word in the corpus that behaved in this manner.† What is clear about the word *the,* however, is that it is a very useful feature for distinguishing between British and American texts. Any given text in the corpus with a relative frequency of *the* near 6 percent is far more likely to be an American text than a British text. On the other hand, the word *the* is comparatively useless when it comes to distinguishing between British and Irish texts, and this, for reasons that will be made apparent soon, is the far more interesting problem.

---

* The p-value, calculated based on the t-test, is less than 0.0001, strong evidence against the proposition that 0.382 could have been derived by the variation in random sampling.

† Admittedly, I did not make an exhaustive search. I looked only at the ten or so most frequent words and then abandoned the search in order to return to my primary objective of exploring how style could be used as a discriminator of nationality.

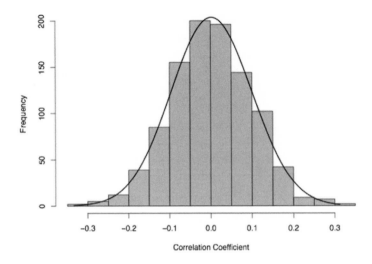

Figure 7.5. Histogram of random correlation coefficients

W. B. Yeats once claimed that he could detect in Irish literature two distinct accents: "the accent of the gentry and the less polished accent of the peasantry" (1979, 9). One nation, two literatures: the first highly influenced by the British tradition and the other a more organic, "pure" style arising out of the native tradition. Could fluctuations in the use of a common word, such as *the,* be dependent upon whether an Irish writer was of the gentry or the peasantry? I am not inclined to make the same class distinctions as Yeats; I do not have the ear for accents that he did, and the business of defining who is of the gentry and who is of the peasantry is one better suited to poets than scholars. Nevertheless, Irish literature presents an interesting case, even as we leave the authors to their respective classes, unsegregated.

With his comments about distinct "accents," Yeats vocalized a sometimes-latent tradition of thinking of true, pure Irish literature as that literature that possesses an authentic "Irish voice" (to use Charles Fanning's term). Yeats, perhaps less consciously, invigorated a practice of valuing or devaluing the merits of the Irish novel in terms of the extent to which the novels were authentically Irish or tainted by some form of "Dickensian" influence. The fault does not lie entirely with Yeats, but Yeats was bolder in his proclamations than other critics.*
Writing of the Irish novel tradition in *Samhain,* he argued that "it is impossible

---

* Margaret Kelleher (2005) makes it clear that there is a tradition of characterizing and criticizing the Irish novel by its failure or success (perceived or otherwise) to match the qualities of the ostensibly superior realist novel that "rose" to prominence in England.

to divide what is new and, therefore, Irish, what is very old and, therefore, Irish, from all that is foreign, from all that is an accident of imperfect culture, before we have had some revelation of Irish character, pure enough and varied enough to create a standard of comparison" (1908, 8). On this point, others, including Thomas Flanagan (1959) in particular and more recently and more generally Katie Trumpener (1997), have sought to define the nineteenth-century Irish novel not in terms of how it differed from or failed to mirror an English realist tradition but in terms of how it "anticipated" and "enabled," as Joe Cleary writes, the twentieth-century modern novel and Joyce's *Ulysses* in particular (Bélanger 2005). Cleary goes so far as to suggest that the position of the Irish on the colonial periphery may have been the catalyst that compelled Irish novelists to be more innovative, inventive, and experimental than their British counterparts. Regardless of the side one takes in this debate—either that the Irish novel is different and, therefore, better, or that the Irish novel is different and, therefore, inferior—there is general agreement that something unconventional is going on with the novel in Ireland.

Irish literature scholars including Thomas MacDonagh (1916), Thomas Flanagan (1959), John Cronin (1980), and most recently Charles Fanning (2000) have commented upon distinct and specific uses of language that they believe characterize, or "mark," Irish narrative as Irish. For some, this unique use of the language in Ireland is thought to be a by-product of the manner in which the Irish adopted (or were forced to adopt) English as a second language. In support of this contention, Mark Hawthorne has written that the "Irish were not accustomed to the English language and were unsure of its subtleties and detonations" (1975, 11). However, both Fanning and Cronin have argued, separately, that the Irish became masters of the English language and employed, in Fanning's words, a mode of "linguistic subversion" designed to counter or retaliate against forces of British colonization.* Still, none of these scholars gets to the heart of the difference, to the actual linguistic or stylistic data. Thus far, these speculations regarding Irish intonations and "accents" have been of the "you'll know them when you see them" (anecdotal) variety. These are hypotheses in need of testing, in need of macroscale confirmation or refutation, and the devil here is most certainly in the data. Let us see (or compute), then, to what extent a nineteenth-century Irish voice may be heard (or measured) amid a cacophony of 1,030 British and Irish novels.

Using techniques described in the previous chapter, I extracted the word-frequency data from the British and Irish texts in the corpus. I winnowed the

---

* I can think of no better expression of this linguistic subversion in fiction than chapter 4 of Carleton's *Emigrants of Ahadarra*. Responding to the schoolmaster's inflated prose, Keenan replies, "That English is too tall for me. . . . Take a spell o' this [and here he refers to the illicit poteen they have brewed] it's a language we can all understand" (1848, 36).

resulting matrix to exclude words with a mean relative frequency across the corpus of less than 0.025 percent. A classification model was then trained on all of these data, and the word and punctuation features were ranked according to their usefulness in separating the two nationalities. Among the words found to be most useful was a cluster of words indicative of "absolutes" and words expressing "determinacy" or "confidence." More frequent in British novels than in Irish novels are the words *always, should, never, sure, not, must, do, don't, no, nothing, certain, therefore, because, can, cannot, knew, know, last, once, only,* and *right.** The British novels were also seen to favor both male personal pronouns and the first-person *I* and *me.*† Irish novels, on the other hand, were found to be most readily distinguished by words we might classify as being characteristic of "imprecision" or "indeterminacy," words such as *near, soon, some, most, still, less, more,* and *much.*‡ Whereas the British cluster of words suggests confidence, the Irish cluster indicates uncertainty, even caution.

Equally instructive are the classes of words that are negatively correlated to nationality, that is, words that are relatively underutilized. Among the most underutilized words in Irish fiction are the words *I, me, my, if, should, could, sure,* and *must.* These are words in the first person and modal words suggestive of possibility or perhaps even certainty about the future. The comparative underutilization of first-person pronouns signals a preference for third-person narration but may also signal a concomitant lack of self-reflective narrative. The absence of the modal words seems to imply not only uncertainty about the future but also an inability to conceive of the future and its possibilities. What is comparatively absent, then, are words that would allow Irish authors to consistently express what "should" or "could" happen, what might happen "if," and what "must" happen to "me." This suggests, perhaps, that the narrative world of the Irish novel is one possessed of a general lack of agency, an observation lending credibility to several more impressionistic assertions made by Terry Eagleton. Among other things, Eagleton argues, the British realist novel is characterized by "settlement and stability," whereas the "disrupted course of Irish history" led to Irish novels characterized by "recursive and diffuse" narratives, with multiple story lines and an "imperfect" realism (as cited in Bélanger

---

* A separate analysis determined that these words were also more frequent in British novels than in American.

† The significance of this fact will not be lost on postcolonial scholars who have argued that the colonial British tended to conceive of the Irish in feminine terms. See, for example, Howe 2000; McKibben 2008; Stevens and Brown 2000.

‡ Separate analysis revealed that American novels are distinguished from Irish and British novels by a higher frequency of concrete nouns and adjectives rather than abstractions: words such as *heart, death, eyes, face, young, life, hand,* and *old* are all more frequent in the American texts.

2005, 14–15). "Imperfect realism": this makes me uncomfortable because it is a purely subjective observation, but even more so because the "imperfect" implies that "perfect" realism—whatever that might be—is the goal. The underlying assumption is that if Irish authors were not striving for perfect realism, then they should have been, and if they were, then they were failing. These are not questions with answers, only speculations. We can, however, observe what is in fact happening with language usage, and if we cannot measure perfection, we can at least measure and quantify the features that mark the two national literatures as different. Success here will lead us back again to the micro scale, where we can then legitimately ask a question such as this: which text in the Irish corpus is most similar to Eliot's *Middlemarch*?

As was seen in the analysis of the word *the*, habits of word usage, conventions of prose style, are not frozen in time; they can fluctuate, and they can be charted. Figure 7.6 shows the aggregated relative frequency of the "British" words: *always, should, never, sure, not, must, do, don't, no, nothing, certain, therefore, because, can, cannot, knew, know, last, once, only*, and *right*. Here the cluster is plotted over the course of 120 years. In addition to upward trending seen in both lines beginning in the 1820s, what is remarkable is the way in which the usage of these features in the two national literatures tends to move in parallel with each other, reminiscent of the behavior of the word *the* in British and American novels. These data indicate that there are both national tendencies and extranational trends in the usage of this word cluster. The British use these words more often, but not necessarily differently from the Irish. Both national literatures are slowly increasing their usage of these "confidence" markers, and they tend to be doing so in parallel—with the Irish always slightly below the British. Unlike the word *the*, however, these are not solely function words. These words carry thematic, semantic baggage. What it is that is influencing this word usage is trickier to ascertain. Perhaps Irish culture is changing in such a way that Irish authors are writing more self-reflexive narratives. Or perhaps Irish authors are consciously imitating the stylistic shifts of their British counterparts, trying to "catch up," as it were. If this cluster of words is in fact a surrogate, an abstraction, for some degree of stability and confidence, then we might hypothesize that over time, Irish prose is coming to express more confidence. Such a hypothesis makes for an interesting diversion: studying the trends more closely, we see only one place where the Irish line moves considerably in a direction opposite to the British, and this occurs in the 1840s, during the height of the Great Famine.* If Irish prose were to move toward expression of a lapse in confidence, a moment of doubt about the future, the famine would seem a fitting place to see such a shift.

---

* In the 1890s, the Irish achieve usage parity, but unlike the 1840s, there is not a clear movement in opposite directions.

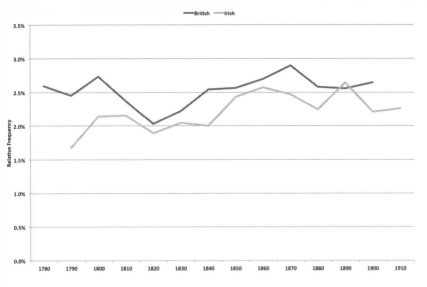

Figure 7.6. The British word cluster over decade and nation

The temptation to "read" even more into these patterns is great. To go further, however, requires acceptance of the initial premise. We must agree that this somewhat arbitrary cluster of words—*always, should, never, sure, not, must, do, don't, no, nothing, certain, therefore, because, can, cannot, knew, know, last, once, only,* and *right*—is a reasonable proxy for some latent sense of confidence in British prose. Some readers will undoubtedly agree and require no further substantiation; others will argue that, when taken out of their context, it is impossible to correlate the frequency pattern of these words with a larger concept such as "confidence." It will seem to some even more egregious to draw connections between these usage patterns and historical events, such as the Irish Famine. Assuming that we are unwilling to make the leap from word cluster to concept, it is nonetheless instructive to see which authors "excel" in the use of these terms. When sorted according to the usage of words in this cluster, we find among the top fifty novels four novels by Jane Austen and nine by Anthony Trollope.* Whether these two authors may be claimed as quintessentially British is a leap I will leave to readers; the data simply tell us that these authors have a particular fondness for words in this particular cluster.

Here I must acknowledge again that this particular cluster of words, although selected by the algorithm as strong distinguishers, was cherry-picked from

* *Lady Susan, Emma, The Watsons,* and *Northanger Abbey* by Austen and *The Duke's Children; The Prime Minister; The Last Chronicle of Barset; Phineas Redux; Can You Forgive Her?; Phineas Finn, the Irish Member; The Way We Live Now; Doctor Thorne;* and *The Small House at Allington,* by Trollope.

among the full list of features the model found to be characteristic of British fiction. My cherry-picking ignored punctuation features, for example, as well as words that I deemed to be less meaningful (or whose meaning I did not immediately understand): *the, this, had,* and *been,* for example. Allow me, therefore, to put the cherries back on the tree, and let us see which novels in the corpus are most tellingly Irish and which most obviously British. The writer with a word-frequency profile that is most characteristically Irish is Charles Johnstone (1719–1800?). At first glance, this seems a surprising distinction; Johnstone was by no means provincial. Though born in Limerick, he traveled widely, living in London and Calcutta and writing books set in India, the Middle East, and Africa. Aileen Douglas argues that, though Johnstone "most strenuously advocates the ideal of Britain" (2006, 32), he is at the same time a satirist in the Swiftian tradition and a writer deeply committed to the critique of colonialism in Ireland. As we saw in the previous chapter, genre choices can often entail certain word-frequency patterns. Perhaps the critique of colonialism naturally results in an increase in the aforementioned "Irish" markers. In the list of most Irish writers, John Banim and William Carleton follow Johnstone in second place and third place. These two writers fit more easily into the prescribed rules for being "authentically" Irish. Banim was of the Catholic middle class and wrote what were essentially regional novels about the peasants in his home county of Kilkenny. Carleton, even more than Banim, was a man of "authentic" Irish bona fides. He was born of poor Gaelic parents in County Tyrone, and his first ambitions were toward the priesthood.

By this metric of word-frequency patterns, the least "Irish" of the Irish authors in the corpus are Maria Edgeworth, Bram Stoker, and Oscar Wilde. Edgeworth, though a pioneer of the Irish regional novel and an influence on Sir Walter Scott—who wished to attempt for his own country "something . . . of the same kind with that which Miss Edgeworth so fortunately achieved for Ireland" (Cahalan 1988, 16–17)—was also keenly aware that her audience was British; her prose is frequently aimed in that direction. The latter two, Stoker and Wilde, are frequently, conveniently, and too often mistakenly remembered as being British writers, not Irish ones.

On the other side of the Irish Sea, the most distinctly British authors were found to be Alan St. Aubyn, Mary Angela Dickens, and Margaret Oliphant. It is worth noting that the more familiar Trollope and Austen are not far down the list. Alan St. Aubyn, a pseudonym for Mrs. Frances Marshall, wrote women's "varsity novels" and was, according to Ann McClellan, quite popular at the end of the century. Her popularity, however, was forged through compromise. McClellan writes that "to get published, she had to appease men's fears; to sell books, she had to fulfill girls' dreams" (2010, 347). In short, she gave the people what they wanted. Mary Angela Dickens, eldest daughter of Charles, was a novelist, a *Londonite,* and a devoted member of London society. Early reviewers are mixed in their opinions of her work: some appear to judge her on the "Dickens standard," while others give her a pass in reverence to her lineage. Whether good or bad, she is most certainly a British author. Last among the top three is Margaret Oliphant, a Scot by birth who moved to Liverpool at the age of ten. Oliphant was prolific, and her work earned her the telling distinction of being "Queen Victoria's favorite novelist" (Husemann 2003, n.p.).

Least British according to this metric is William Hutchinson. Ironically, Hutchinson's most un-British novel is titled *The Hermitage of Du Monte: A British Story.* Hutchinson is followed by the apparently anonymous novel *Llewellin: A Tale.** The book is dedicated to the then eight-month-old Princess Charlotte Augusta of Wales. Louisa Stanhope, a writer of Gothic and historical novels, follows the author of *Llewellin* in third place. Readers, such as myself, who are unfamiliar with these three finalists in the category of "least British of the Brits" may travel just a few steps up the list to find the more recognizable works of Sir Walter Scott: first *Ivanhoe* and then *A Legend of Montrose.* With Scott, a writer frequently corralled among the British (that is, not always thought of as a distinctly Scottish author), it would appear that the method has failed. Though Scott's themes were often British and Saxon, his style remained distinctly, undoubtedly, a by-product of his Scottish heritage and his early preoccupation with the oral traditions of his native Highlands.

Here we hit upon the end point of what this stylistic or linguistic feature analysis can provide in terms of separating writers by nationality. The most frequent words can take us no further. The classification procedure employed in this chapter revealed a number of features that were useful in distinguishing between British and Irish prose, but in the end, classification accuracy never rose above 70 percent. This result is neither surprising nor discouraging; it simply indicates that there are many similarities between the two national literatures and that stylistic habits of word and punctuation usage are an imperfect measure of national style—imperfect, but not entirely useless. They do take us part of the way, and they do reveal elements of prose style that are characteristic of the two nations. At the same time, the results show that the borders of prose are porous: influence knows no bounds. Should Scott, despite his Scottish "accents," still be classed—as my former student Kathryn VanArendonk put it—among those whistling "Rule, Britannia"?† For this answer, we must now move toward thematics: if Scott does not write in a typically British way, does he at least write of typically British topics?

---

* "Apparently" because the author is listed as "Llewellin."

† Ironically, the poem "Rule, Britannia" was written by the Scottish poet James Thomson.

8 THEME

All ideas are second hand, consciously and
unconsciously drawn from a million outside
sources, and daily used by the garnerer with a
pride and satisfaction born of the superstition
that he originated them.

—Mark Twain, letter to Anne Macy (1903)

A typical complaint about computational stylistics is that such studies fail to
investigate the aspects of writing that readers care most deeply about, namely,
plot, character, and theme.* In the previous chapter, we saw how stylistic information can be usefully extracted from texts in a corpus and how the derivative
data can be used to chart linguistic macro patterns and macro trends present
in a century's worth of novels. I also began to address the trickier business of
theme through a discussion of a particularly "British" word cluster, a cluster that
I suggested as a possible surrogate for an expression or thread of "confidence"
that runs through much British prose and much less through Irish prose. My
analysis of this word cluster, selected from among other frequently occurring
word tokens, represented a small and imperfect step in the direction of thematic
discovery. If we are to capture the great richness of thematic diversity in the
corpus, however, then from the small step, a giant leap is now required.

Summarizing the arguments of the Russian "preformalist" Alexander Veselovsky, Victor Erlich writes that "the main concern of the literary historian is not
with assessing the unique contributions of individual writers, but with spotting
the migratory poetic formulae; accounting for their appearance in various ethnic
milieus . . . and tracing them through all vicissitudes back to the starting point"
(1980, 29). Of general types and themes in literature, Alexander Veselovsky explains that a "gifted poet . . . may by chance hit upon this or that motif, produce

* See, for example, Withshire's response (1988) to Burrow's study of Jane Austen,
which was noted in chapter 4.

imitators, create a school of writers . . . [but] these minor details . . . are hardly discernible in the broad alternation of the socio-poetic demand and supply" (as cited in ibid., 29). Veselovsky sought to define a science of literary poetics that would allow him to argue that literature evolves partially—or even completely—independent of individual creativity.* Literary history in Veselovsky's conception should be viewed as a series of recurring narrative plots, motifs, and devices that overshadow and dwarf the minor contributions of individual authors. These recurring elements exist in a larger literary system that is external to, or at least "outside" of, the immediate consciousness of the authors.

In the 1890s, Veselovsky and his brother Aleksey theorized along these lines about the origins of poetry. They attempted to trace the genesis of current poetic themes by adopting the methods of mythographers and linguists who conceived of recurrent themes as the products of external influence (see Polonsky 1998, esp. 16–17). Fascinating work to be sure, but, more generally, the Veselovsky brothers were interested in comparative literature and specifically in understanding and defining the influence of Western culture on Russian literature. Aleksey Veselovsky's study on the subject, *The Western Influence in New Russian Literature*, has not been translated into English, but Rachael Polonsky's rendering of the opening paragraph provides a usable jumping-off point for understanding just how ambitious the goal was:

> "The exchange of ideas, images, fables, artistic forms between tribes and peoples of the civilized world is one of the most important things studied by the still-young science of literary history." This process of exchange is "one of the laws of development of artistic creativity." On its way through history, a people assimilates the tales and myths, ideas and dreams, fables and folk motifs of others; "all this merges [*slivaet*] with its own birthright." "Borrowing [*zaimstvovanie*] can go from people to people . . . moving through time and space so that it becomes indirect . . . peoples can be influenced by peoples they have never touched." The exchange of ideas is an "eternal principle" that will be encountered whether a scholar studies literature by genre or by school. (1998, 18–19; brackets in the original)

These conclusions—hypotheses, really—set forth in the opening paragraph are ambitious, and, regrettably, Veselovsky never manages to take them beyond the anecdotal type of analysis to which we are still accustomed, which is to say a close reading. Hoping to show the broad interinfluences of literature, Aleksey

---

* The brothers Veselovsky, Alexander and Aleksey, may be seen as precursors, or "forerunners," as Erlich writes, of the main formalist movement of the 1920s and 1930s. Although their "preoccupation with genealogy . . . was largely abandoned by the Formalist theoreticians," their conceptions of plot and theme are echoed in works by Shklovsky, Propp, and others. See Erlich 1980, chap. 13.

Veselovsky wrestles with Pushkin and Tolstoy in the context of Rabelais, Goethe, and Cervantes, but in the end, *The Western Influence in New Russian Literature* fails to get beyond the limits of human-scale synthesis. Instead of generating big theories, the work becomes sidetracked by a more political battle that has Veselovsky wrestling his conservative colleagues who wished to reject the entire premise: Russian literature was most certainly too "original" and "pure" to be open to external linguistic and thematic pollution! However unrealized their objectives may have been, the Veselovskys provide nothing short of a call to arms for the modern, digitally equipped, scholar. With big data and computation, we possess the ability to identify and track the "migratory formulae" of literary history that the Veselovskys imagined.*

In terms of giving scholars a means of tracking thematic trends over time, the release of the Google Ngram Viewer in 2011 lowered the bar considerably.† The Ngram Viewer offers users the opportunity to track an n-gram's relative frequency behavior over the course of time and in a corpus of several million books. The Ngram Viewer, however, is not without problems, and users must exercise caution in terms of what can be said about theme based on the relative frequency of individual words. Among the more obvious problems is the issue of metadata, or more precisely the lack of metadata available to users of the Ngram tool. The only metadata provided are publication dates, and even these are frequently incorrect. Different printings, different editions, and the unaccounted-for presence of duplicate works in the corpus complicate matters even further. Even if these issues are resolved, something that the authors of the tool and the accompanying paper in *Science* (Michel et al. 2011) promise to do, other problems remain for scholars wishing to make the interpretive move from word to theme.‡ When we examine a word, or an n-gram, out of the context in which it appears, we inevitably lose information about how that word is being employed. If we are merely interested in stylistic habits, such out-of-context counting can be usefully employed, but when it comes to drawing semantic meaning from a word, we require more than a count of that word's occurrence in the corpus. A word's meaning is derived through context; as the English linguist John Rupert Firth has famously noted, "You shall know a word by the company it keeps" (1957, 11).

---

* I am grateful to my colleague Glen Worthey, who read and translated for me relevant sections of Veselovsky's *Western Influence in New Russian Literature.*

† http://books.google.com/ngrams.

‡ My blog post on December 12, 2010, offers a more specific breakdown of the most obvious problems. See http://www.matthewjockers.net/2010/12/22/unigrams-and-bigrams-and-trigrams-oh-my/.

Douglas Biber's *Corpus Linguistics: Investigating Language Structure and Use* is an excellent primer on many factors complicating word-focused text analysis and the subsequent conclusions one might draw regarding word meanings. As Biber points out, using a concordance program that produces keyword-in-context lists is a good start because such lists offer context, but these lists are hardly practical when it comes to an analysis of anything beyond even a few thousand occurrences of a key word in a given corpus (Biber et al. 2006). For investigations of this scale, the next option is to examine keywords and their collocates: the words that tend to co-occur with a keyword being investigated. Biber notes the "strong tendency for each collocate of a word to be associated with a single sense or meaning" of the word. He adds that "identifying the most common collocates of a word provides an efficient and effective means to begin analyzing senses" (ibid., 36). Biber also describes the problems associated with words that have varying parts of speech and thus "mean" differently depending on how they are being used. The Google Ngram Viewer provides no way of distinguishing between the word *deal* when used as a noun and *deal* when used as a verb (to use Biber's example). Given that the Google Ngram Viewer does allow for bigram, trigram, and so on searching, we are able to take some rough stabs at separating the two meanings by including context words. We may, for example, search for *deal the*, as in "deal the cards," versus *deal of,* as in "a great deal of monkey business." Here again, however, the quality of our results is limited by our ability to anticipate, in advance, the number and variety of potential collocates: for example, *deal to, deal in, deal with,* and so forth. Complicating matters still further, the researcher exploring the Google corpus must also consider the lemmas of the words under investigation. What, for example, of *dealt* and *dealing*?*

This is not to say that the Google Ngram Viewer and its corpus is of no, or even of little, value. On the contrary, there is much to be learned from the way that words "dance through history together."† Nevertheless, the researcher and layman alike must be cognizant of these limitations, especially when making the leap from word frequency to word meaning, or from word frequency to theme. The latter is precisely what many in the blogosphere seemed to be doing in the days following the release of the Ngram tool. I wager, in fact, that to date the vast majority of words entered into the Ngram Viewer have been nouns.

---

* I must acknowledge that the Ngram Viewer was built, at least in part, out of a desire to study these kinds of variants. I do not wish to disparage the larger research project and would point out that the Ngram tool is only the most public manifestation of the research.

† This lovely phrase is from Ryan Heuser, a former student and current coordinator of the Stanford Literary Lab.

Moreover, I suspect that the great majority of users entering these nouns have entered them with the assumption that they have some inherent or tangible meaning in connection with "culture," as if to say that the usage of a word is evidence of its purchase and relevance to the community represented in the corpus, as if a word could fully stand in for a particular concept, a theme. In fact, the Ngram Viewer offers little in terms of interpretive power: it cannot tell us *why* a particular word was popular or not; it cannot address the historical *meaning* of the word at the time it was used (something at which the *Oxford English Dictionary* is particularly good), and it cannot offer very much at all in terms of *how* readers might have perceived the use of the word. Forgetting even these issues, we cannot ignore the life that words have outside of written discourse. When we talk about the Ngram Viewer as a window into culture, or "culturomics," we speak only of written culture; even less so, we speak of written culture as it is curated by librarians at major research universities who have partnered with Google in scanning the world's books. If we believe the Ngram data, usage of the word *cool* peaked in 1940s and then began a precipitous drop that continued at least until the mid-1980s. Forgetting entirely the problem of disambiguating the meanings of *cool* (that is, "cold" versus "interesting"), surely the word's actual frequency in "culture" is not reflected in the Ngram data. *Cool,* as in "That's a cool car, man," remains ubiquitous in spoken dialogue, if not in published work.

The meanings of words are found in their contexts, and the Ngram Viewer provides only a small peephole into context. The size of the digital library, and even of the much smaller Stanford Literary Lab corpus of some thirty-five hundred nineteenth-century novels, makes n-gram viewing, KWIC lists, and collocate studies untenable for all but the most infrequent of words. If our goal is to understand the narrative subjects and the recurrent themes and motifs that operate in the literary ecosystem, then we must go beyond the study of individual n-grams, beyond the words, beyond the KWIC lists, and beyond even the collocates in order to capture what is at once more general and also more specific. Cultural memes and literary themes are not expressed in single words or even in single bigrams or trigrams. Themes are formed of bigger units and operate on a higher plane. If we may know the sense of a word by the company of words that surround it in a sentence, we may know a theme by the sentences, paragraphs, chapters, and even full books that express it. In short, simple word-to-word collocations and KWIC lists do not provide enough information to rise to the level of theme. What is needed in order to capture theme are collocations of collocations on a much larger scale.

Probabilistic latent semantic indexing (Hofmann 1999, 2001) and, more specifically, probabilistic topic modeling employing latent Dirichlet allocation (LDA) take us a very long way toward fulfilling that need (see Blei, Ng, and

Jordon 2003; Blei et al. 2004; Griffiths and Steyvers 2002, 2003, 2004; Steyvers and Griffiths 2007). Topic models are, to use a familiar idiom, the mother of all collocation tools. This algorithm, LDA, derives word clusters using a generative statistical process that begins by assuming that each document in a collection of documents is constructed from a mix of some set of possible topics. The model then assigns high probabilities to words and sets of words that tend to co-occur in multiple contexts across the corpus.*

Aside from the researcher's somewhat arbitrary setting of the number of topics to be "discovered," the entire process is done in an unsupervised fashion. "Unsupervised" means that the machine does not know in advance what themes to look for. With no human input into what constitutes a theme, a motif, a topic, the model collects distributions of co-occurring words and then returns them in a manner that allows us to examine, assess, interpret, and intuit what they all have in common, that is, their shared "theme."† The reality, of course, is that the process is far more complicated, and readers with a high tolerance for equations and plate notation will find satisfying reading in Blei, in Steyvers, and in Newman. Those less concerned with the statistics and more interested in humanistic knowledge, I direct to historian Sharon Block, whose work topic modeling an eighteenth-century newspaper is, to my knowledge, the earliest example of topic modeling in the humanities. Working with David Newman, Block performed an analysis of articles taken from the *Pennsylvania Gazette* in the 1700s. In the paper, Block describes topic modeling as follows:

---

* A layman's explanation of the LDA process can be found online at http://www
.matthewjockers.net/macroanalysisbook/lda/.

† In this chapter, I use the terms *theme, topic,* and *motif* as synonyms for the same general concept: namely, a type of literary material, that is, "subject matter," that recurs with some degree of frequency throughout and across a corpus. This material functions as a central and unifying unit of a text or texts. Despite a long history of studying theme and motif in literature and even more extensively in folklore, these terms do remain ambiguous, terms of convenience. I believe that the word clusters discussed here are self-evidently thematic and that even while the matter of what constitutes a theme or motif is a broad area in which some things are black, some white, and some gray, most readers will recognize in the word distributions the larger thematic category to which these words belong. Although handbooks such as *Themes and Motifs in Western Literature* (Daemmrich and Daemmrich 1987) may help us to understand theme, even these scholarly compilations are open to the charge of being arbitrary—they define by example, not by concise definition. Daemmrich offers the theme of "Death," for example, and I am comfortable accepting "Death" as a theme. But Daemmrich also records a theme called "Eye." To my mind, "Eye" would be more appropriately chronicled in a dictionary of symbols than in a handbook of themes.

Topic modeling is based on the idea that individual documents are made up of one or more topics. It uses emerging technologies in computer science to automatically cluster topically similar documents by determining the groups of words that tend to co-occur in them. Most importantly, topic modeling creates topical categories without a priori subject definitions. This may be the hardest concept to understand about topic modeling: unlike traditional classification systems where texts are fit into preexisting schema (such as Library of Congress subject headings), topic modeling determines the comprehensive list of subjects through its analysis of the word occurrences throughout a corpus of texts. The content of the documents—not a human indexer—determines the topics collectively found in those documents. (2006, n.p.)

Readers who find Block's work on a corpus of newspaper articles useful may find Cameron Blevin's blog post (2010) about topic modeling Martha Ballard's diary equally appealing.* For our purposes here, suffice to say that the model identifies words that tend to co-occur together in multiple places in multiple documents. If the statistics are rather too complex to summarize here, I think it is fair to skip the mathematics and focus on the end results. We needn't know how long and hard Joyce sweated over *Ulysses* to appreciate his genius, and a clear understanding of the LDA machine is not required in order to see the beauty of the result.

The results that I shall describe and explore here were derived from David Mimno's implementation of LDA in the open-source MAchine Learning for LanguagE Toolkit, or "MALLET," software packaged developed by Andrew McCallum (2002) and other contributors at the University of Massachusetts–Amherst. In my experience, the MALLET implementation is the most robust and best-tested topic-modeling software package. The documentation accompanying Mimno's implementation of LDA describes topic modeling as follows: "Topic models provide a simple way to analyze large volumes of unlabeled text. A 'topic' consists of a cluster of words that frequently occur together. Using contextual clues, topic models can connect words with similar meanings and distinguish between uses of words with multiple meanings" (McCallum 2009, n.p.). In short, topic modeling provides a scalable method for word-sense disambiguation that specifically addresses the limitations of traditional collocation and KWIC lists that were discussed above. Unlike KWIC and collocate lists, which require careful human interrogation in order to parse out one word sense from another, topic modeling works in an unsupervised way, inferring information about individual word senses based on their repeated appearance in similar contextual situations. The resulting "topics" in a given collection of texts are not provided to the re-

---

* See also Robert K. Nelson's online commentary "Of Monsters, Men—and Topic Modeling" that appeared in the *New York Times* online opinion pages, May 29, 2011, http://opinionator.blogs.nytimes.com/2011/05/29/of-monsters-men-and-topic-modeling/.

searcher in the form of labeled themes (for example, the theme of "Seafaring"), but rather as sets of words, which are "ranked," or "weighted," according to their probabilities of appearing together in a given topic. The ease with which these resulting word clusters can be readily identified as topics or themes is referred to as topic "coherence" or topic "interpretability." Figures 8.1 and 8.2 use word clouds to visualize two topics that were harvested from the Stanford Literary Lab's collection of 3,346 books. The individual words are weighted, and the weights represent the probability of the word in the given topic.*

It is not difficult for a human interpreter to make sense of the word clouds and to assign labels to the themes represented by these algorithmically derived word lists. Without getting too specific, the first may be labeled "Native Americans" and the second "Ireland."† Within each topic are words that, when taken in isolation, would provide very little in terms of thematic information. Consider, for example, the word *stream* in topic 271, the "Native Americans" topic.

---

* That is, *Indians* is the word most likely to appear in topic 271 followed by *chief* and *Indians*, and so forth. Another topic may also have the word *Indian* with a much smaller emphasis. In this topic, for example, we find the word *party*. In this context, we understand that *party* is being used in the sense of *war party*. Another topic, about celebrations, for example, might have the same word type, *party*, with a different weight and a different sense.

† Obviously, these are generalities: each of the word clusters contains potential subclusters or subtopics, and, given different parameters, the LDA process might be tuned to detect different levels of granularity. Also found in these collections of words are markers indicative of attitudes toward the overarching theme: *savages, scalp*, and perhaps even *death* in the context of the other words found in topic 271 give us an inkling of how the Indians of this topic are being represented in the corpus. Were we interested in pursuing a finer level of granularity—if we were interested, for example, in separating the depiction of Indians as peaceful frontiersmen from the depictions of Indians as scalping savages—we might rerun the topic model and set the parameters so as to define a larger number of topics, or we might use text segmentation to create smaller units of text for processing. These techniques will be described in more detail below.

Likewise, it appears that topic 25 contains the seeds of what might be two separate themes under the larger heading of "Ireland." Consider how a sublist of words including *heart, cabin, bog, county, mountains, Derry, house, air, evening, turf, friends,* and *heaven* presents a picture of the native Irish with perhaps some idealization of the Irish countryside. Contrast that with a sublist of words containing only *night, land, cabin, bog, sorrow, divil, peasantry, whiskey, manner, officer, barracks, agent,* and *officers,* and we can conjecture the presence of a topic with greater negative associations, one that leads us to consider how British rule in Ireland impacted the depiction of Ireland and provided a contrast to the more idealized Ireland. Taken together, the two sublists offer a broad view and capture the idea of Ireland as a bifurcated country: *One Island, Two Irelands*, as the title of a documentary film portraying the "Troubles" puts it, or *The Two Irelands*, as in David Fitzpatrick's study of Irish partition from 1912 to 1939.

Figure 8.1. "Native Americans" theme

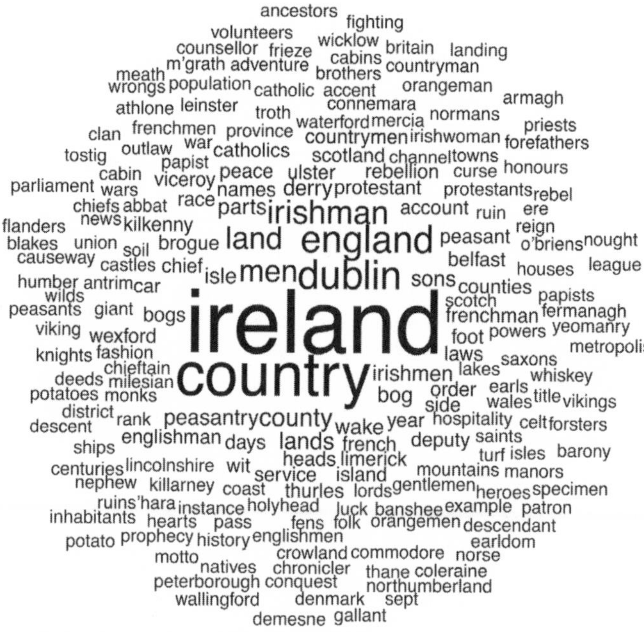

Figure 8.2. "Ireland" theme

In conjunction with the much larger company of other words that the model returns, it is easy to see that this particular use of *stream* is not related to the "jet stream" or to the "stream of immigrants" entering the United States in the 1850s. Nor is it a word with any affiliations to contemporary "media streaming." This *stream* refers to a body of flowing water. Its contextual relationship to other words such as *wilderness* and *prairie*—not to mention the more obvious *Indians* and *chiefs*—leaves us knowing with no uncertainty that the larger "theme" of which *stream* is one component is Native Americans. The words returned from the model paint both setting and subject; the result is a useful and quantifiable representation of a very particular theme. Importantly, though, note further that *stream* is not a word likely to arise in one's consciousness upon hearing the words *Native American*. *Stream* is, however, entirely appropriate in the context of these other words because it fits with and belongs in the theme. Were we conducting a traditional scholarly analysis of the "theme" of Native Americans in nineteenth-century fiction, would we have even thought to include streams? Consider the following passage from Mayne Reid's 1851 novel *The Scalp Hunters*. The first occurrence of the word *stream(s)* is located 225 words away from the occurrence of the word *Indians,* approximately the distance between the top and bottom of a standard book page:

> The scenery was altogether new to me, and imbued me with impressions of a peculiar character. The *streams* were fringed with tall groves of cottonwood trees, whose column-like stems supported a thick frondage of silvery leaves.
> . . . [199 words removed here] . . .
> As we approached the Arkansas, we saw mounted *Indians* disappearing over the swells. They were Pawnees; and for several days clouds of these dusky warriors hung upon the skirts of the caravan. But they knew our strength, and kept at a wary distance from our long rifles.

The word *stream* does not occur "close" enough to the word *Indian* to have been picked up in a KWIC list, and even a collocation concordance would be unlikely to identify *stream* as an important word in the context of Indians, since *stream* is not going to be a very frequent collocate. Yet the topic-modeling methodology, which treats documents as "bags" of words, is not restricted from recognizing that there is something important and contextually homogeneous about *stream* and *Indians*.

The two topics described above were produced during a run of the MALLET topic modeler that sought to identify five hundred topics in a corpus of 3,346 nineteenth-century books. When running an LDA model, the researcher sets a variety of parameters to determine how the model is constructed. The primary parameter, and the one that causes no small amount of discussion and confusion, is the parameter determining the number of topics to be harvested from these data. There is neither consensus nor conventional wisdom regarding a perfect number of topics to extract, but it can be said that the "sweet spot" is largely dependent upon and determined by the scope of the corpus, the diversity of the corpus, and the level of granularity one is seeking in terms of topic interpretability and coherence. As noted previously, the "interpretability and coherence" of a topic mean specifically the ease with which a human being can look at and identify (that is, "name" or "characterize") a topic from the word list that the model produces. Setting the number of topics too high may result in topics lacking enough contextual markers to provide a clear sense of how the topic is being expressed in the text; setting the number too low may result in topics of such a general nature that they tend to occur throughout the entire corpus. Chang et al. (2009) have conducted one of the most compelling studies of topic interpretability. The authors test statistical and unsupervised approaches designed to evaluate topic coherence against qualitative human evaluations. Their conclusion is that automated methods for assessing topic interpretability are negatively correlated with human evaluations of interpretability. In other words, though the machine does a very good job in identifying the topics latent in a corpus, the machine does a comparatively poor job when it comes to auto-identifying which of the harvested topics are the most interpretable by human beings.

Interpretability is of key concern to us since we are most interested in investigating and exploring themes that we understand and recognize. This is an important point to dwell on because one criticism of unsupervised models is that they are black boxes. In one sense, it is true that with no, or very little, input from the human operator, the machine churns through a corpus and harvests out what it "believes" to be the "n" most important or prevalent topics in the corpus. From an information-retrieval perspective, this may be all that is required. If our goal is only to find documents with similar content, then the results of the topic model can be further processed so that texts with high proportions of "topic A" are grouped in one pile and those with strong proportions of "topic B" in another. This method has proven to work extremely well when it comes to document clustering and information retrieval (see, for example, Cohn and Hofmann 2001; Hofmann 2001; Wei and Croft 2006). For literary scholars, however, it is the interpretability and coherence of the topics that ultimately count. For illustrative purposes, figure 8.3 shows the word cloud generated for topic 123. Although it is true that an uninhibited reader might be able to make an argument for the interpretability of this topic, this set of words is clearly something other than what was seen in the topics of figures 8.1 and 8.2. Out of five hundred topics derived in this research, I identified fourteen as being "uncertain" or "unclear."* What, then, does this mean—that

---

* Word clouds for all five hundred topics can be found online at http://www .matthewjockers.net/macroanalysisbook/macro-themes/.

Figure 8.3. An incoherent theme

some topics lack clarity—and how are we supposed to trust the algorithms if alongside two homogenous, pristine, interpretable topics we also find these impenetrable juggernauts?

For computer scientists and linguists working in the field of topic modeling, this is an active area of research, but it is not a problem for us to dwell upon here. Ideally, all of the topics the machine produces would be perfectly interpretable; the presence of uninterruptable topics, however, does not undermine the usefulness of the topics that are interpretable.* If we choose to ignore some topics, say the ambiguous one, and focus our attention on others, say only the most interpretable, we do no disservice to the overall model, and we in no way compromise our analysis. Choosing to examine only some of the machine's

---

* For information-retrieval researchers and scholars working in machine learning, the problem of uninterruptable topics is a nut to be cracked, and a variety of approaches are being explored: for example, approaches that attempt to automatically score topic coherence. It is fair to say that the more interpretable the resulting topics, the better the model's use, and so there is legitimate motivation to improve the modeling algorithms to a point where they turn out only pristine topics. See, for example, Lau, Newman, et al. 2010; Lau, Grieser, et al. 2011; Newman, Lau, et al. 2010; Newman, Noh, et al. 2010.

topics and not others is a legitimate use of these data and should not be viewed with suspicion by those who may be wary of the "black box." Indeed, as literary scholars, we are almost constantly focusing our gaze on the specific elements of a text that we consider to be the interpretable elements. That we may do so at the expense of some other valuable insight we might gain by focusing our attention elsewhere is understood. Put simply, not everything in a book can be studied at once: *Moby Dick* explores both whaling and religion, but a scholar writing of religion in *Moby Dick* cannot be faulted for failing to discuss cetology. The place where error, or more correctly "debate," can creep into the topic-modeling process is in the assignment of thematic labels, that is, in the human interpretation of the machine-extracted topics. Some interpreters will disagree over the appropriate label to assign to a given word-topic distribution, but these disagreements will almost always be over the precision, or imprecision, of the human-generated topic labels and not over the underlying theme represented by the words in the topic. For this research, I have found it useful to visualize the topic-word distributions as word clouds. This has the effect of accentuating those words that are most central to the topic while pushing the related but less central words to the periphery of the visualization. In general, the labels that I have assigned to the five hundred topics I explore in this research are derived from the primary, or "key," words revealed by these topic clouds. In some cases, however, my labels are a synthesis of the words, that is, they are labels that use words not necessarily found in the topic, labels designed to offer a more general summary: the label "Native Americans," for example, is what I use to describe the cluster of words in figure 8.1.* As noted above, the labeling of topics is subjective and can be contentious; for this reason, I have placed all five hundred topic clouds online. Readers wishing to verify my labeling choices are encouraged to study the topic-cloud visualizations.

With that said, let us unpack the topic-model results a bit further. In addition to outputting the word clusters seen in the figure, the model also provides output indicating the percentage or proportion of each topic assigned to each document. Remember that each document contains a mixture of topics in different proportions, like a pie in which some pieces are larger than others. The model provides similar information for the corpus as a whole. Figure 8.4 shows the distribution of the top-ten topics found in *Moby Dick* alongside the same topics in the entire corpus. The presence of topic 347 ("Seas and Whaling"), a theme dealing with islands, whaling, and sea voyages, is prominent in *Moby Dick:* according to the model, about 20 percent of the novel. This seafaring theme is followed by theme 85, which deals with ships. Next is theme 492 about boats

---

* This is a particularly useful label, given that another topic deals with India and another set of "Indians."

and water, and then 455, a theme that deals with captains and crews. In *Moby Dick,* these are big themes—in the entire corpus, however, they are barely noticeable, as seen in the darker gray bars representing the corpus mean for these themes. Figure 8.5 shows the top-ten topics from the overall corpus alongside those same topics in *Moby Dick.* With the exception of the themes associated with morning and night, the themes that dominate the overall corpus are comparatively foreign to *Moby Dick.* Indeed, *Moby Dick* is very much an outlier in terms of the themes that dominate this nineteenth-century corpus.

With a basic sense of how topic modeling works and what it produces, we can now delve into my specific application of LDA to this corpus of 3,346 nineteenth-century books. When running a topic model, a researcher has the option of excluding "stop words" from the analysis. Most commonly, stop words are defined as high-frequency "function" words such as articles and prepositions. The MALLET software provides a setting that will ignore a standard list of very common English adverbs, conjunctions, pronouns, and prepositions. Unlike the stylistic analysis of the previous chapter, where we sought to exclude context-sensitive words, in topic modeling we want to do the exact opposite: we want to remove words that carry no thematic weight and concentrate on those words that best convey meaning. For this analysis of theme, I determined that even the standard stop list in MALLET was unsatisfactory. In addition to the usual set of common words, many other word types can "pollute" an otherwise pristine thematic signal. The repeated use of a common name in multiple books, "John," for example, can come to dominate a topic that would otherwise be purely topical in nature ("John" from one book being not the same as "John" from another). Prior to topic modeling the texts for this research, therefore, I employed the Stanford Named Entity Recognition software package (Finkel, Grenager, and Manning 2005) to identify named entities in the corpus. These character and personal names, identified by the NER software package, were then added to the list of common stop words. Ultimately, the stop-word list totaled 5,631 distinct word types.* Marks of punctuation and numbers were also specifically excluded.

Through experimentation it was observed that even finer-grained and more interpretable topics could be derived through a further reduction of the vocabulary being modeled. For modeling theme, I discovered that highly interpretable and thematically coherent topics could be derived through a model built entirely from nouns.† Constructing a noun-based model required preprocessing all of

---

* See http://www.matthewjockers.net/macroanalysisbook/expanded-stopwords-list/.

† Depending on what one wishes to analyze in the topics, the exclusion of certain word classes could be viewed as a controversial step. By eliminating adjectives, for example, the resulting topics may lack information expressive of attitudes or sentiments. Likewise, the

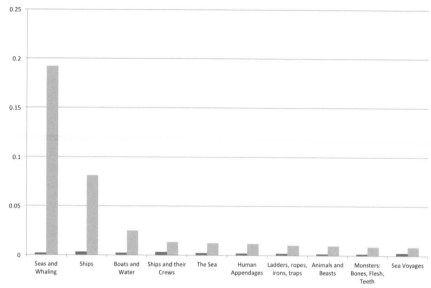

Figure 8.4. Top-ten topics in *Moby Dick*

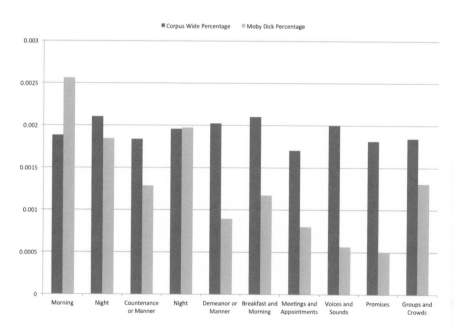

Figure 8.5. Top-ten topics in corpus

the texts in the corpus with a part-of-speech (POS) tagger.* In this manner, Austen's "It is a truth universally acknowledged, that a single man in possession of a good fortune, must be in want of a wife. However little known the feelings or views of such a man may be on his first entering a neighbourhood, this truth is so well fixed in the minds of the surrounding families, that he is considered as the rightful property of some one or other of their daughters" is transformed into "truth man possession fortune want wife feelings views man neighbour-hood truth minds families property other daughters." Once the 3,346 texts in the corpus were tagged for part of speech, a custom script chunked each text into 1,000 word segments and then extracted the words identified as nouns from each segment and created a new corpus of text segments composed entirely of

------

elimination of verbs may result in topics that fail to capture the actions associated with the novels. I must offer the caveat, therefore, that the noun-based approach used here is specific to the type of thematic results I wish to derive; I do not suggest this as a blanket approach. In my experiments, I have often found that a combination of specific parts of speech can reveal aspects of narrative and narrative style that are not captured by nouns alone. Nevertheless, the noun-based approach that I describe here proves to be extremely effective in generating coherent topics that can be easily identified and interpreted. The effectiveness of nouns for this purpose was determined through an iterative process of trial and experimentation. Various combinations of different parts of speech were tried and examined. Each combination had certain advantages and disadvantages. For the purpose of modeling theme, nouns produced the best results. This will be made clear in the analysis that follows. Verbs were discovered to have only limited value, and though adjectives were found to be highly effective in capturing sentiment, they were not effective in capturing or further elucidating theme. The development and use of an adjective-based model for detecting sentiment alongside theme is a current area of experimentation in a project of the Stanford Literary Lab that is funded by the Mellon Foundation.

* There are a variety of POS taggers available for this kind of work, and all of them have advantages and disadvantages. The Stanford POS tagger, for example, that was used in this research is known to be highly accurate, but since it is trained on hand-tagged samples of journalistic prose from the *Wall Street Journal,* it may not be as sensitive to literary prose as another tagger trained on a corpus of nineteenth-century fiction. Modern part-of-speech taggers rely on supervised machine learning and machine classification. In simple terms, the tagger is given a training corpus of documents that have been marked up by a human coder, and once "trained" on this corpus, the tagger is then given new, unmarked, text for which it assigns part-of-speech tags based on what it has learned from the training data. I have not done extensive comparisons to determine whether one or the other tagger is "better." Matthew Wilkins provides a useful review of several taggers on his blog at http://workproduct.wordpress.com/2009/01/27/evaluating-pos-taggers-conclusions/. See also http://nora.hd.uib.no/corpora/1997–3/0161.html and Boggess et al. 1999.

nouns. MALLET was then employed to model the corpus and extract 500 latent topics from this noun-based and segmented corpus of 631,577 novel chunks.*

Text segmentation was done in order to improve topic quality and interpretability. Topic modeling treats each document as a "bag of words" in which word order is disregarded. Without segmentation, a single novel would be processed as a single "bag." Since the topic model works by identifying words that tend to co-occur, the bigger the bag, the more words that will tend to be found together in the same bag. If novels tended to be constrained to only a very small number of topics or themes, then treating an entire novel as one bag might be fruitful. In reality, though, novels tend to have some themes that run throughout and others that appear at specific points and then disappear. In order to capture these transient themes, it was useful to divide the novels into "chunks" and run the model over those chunks instead of over the entire text. There appears to be no conventional wisdom regarding ideal text-segmentation parameters. David Mimno—author of the MALLET topic-modeling software—reports in email correspondence that he frequently chunks texts down to the level of individual paragraphs. For the books in this corpus, I found through experimentation that 1,000-word chunking was effective.† Knowledge of the scope and variety of the corpus, along with a sense of the research questions to be investigated, proved to be the most useful guides in determining an ideal number of topics and ideal degree of text segmentation. Until new research provides an algorithmic

* In work sponsored by the Mellon Foundation, this process was later formalized by Loretta Auvil and Boris Capitanu as a SEASR workflow.

† Other experiments included building models based on dividing each novel into ten equal-size chunks, page-based chunks, paragraph chunks, and 250-consecutive-noun chunks. None of these produced topics of greater quality (interpretability) than what was observed in the 1,000-word chunking. In fact, some topics that represent major themes in specific novels were "lost" when segmentation became too fine grained. It was observed, for example, that the theme "Whaling Ships" disappears from the topic results when the chunk size becomes too small. This is because the theme of whaling in *Moby Dick,* for example, tends to get expressed across the breadth of the entire text and to a lesser degree in specific sections. If the chunks get too small, the concurrence of whaling terms within a chunk do not rise to a level worthy of "topic status"; instead, the whaling terms gets absorbed into larger themes associated with "seafaring." For this corpus, segmentation of each text into 1,000-word chunks produced high-quality results. Undoubtedly, these results could be improved still further, but ultimately it is the interpretability of the topics that is important. In this research, experiments that made small adjustments to text chunk size or number of topics, or both, resulted in trivial or unperceivable change. Experimentation with segmentation revealed very little difference between 500 topics generated using texts that are segmented into 1,000-word chunks versus using 1,500-word chunks.

alternative, trial and experimentation augmented by domain expertise appear to be the best guides in setting segmentation and topic-number parameters.*

MALLET output includes two derivative files: a file containing topic "keys" and a file containing the proportions of each topic found in each text, or each text segment in this case. The keys file is a simple matrix in which the first column of data contains a unique topic identifier, and a second column contains the top words assigned to the topic. A researcher examines these topic-word distributions and assigns them a label. In this work, I have found it useful to visualize the topics as word clouds. In some cases, an appropriate label can be difficult to determine. In this research, I labeled ambiguous topics as "uncertain," and then as a check to the legitimacy of my other labels, I consulted with members of the Stanford Literary Lab to confirm the appropriateness of my choices. There was general consensus about the interpretability and labeling choices I had made. Of the 500 topics, I labeled four as "Bad Data." These were topics that resulted from the poor quality of optical character recognition of some texts in the corpus. Another four topics were labeled "Book Metadata." These topics were obviously derived from the words found in the title pages and metadata of the electronic files. I identified 18 topics as "uncertain." The remaining 474 were found to be interpretable and were given thematic labels.† The second derivative file that MALLET produces provides data regarding the amount (proportion) of each topic found in each text segment. The modeling process assumes that every document is a "mixture" of all of the 500 possible topics in the corpus. Thus, each document is composed of some proportion of each of the 500 topics.‡

Motivated by the work of the Veselovsky brothers and their interest in studying literary evolution in terms of recurring motifs and national literatures, I began my analysis by plotting the mean proportions of every topic, in every year, separated first by nation, then by gender, and finally by nation and gender combined. Linking all of the thematic and topical data to the metadata facilitated

---

* David Mimno and others are presently working on exactly this sort of research. Tuning the algorithm to automatically identify the best parameters requires training data for which the topics have been manually vetted for quality. In the course of my research, I have produced, studied, and labeled several dozen topic models, and I have given many of these results to Mimno for analysis. Using my labeled models, Mimno is able to study the differences between topics that I have identified as interpretable versus ambiguous and look for patterns in the word distributions of the two. In time, Mimno hopes to develop an algorithmic solution for generating the most coherent results.

† www.matthewjockers.net/macroanalysisbook/macro-themes/

‡ This proportions file is a table in which each row is a text segment and each column a topic. The proportions of each topic in each text segment are the values held in the individual cells.

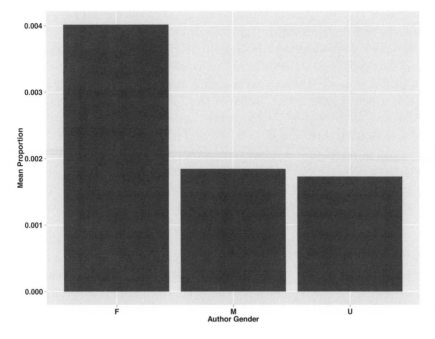

Figure 8.6. "Affection and Happiness" theme by gender

the identification of thematic and topical patterns at the level of the corpus, at the level of the individual book, and across facets of time, gender, and nationality. All 474 interpretable themes were plotted across each metadata facet; the resulting charts can be found on the companion website.*

Examining the charts, a number of things were obvious, not the least of which was that nations and genders have clear thematic "preferences" or tendencies. Some of these preferences correspond rather closely to our expectations and even our stereotypes. For example, a theme associated with strong emotions and feelings that I labeled "Affection and Happiness" appears more than twice as often in female authors as in male authors (figure 8.6). Female authors also tend to write more about women's apparel, as evidenced by their greater usage of topic 29 (figure 8.7), which is a theme I have labeled "Female Fashion." And women are at least twice as likely to write about the care of infants and children as their male counterparts. Figure 8.8, labeled "Infants," shows this topic distribution by author gender.

Not surprisingly, women also appear to have the market cornered when it comes to even more specific expressions of strong emotion. Whether these are expressions of "Happiness" (topic 109), "Passion" (topic 316), or "Grief and

_____

* www.matthewjockers.net/macroanalysisbook/macro-themes

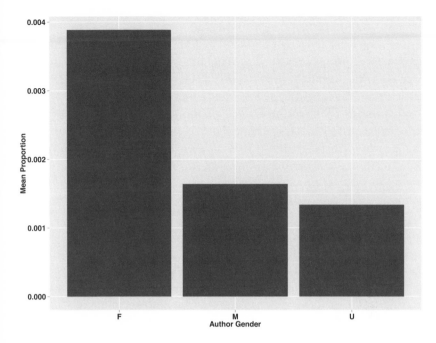

Figure 8.7. "Female Fashion" theme by gender

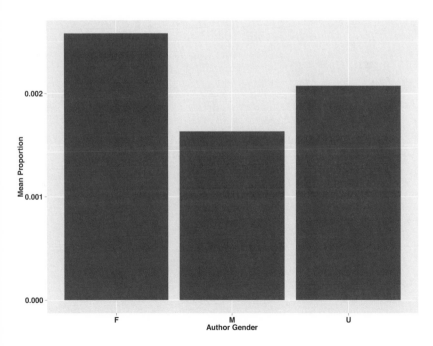

Figure 8.8. "Infants" theme by gender

Sorrow" (topic 43), female authors tend to deal with expressions of feeling and emotion far more often than males. Male authors, on the other hand, are about twice as likely as women to write about "Villains and Traitors" (figure 8.9), about "Quarrels and Dueling" (figure 8.10), and about "Enemies" (figure 8.11).

Other themes in the corpus are not specifically gendered. The use of a rural theme associated with scenes of natural beauty (topic 471) is equally distributed among male and female authors. So too is a related theme of "The Land" (topic 190). And three themes associated with wealth, business affairs, and social rank (topics 338, 359, 375) are all equally distributed across genders. Male and female authors in this corpus are also equally likely to write of humor, jesting, laughter, and joking (topic 381).

The works in this corpus include 1,363 by female authors, 1,753 by males, and 230 of unknown authorship (the "unidentified" gender class labeled as U in the figures). It turned out that these anonymous works are quite interesting. Indeed, several themes in the corpus are overrepresented in works of anonymous authorship, and these themes often relate to sociopolitical institutions such as the monarchy, as seen in topics 97, 108, and 239; or to religious institutions, as in the "Convents and Abbeys" theme found in topic 31; or the theme of "Religion"

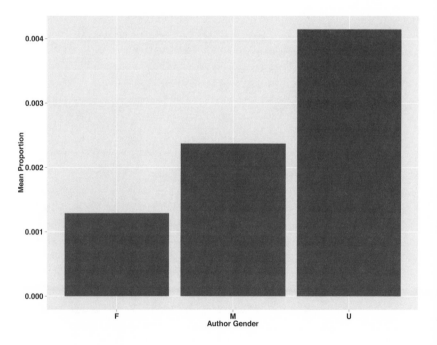

Figure 8.9. "Villains and Traitors" theme by gender

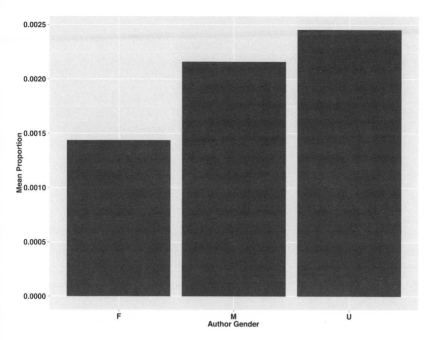

Figure 8.10. "Quarrels and Dueling" theme by gender

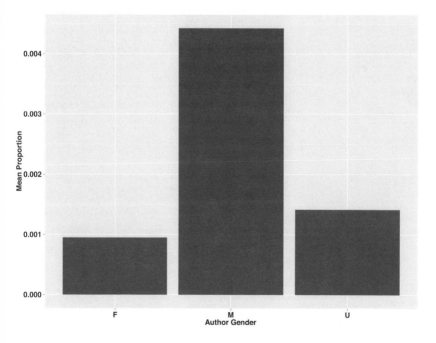

Figure 8.11. "Enemies" theme by gender

found more generally in topic 448. At the same time, these anonymous works are also very high on a theme dealing with the expression of opinions, topic 28. All of this makes perfect sense if we believe that these authors felt the need to conceal their identities in order to present a more candid portrait of politics or religion or both. This is an undoubtedly rich area for further research, and a closer probing of this data led me to a further observation that these anonymous writers have a higher usage of topics 25 and 324, which are "Ireland" and "Scotland," respectively. Taken together, this evidence suggests a class of writers generating thinly veiled narratives that express opinions about religious and nationalistic matters that would have likely been awkward or impossible to express without the use of a pseudonym.

Such an observation naturally leads us to inquire about other correlations between nationality and theme. Sadly, for these unidentified authors we know neither their genders nor their nationalities, and thus it is impossible to know if these writers were themselves Irish or Scottish. For the majority of authors in this corpus, however, we do have information about nationality, and this data can be used much in the same way that gender was used to plot the thematic preferences of male and female authors. When it comes to nationality, some themes were discovered to be predominantly American, others British, and some distinctly Irish.* Prominent in American writing, for example, is a theme associated with slavery† (figure 8.12) and another associated with American Indians (figure 8.13).

An especially Irish theme, which I have labeled "Tenants and Landlords," is found most often in Irish novels and is, in fact, the most prominent theme (that is, the topic given the greatest proportion) in 34 percent of the Irish novels in this corpus (figure 8.14). This theme will be familiar to scholars of Irish literature as the "Big House" theme that was made popular by writers exploring the relationship between ascendancy landlords and their typically poor, Catholic tenants. Topping the list of Irish authors who deploy this theme are Maria Edgeworth (whose *Castle Rackrent* registers 5.2 percent) and William Carleton (whose *Poor Scholar* scores 5 percent). In other words, according to the model, fully 5 percent of each of these books is concerned with the relationships between tenants and landlords. And should we wish to interrogate the usage of this theme at the smaller scale of the individual novel, it is possible to plot the progression, or "incidence," of the theme across the 1,000-word segments of each text. Figures 8.15 and 8.16 plot the usage of the "Tenants and Landlords" theme across "novel time" in the two books.

* Unless specifically noted, Scottish and Welsh authors are generally treated as part of the "British" corpus.

† Two themes in this corpus deal with slavery: one with an American context and the other Persian.

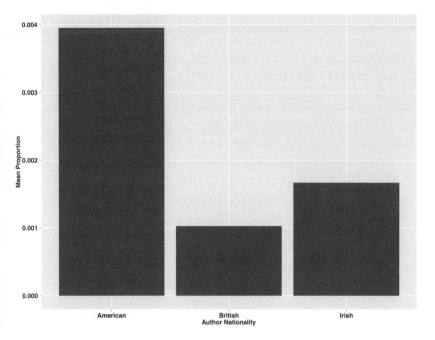

Figure 8.12. "American Slavery" theme by nation

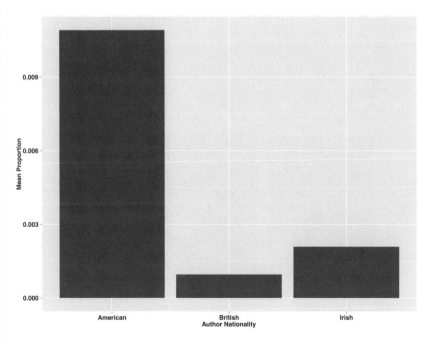

Figure 8.13. "Native Americans" theme by nation

By comparison, this Big House theme, which appears as most important, or most dominant, in 34 percent of Irish-authored novels, appears as dominant in just 0.007 percent of British novels and just 0.003 percent of American novels. Although it is a defining theme of the nineteenth-century Irish novel, it is not omnipresent throughout the entire century. Figure 8.17 shows the "Tenants and Landlords" theme separated by nation and plotted across time. To reduce noise, a five-year moving average was applied to the data. Among the Irish-authored texts in the corpus (the light-gray line), this theme experiences four distinct spikes. The first spike occurs around 1810; this is the time frame within which Maria Edgeworth's *Castle Rackrent* (1800) and Lady Morgan's *Wild Irish Girl* (1806) were published: we would expect to find the theme well represented in these texts. A second, smaller, spike appears in 1835. Then the topic peaks in the 1840s during the years of the Great Famine and a time when writers including Carleton, Lever, and Lytton were active. Whether the famine was also the catalyst for the simultaneous spike seen in American writers of the same period is a question for further investigation. Certainly, the influx of famine immigrants to America would have been very hard to ignore. That this catastrophe may have served as specific fuel for the American literary imagination is another

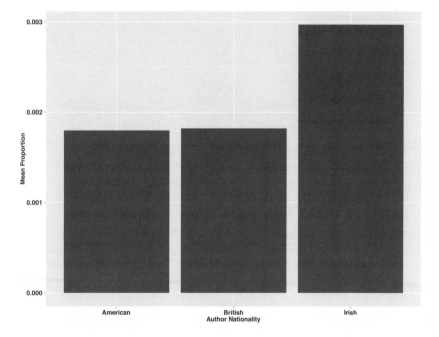

Figure 8.14. "Tenants and Landlords" theme by nation

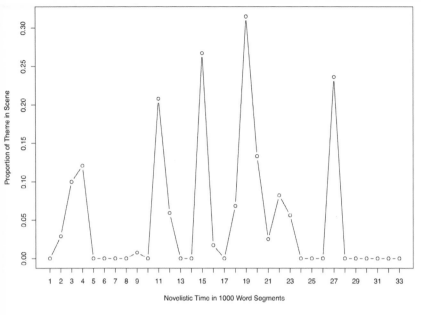

Figure 8.15. "Tenants and Landlords" in *Castle Rackrent*

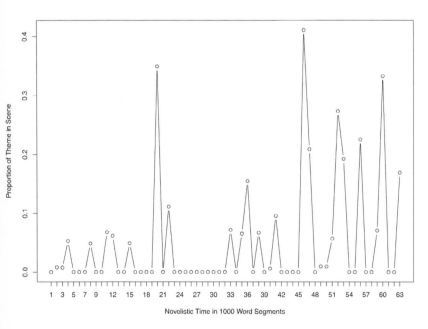

Figure 8.16. "Tenants and Landlords" in *The Poor Scholar*

matter. With James Fenimore Cooper, at least, we know of a looming dissat-
isfaction with the American aristocracy and a desire to avoid in America the
kinds of disparity he witnessed in Europe in the '30s. One Cooper novel from
this period, *The Redskins,* goes to the heart of "tenant-landlord" systems, and
readers cognizant of the situation in Ireland at the time cannot help but note
that Cooper's fictional footman, Barney, is just thirteen weeks out of Ireland.*

This spike of the 1840s is followed by a steep decline into a trough that runs
from the 1850s until the late 1860s. Such a decline may very well be attributable
to the aftermath of the famine. This was, after all, a national catastrophe that
would have made writing fiction about strained tenant-landlord relationships
seem almost cruel and unusual punishment for a devastated population. A final
spike of increased writing about tenants and landlords is seen in the 1860s, where
again it seems to have parallel currency in the American context.

In *The Irish Novel: A Critical History,* James Cahalan asserts that even in the
work of Irish writer Laurence Sterne—who did not write novels specifically
about Ireland—he, Cahalan, can identify the "features of a particular kind of
Irish novel" (1988, 7). Cahalan argues that Irish novels are often unified and
identifiable by distinctly "Irish" themes, even if those themes are not exclusively
Irish. He argues, for example, that a theme of subjugation runs through Irish
prose. Certainly, this "Tenant and Landlords" theme, which includes such terms
as *rights, conditions, rents, landlord, servant, tenants, agents, grievance, com-
plaints, taxes, neglect,* and *bailiff* could be seen as related to subjugation along
the lines that Cahalan hypothesizes. And although Irish authors dominate this
corpus when it comes to use of this theme, there are other themes of subjugation,
which also find expression in the Irish corpus. The theme "American Slavery"
is especially interesting. It is a theme most often found, as we would expect, in
American prose. Nevertheless, the theme gets expressed rather profoundly in
the Irish corner of the corpus, especially during the late 1850s and 1860s. This

---

* Michael J. Pikus has a revealing essay on this subject titled "*The Redskins; or, Indian
and Injin* and James Fenimore Cooper's Continuing Historical Paradox." Pikus writes,
"Despite his appreciation of the American aristocracy and landholding classes, the power
of these classes in Europe dismays Cooper" (1997, n.p.). He cites Cooper as follows: "In
America property is taxed as it should be . . . ; but in Europe as much is extorted as is
possible from the pittance of the laborer, by means of excises. It is not unusual to term
the political contests of the world, the struggle of the poor against the rich; but in Europe
it is, in fact, the struggle of the rich against the poor. Governments, in this quarter of
the world, are in fact degenerating into stock-jobbing companies, in which the mass are
treated as so many producers to enable the few to get good securities for their money"
(*The Letters and Journals of James Fenimore Cooper,* 2:345–46, cited in ibid., n.p.). Pikus
goes on to write that the "sensitivity [Cooper] displays toward the European working
classes reflects a benevolent republicanism" (ibid., n.p.).

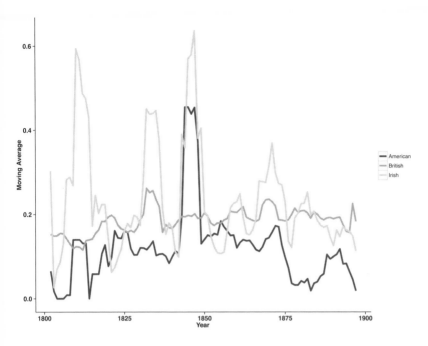

Figure 8.17. "Tenants and Landlords" across time and nation

surge is due almost entirely to the works of the very prolific Irish author Mayne Reid. Reid's books from this period include the renowned antislavery novel *The Quadroon* (1856), which was somewhat shamelessly adapted for the stage by the more famous Irish author and playwright Dion Boucicault and retitled *The Octoroon*. Boucicault's play, more so than Reid's novel, was responsible for fueling debate in Ireland about abolition and the morality of slavery.* The American slavery theme is most prominent in the American part of the corpus, but it shows up twice as often in Irish books than it does in British books, as was seen in figure 8.12.

Thus far, my focus has been on describing thematic *presence,* but the thematic tendencies of nations and of genders may be seen not only in the themes that are overrepresented in their novels but also in those that are conspicuously absent. Despite the significant role played by ships and seafaring in Ireland, for example, the Irish novels in this corpus are almost completely lacking when it comes to themes associated with the sea. And Irish novels have much less than their British contemporaries when it comes to themes associated with the leisure activities of

---

* Irish writers, if not Irish American writers, were generally sympathetic to abolition and appeared to identify with the plight of black slaves in America.

the upper class. Somewhat ironically for a largely rural nation, the Irish authors in this corpus also have little to say about sheep, cattle, and livestock.

To be sure, there is much more that could be said about the general trends and tendencies of themes in this corpus of novels. The aforementioned themes are cited primarily as examples, as a way to give a fuller sense of the data, but they are also noted to serve as provocations for further thought. The thematic distributions are revealing; they incite all manner of questions about the relationships and the correlations between themes and historical events, between themes and author nationality, between theme and author gender, and more. The macro trends visualized here provide context, not on a keyword scale, but on a massive corpus-size scale.

• • •

What, then, can we learn of literary history from these trends? Surely, the things that writers choose to write about are in some sense tied to time and place. A good deal of literary criticism is invested in precisely this argument, that literary texts are historical artifacts, that literary texts are, whether overtly or more subtly, representative of the times in which they are produced. Where we may have been surprised to find that there are clear and measurable differences in word usage among British, Irish, and American writers, we are less surprised to learn that these authors write about different things, or that they write about similar things to differing degrees. Some themes are endemic to particular nations or to particular author genders; other themes cross both geographic boundaries and gender lines. Although this may not come as an incredible surprise to readers, and even less so to scholars of these three national literatures, an examination of exactly how connected the thematic signals are to factors such as gender and nationality turns out to be quite shocking.

The thematic data harvested here provide five hundred thematic data points, that is, five hundred measurements of thematic content for every novel in the corpus. Each of the five hundred variables is measured on a scale from 0 to 1, and each measurement represents a proportion of that thematic variable, or "topic," in a given text: in other words, the sum of all five hundred features for a given text will always equal one. In cases where the value of a topic is very low, or even zero, we can assume the theme is absent, or comparatively absent, from the text. In cases where the value is high, such as the 20 percent value assigned to the "Seas and Whaling" topic in *Moby Dick,* we can assume that the theme is prominent. Importantly, though, all the thematic values in between the maximum and the minimum values provide useful, even essential, information about the contextual makeup of the texts. A child may have only one freckle, but that freckle may carry valuable identifying information. Whether a genetic mutation, a paternal inheritance, or the result of too many hours spent at the beach, that freckle is a part of the person and tells some part of a larger story. Recalling the "LDA Buffet" fable from the website,* consider how a single thematic variable is like one item in a buffet of themes. Altering the quantity and type of one item changes the resulting meal: add one part of topic X, two parts of topic Y, and you get *Persuasion;* double the amount of topic X, and you get *Sense and Sensibility;* add several parts of topic Z, and you get *The Woman in White* by Wilkie Collins. This is a simplification, but conceptually it is a useful one.

The previous chapter's analysis of style has shown that there is more to novels than their thematic content; content is but one component in a complex, creative recipe that includes technique, language, theme, and other factors we have not yet analyzed (including, for example, plot, character, sentiment, and so on).† Like the cook who employs only locally grown ingredients, however, the elements of style and theme employed by nineteenth-century novelists turn out to be largely contingent upon and even determined by local conditions. This is not to say that writers cannot and do not import exotic elements into their fiction; they do. However, as we shall see shortly, the extent and degree (a teaspoon or a cup) to which an author employs a particular theme or writes in a particular style are closely correlated to the "raw materials" available in that author's local literary ecosystem.

Using the thematic data from the LDA model, an experiment was designed to assess the degree to which author nationality, author gender, and date of publication could be predicted by the thematic signals expressed in the books. In a series of tests, a classifier was repeatedly trained on data from a random sample of two-thirds of the novels in the corpus and then tested on the remaining one-third.‡ When it came to detecting, or classifying, nationality, the results were impressive. Using only this thematic data, the classifier was able to differentiate among British, Irish, and American texts with an average accuracy of 67 percent.§ In cases where the model erred, the error often involved a text by

---

* http://www.matthewjockers.net/2011/09/29/the-lda-buffet-is-now-open-or-latent-dirichlet-allocation-for-english-majors/.

† At the time of this writing, two projects of the Stanford Literary Lab are attacking the matter of novelistic "affect," or "sentiment," and the matter of character. The former project employs topic modeling and opinion-mining software to extract dominant shifts in emotional language. The second project is using Named Entity Recognition and Social Network Analysis to track character interactions. See http://litlab.stanford.edu.

‡ As in previous chapters, I have employed the NSC classifier.

§ The experiment was constructed such that in each run of the classifier, an equal number of samples were selected for training and testing. In this way, the probability of a chance assignment could be held constant at 33.3 percent. The observed F-measure, or "harmonic mean of precision and recall," of 67 was significantly better than what could be expected by mere chance.

a writer whom we may consider "cross-national." The cases in point are James McHenry and Mayne Reid, two Irish authors who traveled in and wrote almost exclusively about the United States. When Scottish writers were added to the corpus, the overall model accuracy dropped to 52 percent. That said, this was still a big improvement beyond the expected accuracy of 25 percent. Given the close geographic proximity between Ireland, England, and Scotland as well as the long history of cross-cultural pollination, I was not surprised to find that English, Irish, and Scottish authors were hardest for the classifier to separate. When only English, Scottish, and Irish texts were included, a mean accuracy of 60 percent was observed across one hundred runs of the model—not a bad result given the three-class chance probability of 33 percent. Nevertheless, it was the Americans who proved to be the easiest to distinguish from the rest. For each possible pairing (that is, English and Irish, English and American, English and Scottish, and so on), I performed a series of one hundred independent two-class training and testing experiments. In each series, the mean performance was recorded. In these tests, we may assume that when the classifier's overall accuracy is higher, the two national literatures being tested are more distinct from each other. Put another way, when classification accuracy is high, the classes are most dissimilar; when classification accuracy is low, the machine is having a harder time distinguishing between the two literatures because they are more similar. Sequentially testing each pair provides an estimate of the thematic similarity of the three nations. The best accuracy, an 85 percent f-measure, was achieved when classifying American and Irish books. The next best result was seen in Scottish-versus-American authors, with an f-measure of 83. The American-versus-English test and an f-score of 81 followed this. The most difficult task was distinguishing English from Irish authors. Here the model achieved an f-score of only 62 (an f-score of 66 was observed when classing English and Scottish novels).

More interesting than these classification scores, however, are the data the classifier returns about which features, which themes in this case, were most useful in separating the national literatures. When all four nations are included, the most useful themes are the ones involving dialectical terms. Not too surprisingly, these linguistically potent themes are strong indicators of Irish, American, and Scottish authorship, a fact that returns us in some interesting ways to Yeats's notion of Irish accents and to Fanning's ideas about Irish authors engaging in a type of "linguistic subversion." The data from the classifier provide us a way of exploring exactly which thematic ingredients, in which proportions, best define the three national literatures. They give us a way of backward engineering the thematic recipes favored by the authors of a given nation, and from this we may also readily identify the outliers, those writers and books that are most atypical of the general tendencies. Figures 8.18, 8.19, 8.20, and 8.21 show the twenty-five themes that the classifier identified as being the most positively associated with

children girls
paintings and drawings
english dialect mums and missus
governesses and education of children
evening   knights and chivalry
convents and abbeys
virtue and vice   sorrow   women and men
music horses and riding
hounds and shooting sport
affection and happiness
english places   royalty afternoon and tea time
times of day   gods greek and egyptian
letters correspondence   dinner and food
letters correspondence
death despair and torture
air birds lights outdoors
streets and thoroughfares

Figure 8.18. Dominant British themes

patients and their doctors
health and disease
misfortune grief and sorrow
feelings dear girls children creatures
doors and passages
vanity wit and humor
bedrooms dialect terror
entreaties
maids ireland silence
lords and ladies   genius and talent
tears and sorrow
france french people and language
latin words   tenants and landlords
science and nature
personal character
spirits i e gloomy happy

Figure 8.19. Dominant Irish themes

property and possessions
convents and abbeys
hounds and shooting sport
cases as in the legal sense
guests and company
nephews and nieces   royalty   habits and customs
outlaws and robbers   knaves rogues and asses
matters and affairs   merchants and trade
witches wizards superstition
scottish dialect
scotland   religion
gold and treasure
human appendages   calcutta and india
inheritance ships
ladders ropes irons traps
minister protestant
knights and chivalry
monarchs and their empires

Figure 8.20. Dominant Scottish themes

extremes of weather
cavaliers and spanish mexican locals
governors and other colonial magistrates
sea voyages
ships and their crews
islands
distances and directions   ships cities
trees wilderness frontier
us dollars and us cities
spain indians the sea
folk dialect enemy forces
boats and water
preachers and sermons soldiers and war
rocks valleys summits paths
rivers and streams animals and beasts
moments of confusion in battle
mountains and valleys

Figure 8.21. Dominant American themes

each of the four national classes. In other words, it was the comparatively high presence of these themes in each nation that the machine found most useful in distinguishing the classes. The importance of the themes is registered by their size in the word clouds.

The American corpus is typified by a set of themes largely about the natural world: "Wilderness," "The Frontier," "The Sea," "Native Americans," "Trees," and so forth. This cluster of dominant themes is very much in keeping with Long-fellow's call for a uniquely national literature. In his novel *Kavanagh* (1849), he writes of a national literature that would be "commensurate with our mountains and rivers . . . a national epic that shall correspond to the size of the country. . . . We want a national drama in which scope shall be given to our gigantic ideas and to the unparalleled activity of our people. . . . In a word, we want a national literature altogether shaggy and unshorn, that shall shake the earth, like a herd of buffaloes thundering over the prairies." English authors, on the other hand, are unified by themes related to the aristocracy and upper classes: for example, "Royalty," "Music," "Private Education," "Running of Hounds," "Shooting Sports," and "Art." There are very few among the top English themes that we could consider negative: one theme of sorrow and another I have labeled "Death, Despair, and Torture." Contrast this, however, with the themes that characterize the Irish corpus. Along with the more positive "Wit and Humor," we find an abundance of darker themes such as "Doubt and Fear," "Misfortune," "Health and Disease," "Terror," "Silence," "Tears and Sorrow," and "Grief."

The Scottish corpus shares a lot with the English (as we might expect), such as "Monarchs," "Royalty," and "Running of Hounds," but also in contrast to the English, we see more emphasis on the theme "Religion" (especially "Protestant-ism") and the somewhat odd presence of "Witches, Wizards, and Superstition." As noted previously, we may also learn much from the absence of theme. English authors are silent on the matter of "Tenants and Landlords"; they avoid discussion of "Ireland." American authors are disinclined to discuss the themes of "Lords and Ladies," "Servants," "Housekeepers," and "Maids." Surprising to this researcher, Irish authors were found to be far less interested in natural beauty than either the English or the Americans. Compared to the other nationalities, Irish authors avoid prolonged engagement with the themes "Rivers and Streams" and "Mountains and Valleys"; there is no idyllic "Lake Isle of Innisfree" in this nineteenth-century Irish corpus.

The national data confirm some intuitions and challenge others. Irish authors write more about Native Americans and slavery than we might have imagined, and the American authors—who Hemingway once claimed were intent on imitating the English—proved to be far from "English" in terms of both their style and their theme. Much more dramatic, however, are the data related to gender. The gender data from this corpus are a ringing confirmation of virtually

heart and emotion
sewing work
governesses and education of children
drawing rooms
pleasure tears and sorrow
infants   domestic rooms
happiness health and illness
female fashion
children girls
nurses for children pity
children   affection
flowers and natural beauty
tea and coffee
dear girls children creatures
arms and other physical features

Figure 8.22. Female themes

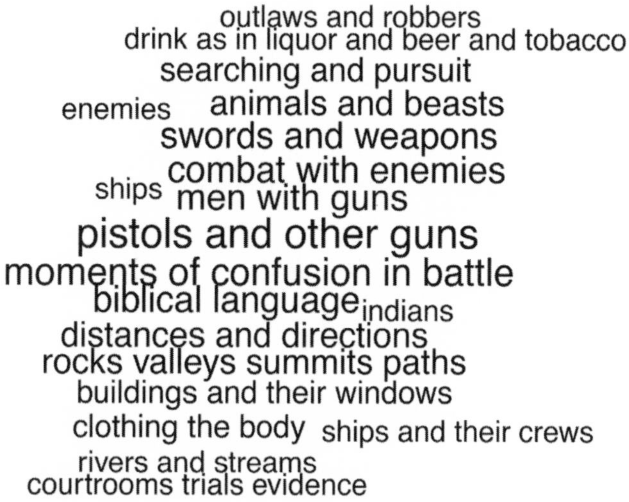

outlaws and robbers
drink as in liquor and beer and tobacco
searching and pursuit
enemies   animals and beasts
swords and weapons
combat with enemies
ships men with guns
pistols and other guns
moments of confusion in battle
biblical language indians
distances and directions
rocks valleys summits paths
buildings and their windows
clothing the body ships and their crews
rivers and streams
courtrooms trials evidence

Figure 8.23. Male themes

all of our stereotypes about gender. Smack at the top of the list of themes most
indicative of female authorship is "Female Fashion." "Fashion" is followed by
"Children," "Flowers," "Sewing," and a series of themes associated with strong
emotions (see figure 8.22). In contrast stand the male authors with their weapons
and war. Topping the list of characteristic themes for men is "Pistols," followed in
turn by "Guns," "Swords," "Weapons," "Combat," and a series of themes related

to the rugged masculine places where such implements of war are most likely to be employed: battlefields, mountains, and so on (see figure 8.23). To be sure, these are not the only things that men and women write about, but so striking are these differences that the classifier achieves 86 percent accuracy when guessing the gender of an author using these thematic data. This 86 percent is a full 6 percent better than what was observed with the stylistic data.

When considering these findings, it is important to remain mindful of the exceptions. These are macro trends we have been exploring, and they provide a generalized view of the whole. These are not necessarily the tendencies of individual authors or even of individual books. Indeed, 33 percent of the books in the nationality experiment and 14 percent of the books in this gender experiment were misclassified: some Irish authors were thought to be American, some male authors to be females, and so on. There are the outliers and the exceptions, and these are the subject of the next chapter.

9 INFLUENCE

> Every work of art is the result of a complex interrela-
> tion of individual features of creative art. The author's
> role is to use these features and to combine them
> into a definite artistic product. The elements of which
> the artwork is created are external to the author and
> independent of him. The author merely uses them for
> his work, with a greater or lesser degree of success.
>
> In every period there is a certain number of artistic
> methods and devices available for creative use.
> Changing these methods and devices is not a matter
> of the individual author's volition, but is the result of
> the evolution of artistic creativity.
>
> —Osip Brik, "Teaching Writers" (1929)

Examining macro patterns in style and theme allows us to contextualize our
close readings in ways that have hitherto been impossible or, at the very minimum, impractical. We see, for example, that while Melville may be best remembered for *Moby Dick, Moby Dick* was only the apex text in a longer tradition of
whaling- and seafaring-themed fiction, a tradition that stretches back at least
to Sir Walter Scott's book *The Pirate* (1821) and through the work of Freder-
ick Marryat.* Along the way, from Scott to Marryat to Melville, other writers
touch upon and help build the themes that ultimately find full expression in
Moby Dick. If we look only at those novels in the corpus containing at least 1
percent of the "Seas and Whaling" topic, we find thirty-six, including books by
James Fenimore Cooper, Edward Augustus Kendall, Edgar Allan Poe, Nathaniel
Hawthorne, J. H. Ingraham, and thirteen others. We know that Melville was a
borrower, and the evidence that he borrowed from Poe's *Narrative of Author
Gordon Pym* and from the Reverend Henry Cheever's book *The Whale and His*

---

* Marryat was a prolific novelist and naval officer who, like Scott, wrote a novel titled
The Pirate (1836). Marryat also developed the maritime-flag signaling code that bears
his name—"Marryat's code."

Captors is fairly well known and easy for close readers of these works to detect (see, for example, Lee 1984; Simon 2005). What is not as clear are the more subtle spheres of influence; consider, for example, an "allusionary" chain. At the opening of *Moby Dick* (1851), Melville cites a line from Hawthorne's *Twice Told Tales* that reads: "I built a cottage for Susan and myself and made a gateway in the form of a Gothic Arch, by setting up a whale's jaw bones." Hawthorne may well have picked this up from Scott, for in Scott's *Pirate* (1821), we are told of a Scottish burgh that had been renovated in a Gothic style with an entrance gate "supported by a sort of arch, constructed out of the jaw-bones of the whale." Ten years after Scott's *Pirate*, the narrator of Anna Marie Hall's *Sketches of Irish Character* (1831) tells of a "mysterious arch, composed of the jaw-bone of a whale" upon which she gazed from her "cottage" where she "kept all her favorite books," including, we are told, books by Walter Scott! Thirteen years after that, Eliza Lanesford Cushing's *Fatal Prediction* (1844) describes a similar jaw-bone arch found outside a fortune-teller's "cottage." Is Hall Hawthorne's literary ancestor, or a more distant relative of Melville, or a descendant of Scott? Are recycled elements and allusions such as these a matter of coincidence or design? Or are they, as Osip Brik suggests, part and parcel of an involuntary creative evolution?*

That such arches existed in reality is a matter of fact; why they become a touchstone in a series of "unrelated" literary works is uncertain. Whatever the reason, the presence of recurring themes and recurring habits of style inevitably leads us to ask the more difficult questions about influence and about whether these are links in a systematic chain or just arbitrary, coincidental anomalies in a disorganized and chaotic world of authorial creativity, intertextuality, and bidirectional dialogics. This kind of big question takes us beyond single books, beyond recurring allusions, and even beyond the macro patterns and trends that have been graphed and charted in previous chapters. At the very least, they demand that we look for some significance in the apparent chaos.

"Evolution" leaps to mind as a possible explanation.† Information and ideas can and do behave in ways that seem evolutionary. Nevertheless, I prefer to avoid the word *evolution* (even though I have just used it several times, and even though it is a favorite trope of the Russian formalists, whose approach I obviously admire): books are not organisms; they do not breed. The metaphor for this process breaks down quickly, and so I do better to insert myself into the safer, though perhaps more complex, tradition of literary "influence" and to simply investigate literary influence on a grander scale than close observation and anecdotal speculation allow. Before abandoning the word *evolution*

---

* See the epigraph.

† Whereas the dialogic text, in Bakhtin's sense of the word, is in dialogue with works both before and after, allusion and influence, whether intentional or accidental, exist in only one direction. In this sense, *evolution* may be a more appropriate term or analogue.

completely, however, one minor point: evolution is not moving us toward anything in particular. It is only movement and change. There is no end point to
evolution. Nor is there any grand objective behind literary change. This is not
to say that individual authors have no agency or do not strive to create something better or different or new—they do; they strive. Instead, I wish to suggest
that a writer's creativity is tempered and influenced by the past and the present,
by literary "parents," and by a larger literary ecosystem. We cannot argue that
Middlemarch is a great novel, any more than we can argue that *Homo erectus*
was a great man; we can only argue about what makes one different or similar
to its peers. I do, however, accept that in literature, as in nature, there are survi-
vors, thrivers, outliers, mutations, and there is also that which does not survive.
Middlemarch and *Homo erectus* may fit into one of these categories, and it may,
therefore, be entirely appropriate to call attention to these forms as exemplars.
Some forms (of life and of literature) excel and become more common; others
shine just briefly. My interest is in tracing where and when these forms emerge
and then where and when they die. My interest is in finding the context in
which change occurs, for it is only by understanding the larger context that we
might then move to address the deeper question of creation, of how and why
such forms come into being in the first place.

   Attempts to demonstrate literary imitation, intertextuality, and influence have
relied almost entirely upon close reading.* It seems very likely that Melville's
"Call me Ishmael" is a direct echo of Poe's "My name is Arthur Gordon Pym."
And though knowledge of this might add to our understanding of Melville's art
(and perhaps also to our appreciation of Poe . . . that is, Melville could not have
done it without him), this is not the scale of influence about which I am thinking. To chart influence empirically, we need to go beyond the individual cases
and look to the aggregate. Borrowing a whale's jaw or a catchy opening sentence
is neither imitation nor influence, not in the full-throated sense that I mean to
explore. Melville's echo of Poe likely goes deeper; it may be just one among a
hundred similar echoes in a hundred other novels. The existence of such a state
would certainly alter our understanding of what it means to be influenced.

   Within the field of observational learning, there exists a theory of "information cascades." The landmark essay defining these phenomena was published in
1992; it begins as follows: "An informational cascade occurs when it is optimal
for an individual, having observed the actions of those ahead of him, to follow
the behavior of the preceding individual without regard to his own information"
(Bikhchandani, Hirshleifer, and Welch 1992, 992). Information cascades offer a
theory of social behavior that serves as a close, if sometimes imperfect, corol-

---

   * I say "almost" because text searching and tools such as Google's "Popular Passage"
finder have made it possible to employ computational search in place of sustained and
concentrated reading. For more on Popular Passage, see Schilit and Kolak 2007.

lary for the kind of thematic and stylistic change explored in previous chapters. The authors of this landmark paper write that their model of social behavior "explains not only conformity but also rapid and short-lived fluctuations such as fads, fashions, booms and crashes" (ibid., 994). More important for our purposes, they argue, as stated above, that an information cascade occurs when "an individual . . . follow[s] the behavior of the preceding individual *without regard to his own information*" (ibid.; emphasis added). In other words, once a cascade begins, it tends to continue and to create a situation of mass imitation in which individuals repeatedly *avoid* the road less taken. Were a whole series of writers to begin writing whaling novels after the publication of *Moby Dick*, it could be argued that these subsequent authors were caught up in an information cascade in which their own independent ideas about what to write were trumped by some herd instinct.* Likewise, this same theory might offer some manner of explanation for the upward trend in British and Irish usage of the "confidence" markers seen in figure 7.6. At the same time, the theory tells us that cascades are fragile; the introduction of a disruptive force, a new "signal," can cause the cascade to collapse and move in an entirely new direction. Not everyone would follow Melville's lead; some mutant writer would take some other road, and a new cascade would follow. As a way of modeling literary influence and intertextuality at scale, information cascades provide an attractive theoretical framework. Whether the data in the literary record can be explained by this theory of information exchange is worth exploring.†

For every book in the Literary Lab corpus, I have extracted both stylistic (as in chapter 6) and thematic information (as in chapter 8). These data can then be combined into an aggregated numerical representation or "expression" of the stylistic and thematic content of every book in the corpus. The resulting data matrix is 3,346 by 578.‡ In each row, 578 different feature measurements represent a book's thematic-stylistic expression, or "signal."§

---

* The contemporary fascination with vampires may be another and more familiar example.

† Consider the genre trends that Moretti describes in *Graphs, Maps, Trees* (2005). Moretti's graphs show us how genres appear, build steam, and then fade out, in what are essentially twenty- to thirty-year cycles. An alternative to the generational hypothesis is that genres represent a type of "information cascade." Such a model could help explain some of the genre-generation discrepancies explored in chapter 6.

‡ Not included here were the uninterruptable topics and the topics that were clearly derived from either book metadata or from bad optical-character-recognition data. For details, see chapter 8.

§ I cannot resist the great temptation to liken these data to the genome. Still, 578 "genes" does not come close to the 20,000–25,000 genes that are estimated to make up human DNA; at best, it is an incomplete, or partial, *literary* genome.

To explore these data, to test the waters and get a sense of how well this amalgamation of features might approximate or represent the book from which it
was extracted, I trained a classifier and then tested how well nationality and
gender could be predicted from the features. Here I could not test genre prediction because not all of the texts in the full corpus have been coded with genre
metadata, nor did it make sense to try to classify by author given the size of the
corpus and number of authors in it. Gender and nationality, where the number of
classes was limited to two and three, respectively, would be enough. The gender
and nationality results were perfectly consistent with what had been observed in
the classification tests described in the previous chapters. Surprisingly enough,
the combination of stylistic and thematic information neither improved nor
worsened classification accuracy. This result may suggest that theme and style
are to some extent interdependent: perhaps thematic choices entail stylistic
ones. Such a conclusion would be in keeping with, if a slight extension of, the
discovery in "Quantitative Formalism: An Experiment" that Gothic novels seem
to demand a higher proportion of locative prepositions (Allison et al. 2012).
Interesting and inconclusive, this is a fruitful area for further exploration and
one that may have implications for scholars working in authorship attribution
in particular. This is, however, beyond the scope of the present study.

My objective now is not to classify novels into nationalities or genders but
rather to capture for each book a unique book signal and then to look for signs
of historical change from one book to the next. Using the "Euclidian" metric, I
calculated every book's *distance* from every other book in the corpus.* Assume
that we have three books and only two features for each book. Let's calls the
three books b1, b2, and b3 and the two features f1 and f2. Table 9.1 shows these
data and some "dummy values" for each feature in each book. These points can
each be plotted in a two-dimensional space, as in figure 9.1, where books b1
and b2 are closest (least distant) to each other in the lower-right corner. These
simple distances can be perceived visually, measured with a standard ruler, or,
of course, calculated with a simple equation—really just a version of the familiar
Pythagorean equation.

This fairly simple equation, thought of in two dimensions, becomes more
complex when thought of in terms of 578 dimensions. The closeness of items
in this high-dimensional space can, however, still be calculated. Assume a new
data set in which we have just four features (as in table 9.2). Using the Euclidean
metric, the distances "d" between books (b1, b2, b3) are calculated as follows:

$$d(b_1, b_2) = \sqrt{(10-11)^2 + (5-6)^2 + (3-5)^2 + (5-7)^2} = 3.162278$$

$$d(b_1, b_3) = \sqrt{(10-4)^2 + (5-13)^2 + (3-2)^2 + (5-6)^2} = 10.09950$$

$$d(b_2, b_3) = \sqrt{(11-4)^2 + (6-13)^2 + (5-2)^2 + (7-6)^2} = 10.39230$$

Table 9.1. Example feature data, version 1

Book	f1	f2
b1	10	5
b2	11	6
b3	4	13

Note: "*f*" is any arbitrary feature.

Table 9.2. Example feature data, version 2

Book	f1	f2	f3	f4
b1	10	5	3	5
b2	11	6	5	7
b3	4	13	2	6

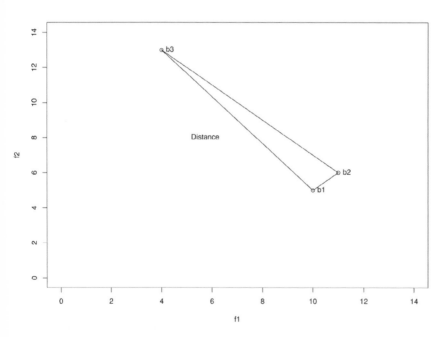

Figure 9.1. Example plotting of distance between books

* In "Textual Analysis," Burrows reports on his own finding that "complete linkages, squared Euclidean distances, and standardized variables yield the most accurate results" when seeking to cluster texts by similarity (2004, 326).

Table 9.3. Euclidean distances from *Pride and Prejudice* based on 578 features

Rank	Author	Title	Distance
0	Austen, Jane	*Pride and Prejudice*	0
1	Austen, Jane	*Sense and Sensibility*	0.042557864
2	Austen, Jane	*Mansfield Park*	0.049754052
3	Austen, Jane	*Emma*	0.050242054
4	Burney, Sarah	*Traits of Nature*	0.056073837
5	Cathcart	*Adelaide: A Story of Modern Life*	0.057314379
6	Waddington, Julia	*Misrepresentation; or, Scenes in Real Life*	0.058382231
7	D'Arblay, Frances	*Cecilia; or Memoirs of an Heiress*	0.058646462
8	Burney, Sarah	*Tales of Dancy*	0.059090054
9	Humdrum	*Domestic Scenes: A Novel*	0.059223492
10	Lister, Thomas	*Herbert Lacy*	0.059397822

In this case, the distance between b1 and b2 (3.162278) is much smaller than the distance between b1 and b3. This indicates that b1 and b2 are more similar to each other in terms of these four features. Using the R statistics package, it is a trivial matter to calculate the distances between every book and every other book in the corpus along all 578 dimensions. The result is a 3,346 × 3,346 distance matrix. Every row of this table represents a single book, as does every column; the values in the individual cells are the calculated distances between them.*

From this "distance matrix," any book in the corpus may be selected, and a ranked list (based on distance) of all of the other books in the corpus can be returned for inspection. The first thing one discovers by going through a few of these lists is that books by the same authors tend to show up at the top of the list. Books by the same author tend to be stylistically and thematically similar. A ranked list of books closest to *Pride and Prejudice,* for example, is shown in table 9.3.

The presence of three other books by Austen at the top of a list, which began with a search for books most similar to *Pride and Prejudice,* confirms much of what we have already learned from the authorship-attribution literature and from what has been reported in previous chapters. Austen wavers only slightly when it comes to her core themes and even less so when it comes to her linguistic signature. Put rather too bluntly, neither Austen's stylistic nor her thematic

---

* As you can imagine, there is a diagonal of "0" values in the cells where the row from book b1 intersects with a column for the same book, b1. There is zero distance between a book and itself.

range is exceedingly vast. It must be kept mind that these rankings of similarity are relative to the corpus as a whole, relative to all 3,346 books. In other words, *Sense and Sensibility* may not ultimately be the most similar book in the universe to Austen's *Pride and Prejudice,* but it is the most similar of the books in this corpus. As the corpus grows, the values may change to greater or lesser degrees. A similar study can be made of Dickens's *Tale of Two Cities.* As with Austen's novel, *Tale* returns several other books by Dickens (table 9.4), but also shows the strong presence of another author, George Payne Rainsford James. James was a close contemporary of Dickens—born thirteen years earlier—and, like Dickens, was prolific, publishing more than forty novels.

Worth noting too is that in the top-ten results for *Pride and Prejudice,* we find only one male-authored book, and all are books by British authors. Excepting *Life's Masquerade,* which is of unknown authorship, in the *Tale of Two Cites* list, we find all male and British authors. The result is much the same when charting books similar to *Moby Dick.* We observe an all-male list that includes at the top other works by Melville (table 9.5) followed by works of his American contemporaries, including most prominently James Fenimore Cooper and Edgar Allan Poe. The two exceptions are Robert Ballantyne and Robert Louis Stevenson, two Scots. The lesser-known Ballantyne spent six years in Canada in the employ of the Hudson's Bay Company and then wrote works largely based on this experience. Interestingly, the work of Ballantyne's identified here, *The Coral Island,* is known to have been an influence upon Stevenson, who included mention of Ballantyne in the introductory poem that prefaces *Treasure Island.**

Table 9.4. Euclidean distances from *Tale of Two Cities* based on 578 features

Rank	Author	Title	Distance
0	Dickens, Charles	*A Tale of Two Cities*	0
1	Dickens, Charles	*Master Humphrey's Clock*	0.046820931
2	Dickens, Charles	*Little Dorrit*	0.0472454
3	James, George Payne Rainsford	*The False Heir*	0.048010961
4	James, George Payne Rainsford	*Lord Montagu's Page: A Historical Romance*	0.048851065
5	James, George Payne Rainsford	*The Vicissitudes of a Life: A Novel*	0.050046016
6	Locker, Arthur	*Sir Goodwin's Folly: A Story of the Year 1795*	0.051164434
7	Collins, Wilkie	*After Dark*	0.051527178
8	Dickens, Charles	*Dombey and Son*	0.051644288
9	Dickens, Charles	*Barnaby Rudge*	0.051970992
10	Unknown	*Life's Masquerade: A Novel*	0.052783311

* Were table 9.5 expanded from the top ten to the top eleven, *Treasure Island* would be the eleventh book in the list.

Table 9.5. Euclidean distances from *Moby Dick* based on 578 features

Rank	Author	Title	Distance
0	Melville, Herman	*Moby-Dick; or, The Whale*	0
1	Melville, Herman	*Omoo: A Narrative of Adventures in the South Seas*	0.057784134
2	Melville, Herman	*Mardi and a Voyage Thither*	0.073077699
3	Cooper, James	*The Crater; or, Vulcan's Peak: A Tale of the Pacific*	0.073798396
4	Cooper, James	*The Sea Lions; or, The Lost Sealers*	0.08339971
5	Melville, Herman	*Typee: A Peep at Polynesian Life*	0.101393295
6	Ballantyne, Robert	*The Coral Island: A Tale of the Pacific Ocean*	0.117425226
7	Poe, Edgar Allan	*The Narrative of Arthur Gordon Pym of Nantucket*	0.13125092
8	Stevenson, Robert	*Island Nights' Entertainments*	0.146050418
9	Williams, William	*The Journal of Llewellin Penrose, a Seaman*	0.176751153
10	Payn, James	*A Prince of the Blood*	0.18207467

These tables listing the distances between books take us in the direction of gauging influence, but they are still too small in scale to give us the broad picture of literary history that we are looking for. Having computed the stylistic-thematic distances among all the books in the corpus, it is possible to move even further away from individual data points and into a larger-scale visualization of the entire corpus. For this, network visualization software is well suited.

In terms of literary history and literary *influence,* our corpus is a type of network. Whether consciously influenced by a predecessor or not, every book is in some sense a descendant of, or "connected to," those before it. Its relationship may be familial, that is, a new book by the same author, or it may be parodic, as in *Shamela,* a book meant to be a direct response to some other book. Or the relationship may be indirect and subtler, as when an author unconsciously "borrows" elements from the book(s) of some predecessor(s), or simply pulls from the same shared pool of stylistic and thematic materials. Previous chapters have shown how writers can draw elements from what is available on their stylistic and thematic "buffets": that is, writers may consciously or unconsciously adopt the habits of prose that are typical to their time period, their gender, their nation, or the genre in which they are writing. Like the master craftsman teaching an apprentice by example, so too does each subsequent generation learn from and then evolve beyond the former, while all the while being constrained by the available resources. The artistry—as Brik and other formalists have argued—comes in the assembly of these resources.

To visualize this corpus as a network, then, and to interrogate my hypothesis of literary progression and influence, I converted the distance matrix described above into a long-form table with 11,195,716 rows and three columns. Each row captures a distance relationship between two books: the first cell contains one book, a "source," and the second cell another book, the "target." A third cell contains the measured distance between the two. I reduced these data by removing all of the records in which the second book was published *before* the first: influence only works in one direction! This reduced the data from around 11 million records to a more manageable 5,548,275 records. The distance measures in this final data set ranged from 0.05946 to 107.44473, with a mean distance of 10.45770.* I then further reduced the data by calculating the standard deviation for the distances from every source book to all of the other books in the corpus.† I then removed those target books that were more than one standard deviation from the source book. This winnowing is done both for computational convenience and for network simplicity. The process has the effect of retaining only those books that are particularly close, or similar, to each other. In the initial distance matrix, every book is connected to every other book; however, at some distance the argument that two works are related or connected breaks down. After this culling, the number of edges or "connections" from one book to another was reduced to 165,770 book-to-book relationships; 5,382,505 weaker connections are ignored. Using custom scripts in R, these data, along with a separate table of metadata for each individual novel, were combined and converted to the "Graph Exchange XML Format" (GEXF). This file was then imported into the open-source network-analysis software package Gephi (Bastian, Hemann, and Jacomy 2009).

Networks (or "graphs," as they are frequently called) are constructed out of two primary elements: nodes and edges. For our purposes, nodes are individual books, and edges are the distances between them. In this data set, the edges are weighted using the distance measure calculated with the Euclidean metric. Nodes with smaller distances are more similar and more closely connected. When plotted, nodes with larger distances will spread out farther in the network diagram. Figure 9.2 offers a simplified example.

Gephi provides a number of layout options and analysis routines for network data. The layout algorithms provide methods for displaying the data, that is, methods for making the intricacies of the network most visible. With a large network such as this, generating and then plotting images that can be displayed, on a standard, book-size, page, are challenging. Despite this challenge, a few

---

* Some readers may find it useful to think of these distances in terms of a familiar measure of distance such as "inches" or "centimeters." The two closest books in the corpus are 0.05 inches apart, and the two that are farthest from each other are 107.4 inches; on average, books are about 10 inches apart.

† It may be easier to consider this process one book at a time. For *Moby Dick,* for example, I calculate the standard deviation from *Moby Dick* to all of the other books in the corpus that were published after *Moby Dick*. I then keep only those books that have a distance less than one standard deviation above the minimum distance.

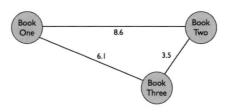

Figure 9.2. Example network graph

useful plots can be shown here. Figure 9.3 shows the entire network laid out using the Force Atlas 2 algorithm. The individual book nodes are the gray-scaled "dots," and the edges are the more visible arching lines.

Gephi provides an option that allows for coloring of the nodes based on the metadata contained in the node records. With the addition of this coloring or gray-scaling, several macrostructures can be made visible in this graph.* In figure 9.3, the book nodes have been colored according to the publication years of the books. The edges that are directed outward from these source nodes have been colored with the same shade of gray. The lighter-gray nodes and edges indicate works from the earlier part of the century; the darker nodes are later. The further back in time we go, the lighter the nodes become. This shading of the nodes by year reveals a clear time signature to the stylistic-thematic data. Beginning in the lighter, western, section of the graph, we move eastward through time. It is critical to bear in mind here that the novels are *not* being clustered in the network based on their publication dates; in fact, dates play no role whatsoever in determining how close the books are to each other or how they are laid out in the network visualization. Books are being pulled together (and pushed apart) based on the similarity of their computed stylistic and thematic distances from each other. The fact that they line up in a chronological manner is incidental, but rather extraordinary.† The chronological alignment reveals that thematic and stylistic change does occur over time. The themes that writers employ and the high-frequency function words they use to build

* Color versions of figures 9.3 and 9.4 can be found online at http://www.matthewjockers .net/macroanalysisbook/color-versions-of-figures-9-3-and-9-4/.

† I say "rather" because some amount of chronological organization is to be expected given that I have removed the possibility that a book in the future could influence a book in the past. Nevertheless, the possibility exists that a book from 1800 is most stylistically and thematically similar to a series of books published in the 1890s and that this book from 1800 will be situated in the network alongside these more similar works that are published ninety years later. This is, in fact, exactly what is observed for some books in the corpus.

Figure 9.3. Nineteenth-century novel network with date shading

the frameworks for their themes are nearly, but not always, tethered in time. At this macro scale, style and theme are observed to evolve chronologically, and most books and authors in this network cluster into communities with their chronological peers. Not every book and not every author is a slave to his or her epoch; there are a few outliers who buck the trend. Before moving to a discussion of the outliers, however, a few more observations about the macro structures of this network are in order.

Figure 9.4 shows the same network layout reshaded according to author gender.* Male nodes and edges are colored lighter gray, and the female nodes are black. A clear boundary can be seen dividing the network into male and female regions. Works by female authors are more stylistically and thematically similar to each other, and they cluster together in the south and southeast portions of the main network. Males are drawn together in the north.

In both renderings of the network, we can see the presence of outliers: in figure 9.3 there are works from earlier in the century that cluster in portions of the network dominated by works from a later period, and in figure 9.4 there are male authors placed firmly in the more female-dominated regions of the graph, and vice versa for several female authors. Without a large screen and an interactive program in which to view this entire network, many of these individual subtleties and outliers are lost. Three slightly larger outlier "communities," however, are clearly visible at this scale. First, at the lower-right corner of the main network is a community of nodes extending outward and down—where Florida would be if this were a map of the United States. These nodes all belong

---

* Anonymous authors have been filtered out of the image.

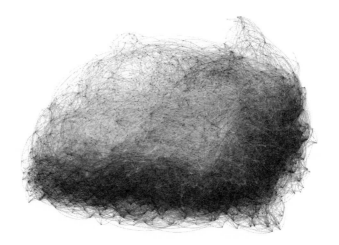

Figure 9.4. Nineteenth-century novel network with gender shading

to books authored by Margaret Oliphant. Remember here that the network has organized itself in this manner independent of any metadata about the books. The graphing software does not know who the authors are. This layout suggests not only that Oliphant's stylistic and thematic "signal" is unique, but that her signal is an extreme within the context of the major subcluster of works dominated by female authors. She is at once connected to the female section of the graph and an isolated peninsula. In other words, Oliphant's signal is unusual both within her gender and to the network as a whole.

Similar to this outlier cluster of works by Oliphant is a similar outcropping of works found farther west and to the north, approximately where Montana would be on a U.S. map. This cluster is made up of six books by Walter Scott alongside works by a series of other Scottish authors, including Robert Louis Stevenson and Henrietta Keddie.* Also present in this "highland" cluster are several works by George P. R. James. James was not Scottish, but he was indebted to Walter Scott. According to James N. MacKenzie (1992), George P. R. James sent his first novel (*Richelieu: A Tale of France*) to Walter Scott for review. It was only after receiving a positive reply from Scott that James found the confidence to send the manuscript off for publication. Scott's approval of James's novel, and

* Keddie, who wrote under the pseudonym Sarah Tytler, was known primarily as a writer of women's fiction. The work of hers that appears in this cluster, however, is atypical of her oeuvre. *Saint Mungs City: A Novel* presents a picture of the Scottish urban world and industrialization. None of her other works appears in this group, a fact that suggests there may be something special or unique about this particular book.

the novel's eventual appearance in this cluster of works similar to Scott's own, is suggestive of an entirely different sort of influence, the influence of endorsement. It is a tantalizing idea, and one that would require a closer reading both of James and of Scott to fully explicate.

The third and final outlier community is found very obviously in the northeast. Unlike the other two, this one is not so easily understood. Indeed, I can offer no unifying thread at all. Table 9.6 provides a listing of the fifteen works that make up this cluster. Aside from all being published within nine years of each other, I find nothing here but noise. Perhaps more knowledgeable scholars will see some link that I have missed.

Beyond these more obvious outlier clusters, there are any number of specific oddities and surprises. What, for example, does it mean that Maria Edgeworth's *Belinda* is mapped to a place in the network that puts her book twenty years ahead of its time? Why are all of Harriet Beecher Stowe's books firmly rooted in the male sections of the network and many of James Payn's in the female half? These are questions that I will not try to answer; they were chosen arbitrarily and are just several among many, and still we have barely sampled the diverse offerings of graph theory and network analysis: Ego networks, for example, can be calculated to explore a single book's sphere of influence. Node-centrality measures can provide a sense of a book's importance to and within the larger network. The Gephi software provides tools for calculating these and many other measures, and through such measures Gephi gives us the power to sift and rank the relative importance of one node versus another. Gephi's PageRank statistic, for example, is based on the algorithms developed by Google founders

Table 9.6. A cluster of books

Author	Title	Publication year
Bates, Emily	*George Vyvian*	1890
Beale, Anne	*Courtleroy*	1887
Davidson, Hugh	*The Green Hills by the Sea*	1887
Deccan, Hilary	*Light in the Offing*	1892
Fitzclarence, Wilhelmina	*Dorinda*	1889
Grant, James	*Colville of the Guards*	1885
Hake, Thomas	*In Letters of Gold*	1886
Harwood, John	*Sir Robert Shirley Bart*	1886
Hayward, Gertrude	*Dulcibel*	1890
Lambert, George	*The Power of Gold*	1886
Linton, Elizabeth	*Through the Long Night*	1889
Spender, Emily	*Until the Day Breaks*	1886
Spender, Lillian	*Mr. Nobody*	1884
Wilkins, William	*The Forbidden Sacrifice*	1893
Woollam, Wilfred	*All for Naught*	1890

Sergey Brin and Lawrence Page. It is designed as a tool for assigning "a numerical weighting to each element of a hyperlinked set of documents, . . . with the purpose of 'measuring' its relative importance within the set" (Wikipedia 2011b). When applied to this nineteenth-century corpus in which the links are measures of stylistic and thematic affinity, the algorithm points us first to Laurence Sterne's *Tristram Shandy,* next to George Gissing's novel *The Whirlpool,* and then to Benjamin Disraeli's *Venetia. Tristram Shandy* is a book frequently lauded as one of the highest achievements of the novel form, and, by all accounts, Gissing was one of the century's most accomplished realists. Disraeli's minor novel *Venetia* is harder to understand. Maybe its presence here is a sign that the method has failed, or perhaps it is a sign that close readers need to reevaluate *Venetia.* In short, these network data are rich—too rich, in fact, to take much further in these pages because they demand that we follow every macroscale observation with a full-circle return to careful, sustained, close reading. This is work for the future. With more than three thousand books, the observations we could make and the questions we might ask about the context in which a title appears are overwhelming. My purpose here has been to describe the landscape and offer a glimpse of the possibilities and a few of the provocations.

At the macro scale, we see evidence of time and gender influences on theme and style. By superimposing these two network snapshots in our minds, we can begin to imagine a larger context in which to read and study nineteenth-century literature. What is clear is that the books we have traditionally studied are not isolated books. The canonical greats are not even outliers; they are books that are similar to other books, similar to the many orphans of literary history that have been long forgotten in a continuum of stylistic and thematic change. Whether these orphans are worth fostering is an entirely different and more complicated question. In terms of their potential influence on those other works that we already know and care about, they are certainly worth our attention, and macroanalysis offers us a way of finding them in the haystack of literary history.

PART III   PROSPECTS

10 ORPHANS

In a revolution, as in a novel, the most
difficult part to invent is the end.
—Alexis de Tocqueville, 1896

I began this book with a call to arms, an argument that what we have today in terms of literary and textual material and computational power represents a moment of revolution in the way we study the literary record. I suggested that our primary tool of excavation, close reading, is no longer satisfactory as a solitary method of literary inquiry. I argue throughout these chapters that large-scale text analysis, text mining, "macroanalysis," offers an important and necessary way of contextualizing our study of individual works of literature. I hope I have made it clear that the macroanalysis I imagine is not offered as a challenge to, or replacement for, our traditional modes of inquiry. It is a complement.* I ended, in chapter 9, with an exploration of literary influence and the idea—just an idea and some preliminary experiments to test it—that literature can and perhaps even must be read as an evolving system with certain inherent rules. *Evolution* is the word I am drawn to, and it is a word that I must ultimately eschew. Although my little corpus appears to behave in an evolutionary manner, surely it cannot be as flawlessly rule bound and elegant as evolution. There are those, of course, who question the veracity of biological evolution. I am not among them; it is a convincing argument. Nevertheless, it is true that there are further dimensions to explore, and it may be prudent to consider evolution as an idea, or alternatively "Darwin's dangerous idea," as Daniel Dennett puts it in the title of his book. In the *Wikipedia* entry for Dennett's book, it is noted that "Darwin's

---

* There remains, of course, a place for close reading, and some tasks demand it. Years ago, in the black-opal mines of Lightning Ridge, Australia, I learned the value of "close mining." To extract an opal, one uses a small hand pick and a delicate touch to carefully chip away at the clay that may conceal a hidden gem. A more aggressive approach will most certainly destroy the delicate opals before they are even seen.

discovery was that the *generation of life worked algorithmically,* that processes behind it work in such a way that given these processes the results that they tend toward must be so" (Wikipedia 2011a; emphasis added). The generation of life is algorithmic. What if the generation of literature were also so? Given a certain set of environmental factors—gender, nationality, genre—a certain literary result may be reliably predicted; many results may even be inevitable. This is another dangerous idea, perhaps a crazy one. Even after writing an entire book about how these "environmental" factors can be used to predict certain elements of creative expression, I am reluctant to reach for such a grand conclusion. There is much more work to be done.*

These ideas about the inevitability of literary change and about the inevitability of the form and shape of creativity are still ideas: ideas supported by 3,346 observations and 2,032,248 data points, but ideas nevertheless. Despite some convincing evidence of systematic organization within my corpus, I am not satisfied with my results. Darwin wasn't either. He writes:

> I look at the natural geological record, as a history of the world imperfectly kept, and written in a changing dialect; of this history we possess the last volume alone, relating only to two or three countries. Of this volume, only here and there a short chapter has been preserved; and of each page, only here and there a few lines. Each word of the slowly-changing language, in which the history is supposed to be written, being more or less different in the interrupted succession of chapters, may represent the apparently abruptly changed forms of life, entombed in our consecutive, but widely separated formations. (1964, 290)

It is ironic, and heartening, to find Darwin likening the evidence for evolution to an incomplete text. My corpus of 3,346 books is similar: incomplete, interrupted, haphazard, and at the same time revealing in ways that first suggest, then taunt, and ultimately demand. The comprehensive work is still to be done. Unlike evolutionary biologists, however, we literary scholars are at an advantage in terms of the availability of our source material. Having cited the same passage from Darwin, Franco Moretti points out that "the 'fossils' of literary evolution are often not lost, but carefully preserved in some great library" (2009, 158). It is fitting, therefore, to follow a chapter on literary genealogies with a few thoughts on digital preservation, orphan works, and the future for macroanalysis.

---

* In a coauthored paper, David Mimno and I begin to tackle some of the work that this present study demands. External factors such as author gender, author nationality, and date of publication affect both the choice of literary themes in novels and the expression of those themes, but the extent of this association is difficult to quantify. In this forthcoming work, we address the extent to which themes are statistically significant and the degree to which external factors predict word choice within individual themes. The paper is under review in the journal *Poetics*.

The fact of the matter is that text miners need digital texts to mine, and "modern copyright law," as Loyola law professor Matthew Sag puts it, "ensures that this process of scanning and digitization is ensnared in a host of thorny issues" (2012, 2). Well, that is a nice way of putting it! Today's digital-minded literary scholar is shackled in time; we are all, or are all soon to become, nineteenth centuryists. We are all slaves to the public domain. Perhaps Google, or the HathiTrust, is the "great library" that Moretti imagines? With some twenty million books, Google certainly seems the likely candidate for this title of "great library."* Yet it is not so great. Google is not a library at all. We cannot study literary history from within the arbitrary constraints of "snippet view." Access to a few random lines from a few random pages is tempting pabulum but not a meal. So here, perhaps, Darwin has the advantage: the artifacts of human evolution are not copyrighted! Sadly, the same cannot be said for the artifacts of creative evolution. The HathiTrust digital repository, a self-described "partnership of major research institutions and libraries working to ensure that the cultural record is preserved and accessible long into the future," offers some hope that the record *will be* preserved.† The associated HathiTrust Research Center offers hope that the record *will be* accessible. For now however, the pages of the HathiTrust Research Center are filled with verbs in the future tense: there *will be* X and there *will be* Y. And of what there *will* be, access to some, at least, *will* most certainly require authentication through a portal.‡ The project is young, and the initial phase focuses on works already identified as being within the public domain. For the time being, access to in-copyright material must be forbidden.§ There are technical challenges to be sure, but the real hurdle is legal.

Figuring out how to jump this hurdle is the preoccupation of many a good lawyer, and this topic was the focus of a recent University of California–Berkeley Law School Symposium titled "Orphan Works and Mass Digitization: Obstacles and Opportunities."¶ The final session of this conference asked this question: "Should data mining and other nonconsumptive uses of in-copyright digital works be permissible, and why?" As a contributor to the panel session, I offered an incomplete answer to the second part of the question: I discussed some of the findings from this book. It is not often that a literary scholar gets to address a crowd of several hundred copyright lawyers, so I ended with an appeal: "After

---

* According to Jennifer Howard's 2012 report in the *Chronicle of Higher Education*, Google claims to have scanned "more than 20 million books."

† See http://www.hathitrust.org/about.

‡ See http://www.hathitrust.org/htrc_access_use.

§ In fairness, there is some language on the website indicating that access to a full-text index of the textual data *may* be provided in the future.

¶ See http://www.law.berkeley.edu/orphanworks.htm.

seven years of digging in this corpus of thirty-five hundred books, I've come to the conclusion that there are still dozens of stones unturned, scores of dissertations and papers still to be written. Not one of these papers or dissertations, however, will be conclusive; none will answer the really big questions. For those questions we need really big data, big corpora, and these data cannot be in the form of snippets. To do this work, we need your help." Ultimately, and fittingly, it was the lawyers at the conference who stole the show. They are a motivated crew; they believe in what they are doing, and they are the ones poised to be the unsung heroes of literary history. Matthew Sag's argument in favor of "nonexpressive" use is most compelling.* Sag prefers the term *nonexpressive* to the competing and more ambiguous and sickly sounding term *nonconsumptive*. For Sag and other legal thinkers, the crux of the entire copyright entanglement can be distilled into a discussion of the so-called "orphan works." Books classified as "orphans" are books in which the copyright status is in question because the owners of the books cannot be easily or economically identified. This is the hard nut to crack. Sag reports several estimates regarding the depth of the orphan-works situation:

- 2.3 percent of the books published in the United States between 1927 and 1946 are still in print.
- Five out of seven books scanned by Google are not commercially available.
- Approximately 75 percent of books in U.S. libraries are out of print and have ceased earning income.

That last bullet point is cause for contemplation—Google's digital holdings are made primarily out of books held in libraries.

Sag's essay highlights one of many ironies in this debate: the expressed purpose of copyright is to "promote the Progress of Science and useful Arts."† Irony indeed. I suspect modern readers are under the impression, as I was, that the aim of copyright is the protection of scientific and creative output, not the promotion of it! I encourage readers to look up Sag's article in the *Berkeley Technology Law Journal*. For those of us seeking to mine the world's books, the arguments are compelling, and we ought to have these arguments in our arsenals. In short, Sag argues, "If the data extracted [from books] does not allow for the work to be reconstructed there is no substitution of expressive value. Extracting factual information about a work in terms of its linguistic structure or the frequency of the occurrences of certain words, phrases, or grammatical

---

* Sag's article, "Orphan Works as Grist for the Data Mill," appeared in the *Berkeley Technology Law Journal*. I am grateful to Professor Sag for allowing me access to his unpublished research. See Sag 2012, available at http://ssrn.com/abstract=2038889.

† Article 1, Section 8, Clause 8 of the United States Constitution.

features is a *nonexpressive use*" (ibid., 21; emphasis added). Despite the clarity and obvious logic of this argument, the matter remains unresolved. We are stuck in a legal limbo, trying to resolve the continuum fallacy: at what point does a nonexpressive work become expressive? Good fodder for lawyers and legal scholars; bad news for humanists. The sad result of this legal wrangling is that scholars wishing to study the literary record at scale are forced to ignore almost everything that has been published since 1923. This is the equivalent of telling an archaeologist that he cannot explore in the Fertile Crescent.

In the opening chapter of this book, I cited Rosanne Potter's comments from 1988. She wrote, "Until everything has been encoded . . . the everyday critic will probably not consider computer treatments of texts." It is a great shame that today, twenty-four years later, everything has been digitized, and still the everyday critic cannot consider computer treatments of texts.* Faced with the reality of copyright, many of my colleagues have simply given up. Recently, I was asked to speak to a group of graduate students and literary scholars about what can be done with a large corpus of texts. As I talked, the familiar lights came on; the excitement in the room was palpable. Shortly after the talk ended, the questions began. I watched this same group move from excitement to despair. Can we study Hemingway? No. Fitzgerald? No. Virginia Woolf? Again, no. Their hopes for enhancing their own research were deflated. From a list of several dozen twentieth-century canonical writers, the library had only a single digital text, a "bootleg" copy of Faulkner's *Sound and the Fury* that could not really be "released" for fear of legal retribution. Released? What would it mean to have a digital copy of *The Sun Also Rises* on my hard drive? Nothing, of course; fair use permits me to make a digital copy and use it for research purposes. The fear is that I might in turn release it again, into the proverbial wild. And so goes the story . . . Despite these challenges, I remain hopeful. Ventures such as the HathiTrust Research Center and the Book Genome Project seem poised to make a difference.† Perhaps this nonexpressive book of mine will help.

---

* No, not everything, but compared to 1988, yes, everything imaginable.

† At the time of this writing, Novel Projects' chief executive officer, Aaron Stanton, is working on a university-affiliated research project to allow academic researchers to access information about books in the corpus of the Book Genome Project. If all goes well, researchers will have access to transformative, nonexpressive data mined from portions of the Book Genome's in-copyright corpus. See http://bookgenome.com/.

REFERENCES

Allison, S., R. Heuser, M. Jockers, F. Moretti, and M. Witmore. 2012. "Quantitative Formalism: An Experiment." *N+1,* no. 13: 81–108.

Alt, M. 1990. *Exploring Hyperspace: A Non-mathematical Explanation of Multivariate Analysis.* London: McGraw-Hill.

Anderson, C. 2008. "The End of Theory: The Data Deluge Makes the Scientific Method Obsolete." *Wired,* June 23, 2008.

Auerbach, E. 1953. *Mimesis: The Representation of Reality in Western Literature.* Princeton, N.J.: Princeton University Press.

Baker, N. 2001. *Double Fold: Libraries and the Assault on Paper.* New York: Random House.

Bastian, M., S. Heymann, and M. Jacomy. 2009. "Gephi: An Open Source Software for Exploring and Manipulating Networks." Paper presented at the Third International AAAI Conference on Weblogs and Social Media. San Jose, Calif., May 17–20.

Bauerlein, M. 2008. *The Dumbest Generation: How the Digital Age Stupefies Young Americans and Jeopardizes Our Future; or, Don't Trust Anyone under 30.* New York: Penguin Group.

Bélanger, J. 2005. *The Irish Novel in the Nineteenth Century: Facts and Fictions.* Dublin and Portland, Ore.: Four Courts Press.

Biber, D., S. Conrad, and R. Reppen. 2006. *Corpus Linguistics: Investigating Language Structure and Use.* Cambridge: Cambridge University Press, 1986.

Bikhchandani, S., D. Hirshleifer, and I. Welch. 1992. "A Theory of Fads, Fashion, Custom, and Cultural Change as Informational Cascades." *Journal of Political Economy* 100, no. 5.

Birkerts, S. 1994. *The Gutenberg Elegies: The Fate of Reading in an Electronic Age.* Boston: Faber and Faber.

Blei, D. M., T. L. Griffiths, M. I. Jordan, and J. B. Tenenbaum. 2004. "Hierarchical Topic Models and the Nested Chinese Restaurant Process." In *Advances in Neural Infor-*

mation Processing Systems 16, edited by S. Thrun, K. Saul, and K. Schölkopf, 17–24. Proceedings of the 2003 conference. Cambridge, Mass.: MIT Press.

Blei, D. M., A. Y. Ng, and M. I. Jordan. 2003. "Latent Dirichlet Allocation." *Journal of Machine Learning Research* 3: 993–1022.

Blessing, P. 1977. "West among Strangers: Irish Migration to California, 1850 to 1880." Ph.D. diss., University of California, Los Angeles.

Blevins, C. 2010. *Topic Modeling: Martha Ballard's Diary.* April 1. http://historying .org/2010/04/01/topic-modeling-martha-ballards-diary/.

Block, S. 2006. "Doing More with Digitization: An Introduction to Topic Modeling of Early American Sources." *Common-place: The Interactive Journal of Early American Life* 6, no. 2. http://www.common-place.org/vol-06/no-02/tales/.

Bloom, H. 1973. *The Anxiety of Influence: A Theory of Poetry.* New York: Oxford University Press.

Boggess, L., J. S. Hamaker, R. Duncan, L. Kimek, Y. Wu, and Y. Zeng. 1999. "A Comparison of Part of Speech Taggers in the Task of Changing to a New Domain." Paper presented at the 1999 International Conference on Information Intelligence and Systems, Bethesda, Md.

Budgen, F. 1934. *James Joyce and the Making of Ulysses.* New York: Harrison Smith and Robert Haas.

Burrows, J. F. 1987. *Computation into Criticism: A Study of Jane Austen's Novels and an Experiment in Method.* Oxford: Clarendon Press.

———. 1989. "'An Ocean Where Each Kind . . . ': Statistical Analysis and Some Major Determinants of Literary Style." *Computers and the Humanities* 23, nos. 4–5: 309–21.

———. 2002. "'Delta': A Measure of Stylistic Difference and a Guide to Likely Authorship." *Literary and Linguistic Computing: Journal of the Association for Literary and Linguistic Computing* 17, no. 3: 267–87.

———. 2004. "Textual Analysis." In *A Companion to Digital Humanities,* edited by S. Schreibman, R. G. Siemens, and J. Unsworth. Malden, Mass.: Blackwell.

Cahalan, J. 1988. *The Irish Novel: A Critical History.* Boston: Twayne.

Carleton, W. 1848. *Emigrants of Ahadarra.* London: Simms and M'Intyre.

Casey, D. J., and R. E. Rhodes. 1979. *Irish-American Fiction: Essays in Criticism.* New York: AMS.

Chang, J., J. Boyd-Graber, S. Gerrish, C. Wang, and D. Blei. 2009. "Reading Tea Leaves: How Humans Interpret Topic Models." In *Advances in Neural Information Processing Systems 22,* 288–96. Proceedings of the 2009 conference. Norwich, UK: Curran Associates.

Cohn, D., and T. Hofmann. 2001. "The Missing Link: A Probabilistic Model of Document Content and Hypertext Connectivity." In *Advances in Neural Information Processing Systems 13,* edited by T. K. Leen, T. G. Dietterich, and V. Tresp, 430–36. Proceedings of the 2000 conference. Cambridge, Mass.: MIT Press.

Cronin, J. 1980. *The Anglo-Irish Novel.* Totowa, N.J.: Barnes and Noble Books.

Daemmrich, H. S., and I. Daemmrich. 1987. *Themes and Motifs in Western Literature: A Handbook.* Tübingen: Francke.

Darwin, C. 1964. *On the Origin of Species.* Cambridge, Mass.: Harvard University Press.

Deresiewicz, W. 2006. "Representative Fictions." *Nation,* December 4.

———. 2008. "Professing Literature in 2008." *Nation,* March 24.

Dickens, C. 1850. *The Personal History of David Copperfield, by Charles Dickens: With Illustrations by H. K. Browne.* London: Chapman and Hall. Nineteenth-Century Fiction Collection. Stanford, Calif.: Stanford University Library. http://collections.chadwyck.com/marketing/index.jsp.

———. 1854. *Hard Times, for These Times, by Charles Dickens.* London: Bradbury and Evans. Nineteenth-Century Fiction Collection. Stanford, Calif.: Stanford University Library. http://collections.chadwyck.com/marketing/index.jsp.

Diederich, J., J. Kindermann, E. Leopold, and G. Paass. 2000. "Authorship Attribution with Support Vector Machines." *Applied Intelligence* 19, nos. 1–2: 109–23.

Douglas, A. 2006. "The Cambridge Companion to the Irish Novel." In *Cambridge Companions to Literature,* edited by J. W. Foster. Cambridge: Cambridge University Press.

Dowling, P. J. 1988. *California, the Irish Dream.* San Francisco: Golden Gate Publishers.

———. 1998. *Irish Californians: Historic, Benevolent, Romantic.* San Francisco: Scottwall Associates.

Ebest, R. 2005. *Private Histories: The Writing of Irish-Americans, 1900–1935.* Notre Dame, Ind.: University of Notre Dame Press.

Emmons, D. M. 1989. *The Butte Irish: Class and Ethnicity in an American Mining Town, 1875–1925.* Statue of Liberty-Ellis Island Centennial Series. Champaign: University of Illinois Press.

———. 2010. *Beyond the American Pale: The Irish in the West, 1845–1910.* Norman: University of Oklahoma Press.

Erlich, V. 1980. *Russian Formalism: History, Doctrine.* 4th ed. The Hague: Mouton.

Fanning, C. 2000. *The Irish Voice in America: 250 Years of Irish-American Fiction.* 2nd ed. Lexington: University Press of Kentucky.

Fernández-Armesto, F. 1997. *Truth: A History and Guide for the Perplexed.* New York: St. Martin's Press.

Finkel, J. R., T. Grenager, and C. Manning. 2005. "Incorporating Non-local Information into Information Extraction Systems by Gibbs Sampling." In *Proceedings of the 43rd Annual Meeting of the Association for Computational Linguistics,* 363–70. Ann Arbor, Mich., June 25–30. http://acl.ldc.upenn.edu/P/P05/P05-1045.pdf.

Firth, J. R. 1957. "A Synopsis of Linguistic Theory, 1930–1955." In *Studies in Linguistic Analysis.* Oxford: Blackwell.

Fischman, J. 2008a. "Digital Humanities Gets Federal 'Office' Space." *Chronicle of Higher Education,* March 25.

———. 2008b. "A Supercomputer Takes Humanities Scholars into the 21st Century." *Chronicle of Higher Education,* April 22.

Flanagan, T. 1959. *The Irish Novelists, 1800–1850.* New York: Columbia University Press.

Flanders, J. 2005. "Detailism, Digital Texts, and the Problem of Pedantry." *TEXT Technology* 2: 41–70.

Forsyth, R. S. 1997. "Towards a Text Benchmark Suite." In *Proceedings of the 1997 Joint International Conference of the Association for Computers and the Humanities and the Association for Literary and Linguistic Computing (ACH/ALLC).* Kingston, On-

tario, June 3–7. http://67.207.129.15:8080/dh-abstracts/view?docId=1997_paper_026
_forsyth.xml;query=Forsyth,%20R.%20S.;brand=dh-abstracts.

Gaskell, E. C. 1849. *Mary Barton: A Tale of Manchester Life.* 2 vols. 3rd ed. London: Chapman and Hall. Nineteenth-Century Fiction Collection. Stanford, Calif.: Stanford University Library. http://collections.chadwyck.com/marketing/index.jsp.

Goodall, H. 2008. "How Digital Technology Is Changing the Liberal Arts." *Chronicle of Higher Education,* January 18.

Gottschall, J. 2008. *Literature, Science, and a New Humanities.* New York: Palgrave Macmillan.

Grieve, J. 2007. "Quantitative Authorship Attribution: An Evaluation of Techniques." *Literary and Linguistic Computing: Journal of the Association for Literary and Linguistic Computing* 22, no. 3: 251–70.

Griffiths, T. L., and M. Steyvers. 2002. "A Probabilistic Approach to Semantic Representation." In *Proceedings of the 24th Annual Conference of the Cognitive Science Society.* Fairfax, Va., August 7–10. http://psiexp.ss.uci.edu/research/papers/semrep.pdf.

———. 2003. "Prediction and Semantic Association." In *Neural Information Processing Systems 15.* Cambridge, Mass.: MIT Press.

———. 2004. "Finding Scientific Topics." *Proceedings of the National Academy of Science* 101 (April 6): 5228–35.

Guillén, C. 1971. *Literature as System: Essays toward the Theory of Literary History.* Princeton, N.J.: Princeton University Press.

Hacking, I. 1983. *Representing and Intervening: Introductory Topics in the Philosophy of Natural Science.* Cambridge: Cambridge University Press.

Hawthorne, M. D. 1975. *John and Michael Banim (the "O'Hara Brothers"): A Study in the Early Development of the Anglo-Irish Novel.* Salzburg Studies in Romantic Reassessment, vol. 50. Salzburg: Institut für Englische Sprache und Literatur, Universität Salzburg.

Hockey, S. 2000. *Electronic Texts in the Humanities: Principles and Practice.* Oxford: Oxford University Press.

———. 2004. "History of Humanities Computing." In *A Companion to Digital Humanities,* edited by S. Schreibman, R. Siemens, and J. Unsworth. Malden, Mass.: Blackwell.

Hofmann, T. 1999. "Probabilistic Latent Semantic Indexing." In *Proceedings of the Fifteenth Conference on Uncertainty in Artificial Intelligence.* Stockholm, July 30–31. San Francisco: Morgan Kaufmann.

———. 2001. "Unsupervised Learning by Probabilistic Latent Semantic Analysis." *Machine Learning Journal* 42, no. 1: 177–96.

Hoover, D. L. 2003a. "Another Perspective on Vocabulary Richness." *Computers and the Humanities* 37, no. 2: 151–78.

———. 2003b. "Multivariate Analysis and the Study of Style Variation." *Literary and Linguistic Computing: Journal of the Association for Literary and Linguistic Computing* 18, no. 4: 341–60.

Hope, J., and M. Witmore. 2004. "The Very Large Textual Object: A Prosthetic Reading of Shakespeare." *Early Modern Literary Studies* 6: 1–36.

Howard, J. 2008a. "Humanities Publishing at the MLA: Digital and Posthuman." *Chronicle of Higher Education*, January 11.

———. 2008b. "Landmark Digital History Monograph Project Goes Open Access." *Chronicle of Higher Education*, February 26.

———. 2008c. "Literary Geospaces: Digital Tools Help Put Literature in Its Place." *Chronicle of Higher Education*, August 1.

———. 2012. "Google Begins to Scale Back Its Scanning of Books from University Libraries." *Chronicle of Higher Education*. http://chronicle.com/article/Google-Begins-to-Scale-Back/131109/.

Howe, S. 2000. *Ireland and Empire: Colonial Legacies in Irish History and Culture*. Oxford: Oxford University Press.

Hunt, L. 1986. "French History in the Last Twenty Years: The Rise and Fall of the *Annales* Paradigm." *Journal of Contemporary History* 21: 209–24.

Husemann, M. M. 2003. *Margaret Oliphant Wilson Oliphant (1828–1897): A Brief Biography*. October 20. http://www.victorianweb.org/authors/oliphant/bio.html (accessed April 19, 2012).

Hutton, P. H. 1981. "The History of Mentalities: The New Map of Cultural History." *History and Theory* 21: 209–24.

Jockers, M. 1997. "In Search of Tir-Na-Nog: Irish and Irish-American Literature in the West." Ph.D. diss., Southern Illinois University.

———. 2004. "A Window Facing West: Charles Driscoll's Kansas Irish." *New Hibernia Review* 8, no. 3.

———. 2005. "A Literature of Good Fortune." In *The Irish in the San Francisco Bay Area: Essays on Good Fortune*, edited by D. Jordan and T. O'Keefe. San Francisco: Irish Literary and Historical Society.

———. 2009. "West of Éire: Butte's Irish Ethos." In *All Our Stories Are Here: Critical Perspectives on Montana Literature*, edited by B. Harrison. Lincoln: University of Nebraska Press.

Jockers, M., and D. M. Witten. 2010. "A Comparative Study of Machine Learning Methods for Authorship Attribution." *Literary and Linguistic Computing* 25, no. 2: 215–23.

Jockers, M., D. M. Witten, and C. S. Criddle. 2008. "Reassessing Authorship in the Book of Mormon Using Nearest Shrunken Centroid Classification." *Literary and Linguistic Computing: Journal of the Association for Literary and Linguistic Computing* 23: 465–91.

Kearns, C. 1997. *Cabbage and Bones: An Anthology of Irish American Women's Fiction*. New York: Henry Holt.

Kelleher, M. 2005. "'Wanted an Irish Novelist': The Critical Decline of the Nineteenth-Century Novel." In *The Irish Novel in the Nineteenth Century*, edited by J. Bélanger. Dublin: Four Courts.

Kirschenbaum, M. G. 2010. "What Is Digital Humanities and What's It Doing in English Departments?" *ADE Bulletin*, no. 150: 55–61.

Koppel, M., S. Argamon, and A. R. Shimoni. 2002. "Automatically Categorizing Written Texts by Author Gender." *Literary and Linguistic Computing* 17, no. 4: 401–12.

Lau, J. H., K. Grieser, D. Newman, and T. Baldwin. 2011. "Automatic Labelling of Topic Models." In *Proceedings of the 49th Annual Meeting of the Association for Computational Linguistics*, 1536–45. Portland, Ore., June 19–24. http://www.aclweb.org/anthology/P11–1154.

Lau, J. H., D. Newman, S. Karimi, and T. Baldwin. 2010. "Best Topic Word Selection for Topic Labelling." In *COLING '10: Proceedings of the 23rd International Conference on Computational Linguistics Posters*, 605–13. Beijing, August 23–27. http://aclweb.org/anthology-new/C/C10/C10–2069.pdf.

Lee, A. R., ed. 1984. *Herman Melville: Reassessments*. Critical Studies Series. London: Vision Press.

Lenoir, T. 1997. *Instituting Science: The Cultural Production of Scientific Disciplines*. Writing Science. Stanford, Calif.: Stanford University Press.

Longfellow, H. W. 1849. *Kavanagh: A Tale*. Boston: Ticknor, Reed, and Fields.

Macdonagh, T. 1916. *Literature in Ireland: Studies Irish and Anglo-Irish*. London: T. F. Unwin.

Mackenzie, R. N. 1992. "George P. R. James." In *Dictionary of Literary Biography*, edited by B. K. Mudge. Farmington Hills, Mich.: Gale Group.

Martindale, C. 1990. *The Clockwork Muse: The Predictability of Artistic Change*. New York: HarperCollins.

Martindale, C., and D. McKenzie. 1995. "On the Utility of Content Analysis in Author Attribution: The Federalist." *Computers and the Humanities* 29, no. 4: 259–70.

McCallum, A. K. 2002. "MALLET: A Machine Learning for Language Toolkit." http://mallet.cs.umass.edu.

———. 2009. "Machine Learning for Language Toolkit: Topic Modeling." http://mallet.cs.umass.edu/topics.php (accessed October 13, 2009).

McClellan, A. 2010. "University Women in Frances Marshall's Fiction." *English Literature in Transition, 1880–1920* 53, no. 3: 331–49.

McKibben, S. E. 2008. "Speaking the Unspeakable: Male Humiliation and Female National Allegory after Kinsale." *Éire-Ireland* 43, nos. 3–4: 11–30.

Michel, J.-B., Y. K. Shen, A. P. Aiden, A. Veres, M. K. Gray, W. Brockman, T. G. B. Team, et al. 2011. "Quantitative Analysis of Culture Using Millions of Digitized Books." *Science* 331, no. 6014: 176–82.

Moretti, F. 2000. "Conjectures on World Literature." *New Left Review* 1 (January–February): 54–68.

———. 2005. *Graphs, Maps, Trees: Abstract Models for a Literary History*. London and New York: Verso.

———. 2009. "Style, Inc.: Reflections on Seven Thousand Titles (British Novels, 1740–1850)." *Critical Inquiry* 36, no. 1: 134–58.

Mosteller, R. F., and D. L. Wallace. 1964. *Inference and Disputed Authorship: The Federalist*. Reading, Mass.: Addison-Wesley.

Newman, D., J. H. Lau, K. Grieser, and T. Baldwin. 2010. "Automatic Evaluation of Topic Coherence." In *Human Language Technologies: The 2010 Annual Conference of the North American Chapter of the ACL*, 100–108. Los Angeles, June 1–6. http://www.ics.uci.edu/~newman/pubs/naacl2010.pdf.

Newman, D., Y. Noh, E. M. Talley, S. Karimi, and T. Baldwin. 2010. "Evaluating Topic Models for Digital Libraries." In *Proceedings of Joint JCDL/ICADL 2010*, 214–24. Gold Coast, Australia, June 21–25. http://www.ics.uci.edu/~newman/pubs/jcdl58 -newman.pdf.

Newman, D., P. Smyth, and M. Steyvers. 2006. "Scalable Parallel Topic Models." *Journal of Intelligence Community Research and Development* 5.

NORA. 2006. *The NORA Project: Project Description.* http://nora.lis.uiuc.edu/description .php (accessed October 13, 2006).

Norris, K. T. 1959. *Family Gathering.* Garden City, N.Y.: Doubleday.

Nunberg, G. 2009. "Google Books: A Metadata Train Wreck." In *Language Log.* University of Pennsylvania. http://languagelog.ldc.upenn.edu/nll/?p=1701 (accessed August 20, 2012).

Olsen, M. 1993. "Signs, Symbols, and Discourses: A New Direction for Computer-Aided Literature Studies." *Computers and the Humanities* 27, nos. 5–6: 309–14.

Palantir Technologies. 2011. *Palantir Government.* http://www.palantirtech.com/ government (accessed September 7, 2011).

Pannapacker, W. 2011. "Pannapacker at MLA: Digital Humanities Triumphant?" *Chronicle of Higher Education,* January 8.

Parry, M. 2010. "The Humanities Go Google." *Chronicle of Higher Education,* May 28.

Pennebaker, J. W. 2011. *The Secret Life of Pronouns: What Our Words Say about Us.* New York: Bloomsbury Press.

Piez, W. 2008. "Something Called 'Digital Humanities.'" *Digital Humanities Quarterly* 2, no. 1.

Pikus, M. J. 1997. "*The Redskins;* or, *Indian and Injin* and James Fenimore Cooper's Continuing Historical Paradox." Originally published in *James Fenimore Cooper: His Country and His Art,* edited by H. C. MacDougall, 93–97. Papers from the 1997 Cooper Seminar, no. 11, State University of New York College at Oneonta. http://external.oneonta.edu/cooper/articles/suny/1997suny-pikus.html (accessed August 1, 2012).

Polonsky, R. 1998. *English Literature and the Russian Aesthetic Renaissance.* Cambridge Studies in Russian Literature. Cambridge: Cambridge University Press.

Potter, R. 1988. "Literary Criticism and Literary Computing." *Computers in the Humanities* 22, no. 2.

Ramsay, S. 2007. "Algorithmic Criticism." In *A Companion to Digital Literary Studies,* edited by R. G. Siemens and S. Schreibman. Malden, Mass.: Blackwell.

———. 2011. *Reading Machines: Toward an Algorithmic Criticism.* Topics in the Digital Humanities. Champaign: University of Illinois Press.

R Development Core Team. 2011. "R: A Language and Environment for Statistical Computing." R Foundation for Statistical Computing, Vienna, ISBN 3–900051–07–0. http://www.R-project.org/.

Rommel, T. 2004. "Literary Studies." In *A Companion to Digital Humanities,* edited by S. Schreibman, R. Siemens, and J. Unsworth. Malden, Mass.: Blackwell.

Rose, S. 1992. "So-Called 'Formative Causation': A Hypothesis Disconfirmed, Response to Rupert Sheldrake." *Rivista di Biologia* 85, nos. 3–4: 445–53.

Sag, M. 2012. "Orphan Works as Grist for the Data Mill." *Berkeley Technology Law Journal* 27, no. 4.

Schilit, B., and O. Kolak. 2007. "Dive into the Meme Pool with Google Book Search." In *Inside Google Books.* Blog.

Schreibman, S., R. G. Siemens, and J. Unsworth, eds. 2004. *A Companion to Digital Humanities.* Blackwell Companions to Literature and Culture 26. Malden, Mass.: Blackwell.

Schulz, K. 2011. "Distant Reading." *New York Times,* June 26, 2011.

Shea, C. 2008. "The Geography of Irish-American Lit." *Boston Globe,* July 30.

Sheldrake, R. 1992. "An Experimental Test of the Hypothesis of Formative Causation." *Rivista di Biologia* 85, nos. 3–4: 431–43.

Siemens, R. G., and S. Schreibman. 2007. *A Companion to Digital Literary Studies.* Blackwell Companions to Literature and Culture 50. Malden, Mass.: Blackwell.

Simon, S. 2005. "Did Melville Borrow the Idea for *Moby Dick*? An Interview with Paul Collins." In *Weekend Edition, Saturday,* on National Public Radio.

Sinclair, S. 2003. "Computer-Assisted Reading: Reconceiving Text Analysis." *Literary and Linguistic Computing* 18, no. 2: 175–84.

Smith, C. A., and M. C. Bisch. 1990. "Joyce's *Ulysses.*" *Explicator* 48: 206.

Stevens, L., and S. Brown. 2000. "Gender, Nationality, and Cultural Representations of Ireland: An Irish Woman's Place?" *European Journal of Women's Studies* 7: 405–21.

Steyvers, M., and T. L. Griffiths. 2007. "Probabilistic Topic Models." In *Handbook of Latent Semantic Analysis,* edited by D. McNamara, T. Landauer, S. Dennis, and W. Kintsch. Mahwah, N.J.: Erlbaum.

Tibshirani, R., T. Hastie, B. Narasimhan, and G. Chu. 2003. "Class Prediction by Nearest Shrunken Centroids, with Applications to DNA Microarrays." *Statistical Science* 18: 104–17.

Trumpener, K. 1997. *Bardic Nationalism: The Romantic Novel and the British Empire.* Literature in History. Princeton, N.J.: Princeton University Press.

Tynjanov, J. 1978. "On Literary Evolution." In *Reading in Russian Formalism: Formalist and Structuralist Views,* edited by L. Matejka and K. Pomorska. Ann Arbor: Michigan Slavic Publications.

Uzuner, O., and B. Katz. 2005. "A Comparative Study of Language Models for Book and Author Recognition." *Lecture Notes in Computer Science* 3651: 969–80.

Walsh, J. P. 1978. *The San Francisco Irish, 1850–1976.* San Francisco: Irish Literary and Historical Society.

Watt, I. P. 1957. *The Rise of the Novel: Studies in Defoe, Richardson, and Fielding.* Berkeley: University of California Press.

Wei, X., and W. B. Croft. 2006. "LDA-Based Document Models for Ad-Hoc Retrieval." In *Proceedings of the Twenty-Ninth Annual International ACM SIGIR Conference on Research and Development in Information Retrieval,* 178–85. Seattle, August 6–10. http://ciir.cs.umass.edu/pubfiles/ir-464.pdf.

Wikipedia. 2011a. "*Darwin's Dangerous Idea.*" In *Wikipedia: The Free Encyclopedia.* http://en.wikipedia.org/wiki/Darwin%27s_Dangerous_Idea.

———. 2011b. "PageRank." In *Wikipedia: The Free Encyclopedia.* http://en.wikipedia .org/wiki/Pagerank.

Wiltshire, J. 1988. "Jane Austen: Computation or Criticism?" *Cambridge Quarterly* 17: 369–81.

Witmore, M. A. J. H. 2007. *Shakespeare by the Numbers: On the Linguistic Texture of the Late Plays.* Edited by S. Mukherji and R. Lyne. Early Modern Tragicomedy. London: Boydell and Brewer.

WordHoard. 2006. *WordHoard: An Application for the Close Reading and Scholarly Analysis of Deeply Tagged Texts.* Version 1.1.5. Northwestern University, September 25. http://wordhoard.northwestern.edu/userman/index.html.

Yeats, W. B. 1908. "First Principles." *Samhain* 7: 6–12.

———. 1979. *Representative Irish Tales.* Atlantic Highlands, N.J.: Humanities Press.

Young, J. 2009. "Digital Humanities Scholars Collaborate More on Journal Articles than 'Traditional' Researchers." *Chronicle of Higher Education,* April 27.

Yu, B. 2008. "An Evaluation of Text Classification Methods for Literary Study." *Literary and Linguistic Computing* 23, no. 3: 327–43.

Zhao, Y., and J. Zobel. 2005. "Effective and Scalable Authorship Attribution Using Function Words." *Lecture Notes in Computer Science* 3689: 174–89.

Zimmer, B. 2011. "The Power of Pronouns." *New York Times,* August 26. http://www .nytimes.com/2011/08/28/books/review/the-secret-life-of-pronouns-by-james-w -pennebaker-book-review.html?pagewanted=all.

Zuboff, S. 1988. *In the Age of the Smart Machine.* New York: Basic Books.

INDEX

Note: Page numbers with an *f* or *t* refer to figures or tables.

ADHO (Alliance of Digital Humanities Organizations), 13
"Algorithmic Criticism" (Ramsay), 18
Alliance of Digital Humanities Organizations (ADHO), 13
Allison, S., 69, 77–78
American novel theme prominences, 140, 141f
Annales school of historiography, 19, 27
anonymity-theme analysis, 138–40
Anxiety of Influence (Bloom), 31
Argamon, Shlomo, 93–94
Auerbach, Erich, 7
Austen, Jane: Burrows analysis, 26–27, 29; *Pride and Prejudice* analyses, 160–61, 160t; *Sense and Sensibility* analyses, 54–55, 64–67, 66–67f
author gender analyses: black American drama corpus, 48–50, 49f; classification accuracy, 95–97; genre analyses, 93–96, 94t, 95t; Irish American authors corpus, 39–43, 41–42f; misattribution, 95t; signals analysis, 93–95; nationality prediction goal, 158; signal word lists, 94f; theme relationship analyses, 136–39, 151–53; theme relationship analysis in word clouds, 152f; theme relationship in bar graphs, 136–39f; time period factors, 95–96
author nationality analyses: British vs. American word usage, 105–11; British vs.

Irish, 111–17; gender prediction goal, 158; theme plotted by "novel time" in two Irish novels, 140–42, 143f; theme relationship analyses, 140–53, 141–42f, 145f; theme relationship in bar graphs, 141–42f; theme relationship in word clusters, 149–50f; themes interpreted by nation, 140–45; word usage analyses, 105–11. *See also* Irish American authors corpus
author style features, 63–67, 92–93, 99–104
Automated Learning Group, 21
Auvil, Loretta, 134

Baker, Nicholson, 13
Bauerlein, Mark, 13
"beautiful" usage analysis (British and American novels of the 19th century), 106–9, 107f, 109f. *See also* word usage analyses
Berkeley Technology Law Journal, 174–75
"Beyond Boston: Georeferencing Irish-American Literature" (Jockers), 36
Beyond Search workshop, 22
Biber, Douglas, 121
bibliographical metadata, 5–37, 62
big data, 3–4, 7–8, 120, 174
"Big House" theme. *See* "Tenants and Landlords" theme
Birkerts, Sven, 13
Bisch, M. C., 29
black American drama corpus, 48–50, 49f
black box, 128, 129–30
Black Drama (Alexander Street Press), 49f
Blei, D., 122–23

MATTHEW L. JOCKERS is an assistant professor of English at the University of Nebraska-Lincoln.

Additional material referred to in this book, including confusion matrices, an expanded stop-words list, and additional graphs and color images, can be found at http://www.matthewjockers.net/macroanalysisbook/.

TOPICS IN THE DIGITAL HUMANITIES

THE UNIVERSITY OF ILLINOIS PRESS

is a founding member of the
Association of American University Presses.

Composed in 10.5/13 Adobe Minion Pro
with Trade Gothic display
by Jim Proefrock
at the University of Illinois Press
Manufactured by Thomson-Shore, Inc.

University of Illinois Press
1325 South Oak Street
Champaign, IL 61820-6903
www.press.uillinois.edu